D1588421

The Irish Chartered Accountant

Centenary Essays 1888-1988

...but I've managed to reduce your liability to 37 years...

Centenary Essays 1888-1988

The Irish Chartered Accountant

Centenary Essays 1888-1988

Edited by
David Rowe

Gill and Macmillan

Published in Ireland by Gill and Macmillan Ltd
Goldenbridge, Dublin 8
with associated companies in
Auckland, Delhi, Gaborone, Hamburg, Harare, Hong Kong, Johannesburg,
Kuala Lumpur, Lagos, London, Manzini, Melbourne, Mexico City, Nairobi,
New York, Singapore, Tokyo

© The Institute of Chartered Accountants in Ireland, 1988
Designed by Jan de Fouw
Cartoons by Martyn Turner

Print origination by Graphic Plan, Dublin
Printed by Criterion Press Ltd, Dublin

All rights reserved. No part of this publication may be copied, reproduced or
transmitted in any form or by any means, without permission of the publishers.

British Library of Congress Cataloguing in Publication Data
The Irish chartered accountant.
 1. Ireland. Accountancy, 1888-1988
 I. Rowe, David
 657' .09415

 ISBN 0-7171-1572-0

Centenary Essays 1888-1988

Contents

Centenary Essays 1888-1988

Alan J. Gibson, B.Sc. (Econ.), F.C.A.

Alan Gibson was born in Airdrie, Scotland in 1942, but moved to Northern Ireland with his family at the age of twelve. He was educated at Methodist College, Belfast, where, apart from meeting his future wife, Elizabeth, he also found time for rugby and cricket. He took an economics degree at Queen's University, Belfast.

He qualified as a chartered accountant in 1967 following his training period with the firm of Wilson, Hennessey & Crawford. He was a member and subsequently chairman of the students' group of the Ulster Society of Chartered Accountants. He was elected to the main committee in 1970 and became chairman in 1979.

That same year he was elected to membership of the council of the Institute of Chartered Accountants in Ireland. He served on a number of its committees and working parties, and was chairman of the Disciplinary Committee, and for three years of the Examinations Committee. His particular interest was in education and training.

He became a partner in Wilson, Hennessey & Crawford in 1971, which in 1973 merged with Deloitte Plender Griffith. In 1985 he was appointed partner-in-charge of Deloitte Haskins & Sells. His firm has had a long association with the Institute of Chartered Accountants in Ireland, and including the predecessor firms, he will be the sixth president from that connection.

He is a member of the executive committee of the Northern Ireland Small Business Institute, and was a member of the Industry Year 1986 Northern Ireland Committee. He is treasurer of the Northern Ireland committee of the British Diabetic Association.

He enjoys playing golf and bridge, and family holidays with his wife and three children.

Foreword 1

by Alan J. Gibson, president of the Institute of Chartered Accountants in Ireland, 1987-8

WHETHER you live there, have done business there, have spent a peaceful holiday there, or know it only as a place on the map, you will all have your own visions of Ireland. A green quilted island washed by the gulf stream, the land of saints and scholars, the land of a hundred thousand welcomes — all true, but there is much more to the Ireland of today.

Divided politically but united by the common demands of modern industrial societies within the European Economic Community, Ireland, south and north, is striving to provide its people, and particularly its young population, with opportunities to take their places in the business world today.

Agriculture, tourism, shipbuilding, aircraft manufacturing, linen, textiles — these are some traditional industries which are facing the challenges of the world's market place, but new industries such as computer hardware and software, electronics, pharmaceuticals, printing and financial services provide exciting opportunities for the whole of Ireland to show the world what its people can do.

The first General Meeting of the Institute of Chartered Accountants held on 4 May 1889 records that there were forty-two members of whom only five were not in practice. They all lived and worked somewhere in Ireland. As we approach the 100th year of the Irish Institute the total membership is just over 6,000 with more than half of those working outside practice. Approximately 5,000 live and work in Ireland, both south and north, with the remainder spread throughout the world in at least sixty countries.

The first accounts to 31 December 1888 showed a total income of £331. The largest single expense related to law costs in connection with the drafting of a petition to the Lord Lieutenant and in drafting the charter and bye-laws. These costs amounted to £218 and the excess of income over expenditure at the end of the year was £105. The financial statements to 31 December 1986 show income of £2.5 million and reserves of approximately £700,000.

These are only limited and objective measurements of the progress of the Institute from those humble beginnings. The chairman of that first meeting remarked on the pleasure he had of seeing before him a qualified body representing the accountants of Ireland. The principal objective of those original founders of our Institute was to improve the position of accountants in Ireland

and to set the standards of professional conduct and ethics which they could pass to future generations.

This centenary volume is not a definitive history of the Institute but rather a series of articles highlighting in many ways the variety of challenge and opportunity open to the chartered accountant of the 1990s. Howard Robinson, himself an Irish chartered accountant, has written a detailed history of the first ninety-five years of the Institute. I commend it to all of you who are interested in such things as a most readable and interesting history of our Institute. Throughout that history the Institute has been blessed with men of integrity and foresight who have faced up to the ethical challenges of a profession, whilst at the same time ensuring its development to keep pace with the business world as it has evolved over those years.

The standing of any professional body is only as good as its members; and it is often forgotten that it is the goodwill of those members in giving up their time and efforts on a voluntary basis which ensures the ongoing maintenance of quality.

The education and training of the chartered accountant has changed significantly over the years. We have moved from a solely examining body to one which educates, trains and examines the potential chartered accountant in Ireland. In this field of education the Irish Institute has been at the forefront of many developments. In the belief that the challenges likely to face the aspiring chartered accountant are of the highest order, the entry standards of those hoping to qualify have been for many years equivalent to that for university entry. Although there has not been exclusively graduate entry, the benefits of university education have been such that a significant proportion of those entering to train as chartered accountants in recent years has been graduate.

The recent growth in the requirement of practising offices for trainees with a relevant accounting degree was anticipated, and the development of joint diplomas in accounting with universities in both Dublin and Belfast is unique within the British Isles. Many young people on the other hand choose to leave school and train to be chartered accountants without going to university. These young men and women feel no inferiority when measured against their graduate counterparts and this is in no small part due to the attitude of our members.

The breadth of knowledge and experience required of today's chartered accountant is such as would make the founders of our Institute blanch. The expanding requirements and developments of the profession, business and commerce, not only in Ireland but throughout the world, has meant that the examination of this knowledge has to keep pace. The Irish Institute was the first in the British Isles to evolve a system of examination based on the multi-discipline concept, to test the future chartered accountant and his capability to react to real world situations. As I said earlier more than half of our members work in industry and commerce and these members have played a significant part, not only in the general management of industry but in the development of financial reporting. Many hold senior executive positions in some of the largest enterprises in Ireland, Great Britain and far beyond. Their knowledge and experience and, most importantly, professionalism have brought to commerce and industry a dimension of which we are justifiably proud.

In the field of public practice, the internationalisation of firms outside the country has been mirrored by developments in Ireland whereby external links have been established by a number of Irish firms. However, the dynamism of the indigenous profession has led to the development of a number of major practices with a solely Irish base. When you consider the industrial base and the size of the total population of Ireland this development has been on a scale which is significant, not only in the size of these firms and the numbers of chartered accountants they employ but also in the reputation they have within Ireland and beyond. The great regret is that with few exceptions the names of so many major figures of influence in the development of Irish accounting have been subsumed into those household names of the big international league.

The vision of the chartered accountant is often portrayed as one of both conservatism and male domination. This may have been the case in the first seventy-five years of our Institute. Today nothing could be further from the truth. A sizeable proportion of Irish chartered accountants are aged under thirty-five and approximately thirty per cent of those who train to be chartered accountants are women. The Irish Institute was amongst the first, if not the first, of the leading accountancy bodies to have a woman as president. It would be presumptuous to comment that women have a place in our profession. This goes without saying and long may it continue and develop.

The Institute played its full part in the development of the world accounting scene. Our members who work abroad are held in the highest esteem, playing their full part in the professional and business community in all five continents. The Irish Institute has been at the forefront in developing accounting standards and auditing standards and guidelines throughout the British Isles. Where necessary it has not been afraid to challenge and criticise as an equal member. Our Institute and many of its members have also played their full part in bodies such as the International Federation of Accountants (IFAC) and the International Accounting Standards Committee (IASC). Indeed the current president of the newly established European accounting body, Fédération des Experts Comptables Européens (FEE), is a past president of the Irish Institute, Margaret Downes.

We are also unique in that having been established before Ireland was divided, our Institute has continued in the spirit of co-operation and professional development in both parts of the island. The council is represented by members elected from the whole of Ireland. We have a tradition that our presidency rotates between Northern Ireland and the Republic of Ireland but is elected by and represents the whole of the membership wherever they may be. We have offices both in Dublin and Belfast and it is not without significance that in centenary year, 1988, it is anticipated that the president during the first half will be from Northern Ireland and in the second half from the Republic of Ireland. Moreover the president in the first half will represent the practising side of our profession and in the second half will be from industry.

The Institute of Chartered Accountants in Ireland has evolved from small beginnings into a pre-eminent position within the accountancy and business world. This is in no small part owing to the foundation given by those who decided to establish the Institute and seek a royal charter in 1888. Their successors have carried on the best traditions, looking forward rather than back. The challenges to our profession in maintaining the best traditions of independence, objectivity and integrity in the evolving commercial and competitive world have never been greater. The original signatories to the charter set the standards for us to follow and we must strive to ensure that we hold on to them.

The Institute library in Belfast

Eugene Greene, B.Comm., F.C.A.

Eugene Greene was born in Donegal on 12 February 1940 and lived and went to school there until 1952. In that year his parents sent him to boarding school in Blackrock College in Dublin, where he stayed until 1958.

From 1958 to 1961 he studied commerce in University College Dublin and upon qualifying in the autumn of 1961 he became articled to John Carney, but subsequently transferred to Butler Chance & Co. and qualified out of that office in January 1965.

He worked with Craig Gardner & Co. from 1 February 1965 to 31 July 1967. He joined Ryan Tourist Holdings as financial accountant in August 1967 and moved over as general manager of Ryan Hotels in 1969 and stayed in that position until July 1972.

In April 1973, along with some other partners, he bought Goodalls of Ireland Limited which is a food manufacturing and distribution company based in Dublin. He is now managing director and a fifty per cent shareholder of Goodalls.

He has been a council member of the Institute from May 1979.

Foreword 2

by Eugene Greene, president of the Institute of Chartered Accountants in Ireland, 1988-9

F ROM its foundation in 1888 until today the membership of our Institute has grown by 19,255 per cent. If we take the same rate of growth over the next 100 years then the membership will total 1,161,300 in the year 2088. An unlikely scenario!

I am sure our founding fathers never foresaw either the explosion in the membership of our Institute or the explosion in the range of services now being offered by our members.

Who knows what the future holds? After all in 1888 who could have foretold that the wonders of the ancient world would be surpassed by the wonders of the modern world, such as mass transportation, space travel, heart transplants, and the mighty computer? So who is to say what will happen over the next 100 years?

But, you know, despite all the changes that have taken place since 1888, and amidst all the turmoil that we see around us in society today the fundamental principles of our Institute haven't changed at all. Indeed, they have remained firmly constant.

We have maintained the high ethical standards we've always had, not just in our professional lives but in our private lives as well. We must continue to maintain these high standards.

We have maintained our high levels of professional independence, objectivity and integrity in all matters, great and small. We must continue to maintain these qualities.

Our members always have had a very high regard for the public interest. We must ensure that the public continues to have confidence in the integrity of the chartered accountant.

I am proud of the fact that we are a thirty-two county body and that we in the south of Ireland have lived and worked harmoniously with our members in Northern Ireland over all those years.

I have been involved almost every year of my working life in the affairs and activities of the Institute. I love it. I have great pride in our Institute. I am proud to call myself a chartered accountant.

I have great confidence that our Institute will survive equally as well over the next 100 years as it so obviously has done in the last 100 years. I will try to contribute in my own small way to ensure that it does.

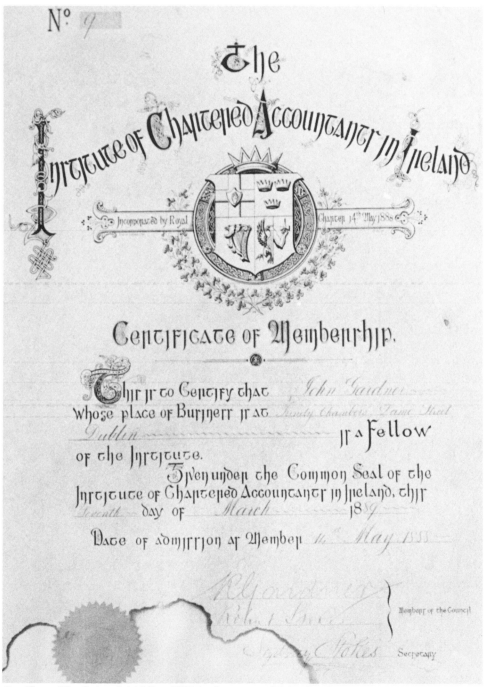

Certificate No. 9 dated 14 May 1888 in the name of John Gardner, found on a rubbish dump recently

Niall W. Deasy, B.Comm., F.C.A.

Niall Deasy was born in Kilkenny in 1943 and moved to Cork some years later where he was educated at the Christian Brothers College. He took a commerce degree at University College Dublin and having served articles in Carthy O'Neill & Co. was admitted to membership of the Institute in 1968. He subsequently joined Peterson Morrison & Co. (now Coopers & Lybrand) and was admitted to partnership in 1975.

He was a member of the DCASS Committee from 1966 to 1968 and was involved in setting up ACASSI in 1968. In 1980-81 he served as chairman of the Leinster Society of Chartered Accountants. He was closely involved in the development of the Leinster Society's Published Accounts Award Scheme which was inaugurated in 1978, and was chairman of the PAA Committee from 1981 to 1985.

He has served on several Institute committees and represented the Irish Institute on the Auditing Practices Committee of CCAB from 1984 to 1987. He was elected to the council of the Institute in 1986.

Amongst his other interests he includes a continuing (but non-participating) interest in rugby, a modest involvement in tennis, a general enjoyment of swimming and a personal commitment to reading. He and his wife Mary-Ellen have three children.

Foreword 3

by Niall W. Deasy, chairman of the centenary committee

A 100th birthday is always a unique occasion and all the more so for the Institute, coming as it has from small beginnings — a point made, I would hasten to add, with the greatest of respect to the founding fathers — to its present substantial status in terms of numbers, influence and the breadth of experience of its membership.

To mark this important occasion my committee and I arranged for the publication of a commemorative volume which would be made available to all of the members of our Institute and other interested parties.

We were keen to avoid simply updating Howard Robinson's excellent history of the Institute, which was published in 1983, and so we decided that the volume would describe the environment in which the Irish chartered accountant works at the present time and also offer an admittedly selective demonstration of the varied roles and guises in which the Irish chartered accountant operates.

The contents of this volume reflect these objectives.

- Cornelius Smith, a distinguished past president of our Institute, has prepared a short chronology of significant events in the Institute's history over the last 100 years.
- Dermot McAleese of the economics department of Trinity College Dublin, a member of the board of the Central Bank and one of the country's most experienced economists has summarised the state of the nation in economic terms, thereby offering the reader the necessary backdrop to the Ireland in which the Irish chartered accountant works.
- The varied influences affecting the work of the Irish professional chartered accountant are described by Timothy Quin and Michael Lafferty. Timothy Quin is a senior member in practice in Belfast and until recently, was a member of the council of the Institute; whereas Michael Lafferty is the London-based publisher of a number of accounting and financial journals including the well-known magazine *The Accountant*. Although Michael Lafferty was born in Ireland, he is paradoxically (perhaps?) a member of the Institute of Chartered Accountants in England and Wales.
- The international influences affecting the Irish chartered accountant are described by Margaret Downes and Alistair Duff. Margaret Downes who describes the European influences, is well remembered as the first woman president of the Irish Institute. She was recently elected the first president of Fédération des Experts Comptables Européens (FEE).

- Alistair Duff, who is a Canadian chartered accountant, is particularly well placed to outline the North American influences which affect the Irish chartered accountant. He was born in Co. Tyrone and educated in Belfast, which adds further relevance, if not feeling, to his comments. He will be president of the Canadian Institute of Chartered Accountants during the Irish Institute's centenary year.

- Women are becoming chartered accountants in increasing numbers and now represent a significant segment of the membership of the Irish Institute. Patricia Barker, who is a member of the Institute and a lecturer in accounting in the National Institute for Higher Education in Dublin, describes the way in which women have responded to the challenges and opportunities which are afforded to an Irish chartered accountant.

- Vivian Nathan, who is a well-known member in practice in Cork, reviews the role of the member in practice who is more typically concerned with smaller clients and their businesses.

- Technology, in particular information technology, is probably the greatest single agent of change facing the role and work of the Irish chartered accountant. Tony Furlong, who is managing director of IBM Ireland and a member of the Chartered Institute of Management Accountants is ideally placed to assess this factor.

- The training of the Irish chartered accountant has always been a matter of priority interest to the Irish Institute and its members. Anthony Walsh, who is head of the School of Accounting and Finance at the National Institute for Higher Education in Dublin, outlines the present state of this highly fluid topic.

- The many and varied roles of the Irish chartered accountant in industry and elsewhere are described by Gerald Dempsey. He was the first president of the Institute drawn from the industrial stream of the Irish chartered accountancy profession and he is presently a director of some of the leading businesses in this country.

- Finally, Diarmuid Ó Cearbhaill, who is a former dean of the faculty of commerce and currently lecturer in economics and commerce in University College Galway, has written in Irish on the matter of the use of minority languages in the EEC.

These essays are of necessity a selective demonstration of the state of the art of the Irish chartered accountancy profession at the time of its 100th birthday. Some members may be aggrieved that their special interest or field of endeavour has not been dealt with and, if so, we apologise for any such omission.

If anything, the range of topics touched on demonstrates the breadth of experience of the members of the Irish Institute and in particular the many ways in which the Institute's professional education and training has enabled our members to achieve their own fulfilment while also contributing to the development of our community.

I believe that these two things — personal fulfilment, and the opportunity for community development — are above all what Institute membership offers, and they are positive and rewarding. The development of our Institute and profession is both a cumulative and on-going process and I have no doubt that the future agenda of the Institute will further strengthen and enhance members' ability to attain these goals.

This volume then is intended to demonstrate where we are now and I hope readers will find it to be both a useful and enjoyable publication in this regard.

In concluding, may I express my thanks to David Rowe for his commitment and dedication to the organisation and development of this volume, and to his hard-working committee members (Eleanor Jenkins, Cornelius Smith, and John Davey) who have also contributed so handsomely to its preparation. May I also express my appreciation to the contributors for their thoughtful and varied essays.

Finally, sincere thanks to our sponsors who are listed on page 255 and without whose support this volume would not have been possible.

---

100 years ago

Absurd public view of accountants' work

Regret may, perhaps, be expressed at what appears to be a want of faith and of hope in the work and the capabilities of the members of that profession of which Mr. Griffiths is so eminent a member. It is perhaps well to disclaim the absurd opinions entertained in some quarters of the nature and scope of an accountant's work, and it is also necessary to protest against the injustice of the wholesale denunciations against auditors indulged in by the press and the public on occasions when an unscrupulous rogue has carried his plans into effect. These are correctives which are now and then required, though perhaps sparingly and on occasions few and far between. But when Mr. Griffiths becomes more specific, and proceeds to refer to bank audits, and gives his estimate of what an auditor can really do, we notice a diffidence, an utter lack of vitality, which we should say cannot be a faithful index to the mind of the speaker.

The Accountant, 2 January 1886

Editorial Introduction

by David Rowe

THIS book is a lasting memento of the centenary of the Institute. We intended that it would be a pleasant book to pick up and browse through, something at once dignified and yet colourful and a little intriguing. We talked of a 'coffee-table' book. It is not quite that, if by that description one thinks of a book too big and awkward to put on your shelf. Nevertheless, it has some of the qualities of the genre.

It was intended also as an historical document. Sometime in the future an historian will be seeking to assess the trends of the late twentieth century, the quality of life and professional practice in those days, the feel and smell and taste of the world of chartered accountancy. I think he will find a lot of what he wants in this book.

But it has turned out to be more than that. I presume that all of the things said herein have been said elsewhere. Gathered together their impact is immense. It is not glib to say again what is said here many times: the changes taking place now are revolutionary, and the Institute and all its members will need to plan for these changes, to face them, and to adapt to them with imagination and flexibility.

Again and again themes come hammering through: the opening up of the financial services world to competition; the invasion of each others' territories by banks, insurance companies, investment advisors, accountants and others; the need for specialisation; the adequacy of self-regulation; the protection of ethics and standards; the impact of technology and so on. It is true to say that a small institute in a small country can be — and indeed in some ways has been — flexible enough to give a lead.

I have been more than impressed at the quality of writing of people who are not professional writers. I feel tempted to pick out a number of essays for particular mention, but if I did so I might end up by picking them all. So I shall confine myself to giving special mention to the 'centenarian' Timothy Quin. His essay is not necessarily the easiest to read, but it is the key essay in this volume, and careful study of it will not be wasted time, for it is incisive, far-reaching, imaginative and challenging.

Finally there are those whom I must thank. In particular I must thank Niall Deasy and the members of his centenary committee who have given me the opportunity of associating my name with this book. I feel like the little bird on the eagle's back, only in this case there are many eagles. Then there are the members of my little advisory group. Nobody will feel that it is invidious if I give special mention to Cornelius Smith, whose erudition, immense knowledge of the profession, incisive analysis of material, and unstinting devotion of his time virtually qualify him to be designated the real editor! Eleanor Jenkins, the Institute librarian, and John Davey, whose experience in the publishing world was invaluable, both gave their time and advice. Ben Lynch, with his background as editor of *Accountancy Ireland* and his in-depth knowledge of the educational scene, gave help and advice. Roger Hussey, director of the Institute, and Robin Donovan, secretary, gave much support, and many useful suggestions. I should mention Bernadette O'Connell, and Patricia Roarke, whose aid was always readily available in the world of typing, telexing, faxing, copying and all the other secretarial support one needs in a venture of this sort. Finally, the patient staff of Gill and Macmillan, under Michael Gill's good humoured leadership; Bobbie Reeners who organised the photographs; and my good friend Jan de Fouw, who designed the book.

PERSONAL PROFILE

David Rowe, F.C.A., A.C.M.A.

Born in Wexford in 1920, David Rowe served articles with Harry H. Forsyth, qualifying in 1942, and becoming a partner in 1943. Subsequently Forsyth & Co. merged with Kennedy Crowley & Co., and then with Stokes Brothers & Pim; David became the technical partner in Stokes Kennedy Crowley & Co. (SKC) until his retirement in 1980.

He then went to Lesotho to help set up the Centre for Accounting Studies there — an Irish bilateral aid project managed by SKC at that time — of which he is still the technical consultant to the Department of Foreign Affairs.

David was chairman of the Dublin Society of Chartered Accountants in 1967-8, and later served as Irish representative on the Auditing Practices Committee of the Consultative Council for the Accountancy Bodies.

He is honorary secretary of An Taisce, the National Trust for Ireland, and chairman of the Agency for Personal Services Overseas. He enjoys cartooning — for the Leinster Society of Chartered Accountants — orienteering, a little mild rock-climbing, and a cottage in Clare. He and his wife Veronica have three children.

Tax evasion — Irish style

Annals of the masters, A.D. 1213

Fionn O'Brolchain, the steward of O'Donnell (Donal More), went to Connaught to collect O'Donnell's tribute [tax]. He first went to Carbury, of Drumcliffe, where he visited, along with his attendants, the house of the poet, Muireagh O'Daly, of Lissadill. On coming into the poet's presence, he betrayed appearances of fear and caution before him, as he was a man of gigantic strength, and as his master had advised him to beware of the poet. O'Daly became enraged on seeing him, and, seizing a sharp axe, he struck him a blow, and slew him on the spot, and then fled into Clanrickard, being afraid of O'Donnell. When O'Donnell obtained intelligence of this, he collected his forces and pursued him, and did not rest until he arrived at the place afterwards called Derry O'Donnell, in Clanrickard (so named because O'Donnell encamped there for the night,) when he began to devastate the country by fire and sword, until, Mac William (de Burgo) at last submitted to him, having previously sent Muireagh into Thomond for refuge. O'Donnell pursued him thither, and proceeded to plunder and lay waste that country also, whereupon Donogh Cairbreach O'Brien sent Muireagh from him for protection to the people of Limerick, to the gates of which O'Donnell pursued him, and, pitching his camp at Moin-ui-Donnell (O'Donnell's Marsh, so called from that circumstance) laid seige to the city, upon which the inhabitants, at the command of O'Donnell, expelled Muireagh, who found no protection, but was sent from place to place, until he arrived at Dublin. O'Donnell after his pursuit, and his visitation of all Connaught, returned home, and having mustered another force with all possible speed, in the same year marched to Dublin, and compelled the inhabitants to banish Muireagh to Scotland; whilst there, the poet composed three poems in praise of O'Donnell, and requesting peace and pardon for his crime. The third poem commences thus: 'Oh! Donal, benevolent hand of peace.' Muireagh obtained pardon on account of his laudatory poems, and O'Donnell afterwards received him into his friendship, and with his usual generosity gave him lands and possessions.

What reason for such wrath can be?
The rascal bandied words with me
I took an axe and hewed him down —
Small matter for a prince's frown.

A Century Young by Cornelius F. Smith

A Comparativ

Cornelius F. Smith, F.C.A., I.C.A.E.W., C.A. Sco.

Cornelius F. Smith — 'Neil' to his friends — was born at Crossdowney, Co. Cavan in 1918 and was educated at Clongowes.

He commenced practice with the late Kevin Briscoe in 1947 and finally retired from Deloitte Haskins & Sells in 1978. His son Martin is a partner there.

He served as president of the Institute of Chartered Accountants in Ireland in 1973-4. He supports the Irish Institute as being a most constructive element for progress and an evolutionary ingredient of that 'Noosphere' identified by Teilhard de Chardin.

Social history research has been an abiding interest. In this he has been assisted as always by his wife Rhona.

Year	Accounting Events in Ireland
B.C. Third Millennium	Astronomical observations.
A.D. 6th century	Brehon Laws codified.
11th Century	Tallysticks and coinage used by Norse traders in Dublin.
15th Century	Audited accounts for city of Dublin.
17th Century	First Irish work on book-keeping. S. Ammonet
1798	Seven accountants practising in Dublin. Bank of Ireland opens.
1840-50	Bankruptcy and Company Acts.
1860s	J. H. Woodworth and Craig Gardner practising in Dublin. Prof. George Boole, Q U Cork, father of computer maths.
1870s	Irish Bankruptcy Act 1872.
1887	Non-Irish auditors appointed for banks and Guinness & Co.

'The essential dates of history may be, for a long time, a secret' J. L. Borges

Chronology of Accounting in Ireland

		General History	Year
Elsewhere	Irish	World History	
Abacus. Accounting records in Babylon.	Great passage tombs constructed in Boyne Valley.	Pyramid in Egypt.	B.C. Third Millennium
Greek banking records.	Brendan the Navigator discovers America.	Justinian code of civil law.	A.D. 6th Century
Domesday Book.	Norse defeated at Clontarf, Dublin.	Norman conquest of England.	11th Century
Fra. Pacioli — treatise on book-keeping.	Development of post-medieval trade and agriculture.	Leonardo da Vinci.	15th Century
First accountant in practice: G. Watson, Edinburgh.	Ulster plantations. Battle of Boyne. Huguenot diaspora.	Halley's Comet. Lloyd's insurance.	17th Century
Income tax first introduced.	Rebellion — Antrim and Wexford. Canals in operation.	Napoleonic wars.	1798
First Charter, Edinburgh CA 1853.	Great Famine — Population halved. Railways constructed.	Crimean War 1854-5.	1840-50
Typewriter invented. (Telephone 1876).	Financial crisis. Overend and Gurney Bank failure.	American Civil War. Federal income tax introduced.	1860s
Institute of Chartered Accountants formed in London. (Charter 1880). Montreal Association of Accounts 1880	Northern industries expand. Land war.	Karl Marx 'Das Kapital'. Franco-Prussian War.	1870s
American Assoc. of Public Accountants formed. (AICPA 1896).	Parnell/Gladstone's Home Rule Bill defeated.	Benz motoring in Mannheim.	1887

Year	Accounting Events In Ireland
1888	ICAI Royal Charter — Signatories
	Belfast 12
	Cork 6
	Dublin 13
	Other associates <u>11</u>
	<u>42</u>
1890s	Partnership Act 1890
	£50 premium for articled clerks deemed appropriate by ICAI.
1900s	Belfast Society of ICAI formed 1906.
	Dublin Accountants Students Society formed 1908 (DSCA 1928).
1912	Ethical Code develops.
1914-18	Higher taxes cause tax consultancy. Michael Collins and McGraths employed by Craig Gardner.
1921-2	Income tax and cost accounts in Syllabus Consumer Price Index 5 (Base 100 — 1982).
1925	Eileen Woodworth — first Irish lady chartered accountant.
1929	ICAI offices at 41-42 Dawson Street 1928-50.
1933-4	Hollerith accounting at ESB.
1938	Jubilee — 50 years a' growing. Membership 41
1939-45	Clery v Shott. Liquidator justified.

I
C
A
I

Ogham writing c. AD 400

Elsewhere	*Irish*	*World History*	*Year*
		General History	
Financial Times published. Leading cases on auditing.	Belfast riots. Munster dairy trade expands. Dunlop re-invents pneumatic tyre.	Inventions alter society — Electrical, chemical, telephones, Kodak, Hollerith.	1888
CPA Act 1896. New York.	Parnell -O'Shea divorce. First Triple Crown. IRFU 1894.	Alfred Marshall 'Economics'. Klondike gold rush.	1890s
Companies Act provided for audit.	Local Government democratised.	Boer War 1899-1902.	
'Journal of Accounting' 1905 published.	Wyndham Acts end Land War.	San Francisco earthquake 1906.	1900s
Companies Consolidation Act 1908 increased demand for audits.	'Titanic' — keel laid (1909).	'Model T' Ford produced 1908.	
Registration of Accountants — Bill failed.	Home Rule Bill and Trade Unions produce turmoil.	Federal income taxes USA now important.	1912
War contracts develop cost accounting.	Ulster Volunteers arm 1914. IRA Rebellion 1916.	World War.	1914-18
Consolidated accounts reporting.	Irish Free State and Northern Ireland established.	Bolsheviks triumph in Russia.	1921-2
Major accounting firms expand.	Shannon electricity scheme planned.	Mussolini and Nazis emerge.	1925
International Congress New York. (A. Muir and G. Brock attended).	De Valera accepts IFS Dáil.	Wall Street Crash. World depression.	1929
Royal Mail S P case established 'true and fair' concept.	Protection of home industries.	Securities and Exchange Act, 1934 (SEC).	1933-4
5th Congress. Berlin.	Chamberlain/De Valera agreement ends 'Economic War'.	Chamberlain visits Hitler.	1938
First accounting 'recommendations'. ICAEW 1942.	'The Emergency'. Eire neutral. N. Ireland prospers.	World War II. Atomic Bombs.	1939-45

Year	Accounting Events In Ireland
1950	Purchased 7 Fitzwilliam Place £8,050. Sold £340,800 in 1984.
1952	6th Congress visitors entertained in Ireland.
1957	Integration — Incorporated Society. Merged membership 1,340.
1963	Gerard O'Brien — first Professor of Accounting in Ireland.
1964	'History of Accountants in Ireland'. H. W. Robinson.
1965	Proposal for fellowship by examination defeated.
1969	'Accountancy Ireland' replaces Members Bulletins (1961).
1970	Integration proposals supported by ICAI (defeated by ICAEW).
1974	CCAB (I) set up.
1976	Ethics Code stresses independence and publicity.
1978	8th Congress UEC in Dublin. 1,400 delegates etc.
1979	Current cost accounting (SSAP 16 — ASC). Inflation 17%.
	Lesotho Accountancy Centre founded by Ireland.
1982	Integration scheme for Ireland deemed impractical.

Elsewhere	*Irish*	*World History*	
Conflict between CPA and US Bar Association.	Recession causes emigration.	Korean War.	1950
UEC founded (1951).	'Welfare State' benefits NI.	Contraceptive pill made.	1952
CA Joint Standing Committee.	Economic Programme — Lemass/Whitaker.	Treaty of Rome signed.	1957
CA bodies join UEC.	Companies Act ROI.	President Kennedy assassinated.	1963
Accountants' 'mega-mergers'.	Free Trade pact — UK/ ROI.	Berkeley Campus disturbances.	1964
Accountants International Study Group (IASC 1973).	O'Neill visits Lemass.	Cultural Revolution in China.	1965
More accounting standards called for.	Civil Rights Movement NI.	US first man on moon.	1969
First SSAP issued by 6 Accounting Bodies (ASC).	Treaty of Accession EEC — 1971-3	US announce withdrawals, Vietnam.	1970
Reciprocal membership agreement — 3 Institutes CA.	Power-sharing executive collapses, NI.	OPEC oil crisis.	1974
Auditing Practices Committee set up. Peer review required for SEC practice.	British ambassador assassinated.	Carter succeeds Nixon.	1976
International Federation of Accountants (IFAC) in Munich.	Norse site excavations at Wood Quay.	Moss/Metcalf congress enquiry AICPA.	1978
American accountants allow advertising. Non-practising officers appointed by AICPA.	Charles Haughey FCA Taoiseach. (Again in 1987).	Margaret Thatcher's Government UK.	1979
Ethics encompasses professional incompetence.	EMS. Ireland breaks link with Sterling.	Islamic fundamentalists rule Iran and hold hostages.	
IASC and IFAC agree at Mexican WA Congress.	De Lorean cars collapse. Triple Crown, IRFU.	James Joyce centenary.	1982

Times Past

The first number of a monthly journal, entitled '£.S.D. – *The Irish Financial Review*', has just been published. The paper as its name implies, is devoted to Irish financial news. Stock Exchange intelligence, company business, and in fact all matters in which Irish capital is concerned, are dealt with in its columns. The issue, which is illustrated, and contains as a frontispiece a photograph of the President of the Dublin Stock Exchange, is extremely creditable; it is published by Messrs. Wilson, Hartnell, and Co., Commercial Buildings, Dublin. A series of articles entitled 'Reminiscences of the Dublin Stock Exchanges,' by Frank E. DeBedet, is commenced in this number. A feature of the publication will be a Bureau of Financial Information.

The Irish Times, 13 February 1897

Where is it?

No copies of £.S.D. – *The Irish Financial Review* have been traced at the National Library of Ireland, Trinity College or the Stock Exchange. What happened to it?

Year	Accounting Events In Ireland
1983	First lady president, Margaret Downes. Training in industry introduced.
1984	Move to Ballsbridge from 7 Fitzwilliam Place. Advertising permitted.
1985	Institute of Accounting Technicians of Ireland first AGM.
1986	IASC meets in Dublin.
1987	Final Admitting Examinatic re-structured.
1988	Centenary celebrations Membership c600 IA Technicians c 22

BELLO: (Squats, with a grunt, on Bloom's upturned face, puffing cigar-smoke, nursing a fat leg) I see Keating Clay is elected chairman of the Richmond Asylum and bytheby Guinness's preference shares are at sixteen three quarters. Curse me for a fool that I didn't buy that lot **Craig and Gardener** told me about. Just my infernal luck, curse it. And that Goddamned outsider *Throwaway* at twenty to one. *(He quenches his cigar angrily on Bloom's ear)* Where's that Goddamned cursed ashtray?

James Joyce, *Ulysses*

Elsewhere	*Irish*	*World History*	
EEC directives regulate accounting.	Shergar is kidnapped.	Lebanon destroyed by civil war.	1983
Three institutes of CA formalise co-operation.	GAA centenary.	President Reagan visits Ballyporeen.	1984
Inflation accounting shelved. CPI + 5%.		Miners strike, UK.	
Reports on fraud. Information technology — first statement.	Anglo-Irish Agreement approved.	AIDS recognised as world health problem.	1985
Professional negligence litigation explodes.	Single European Act envisages tax harmonisation.	Congress/SEC presses auditors to reconsider: (1) Fraud detection. (2) Survivability forecasts. (3) Conflicts of interest (MAS).	1986
HM Government pressures tend towards a more united profession. AICPA Centenary. 240,000 members. Half are women. Half are not in public practice.	Unemployment ROI NI } 19% +		1987
	Millennium Dublin city.	Australia bi-centenary.	1988

The Financial Times.

"Without Fear and Without Favour."
DAILY.
With which is Incorporated the "LONDON FINANCIAL GUIDE."

New Series.—No. 1] LONDON, MONDAY, FEBRUARY 13, 1888. [ONE PENNY.

The Friend OF — THE HONEST FINANCIER. THE BONA FIDE INVESTOR. THE RESPECTABLE BROKER. THE GENUINE DIRECTOR. THE LEGITIMATE SPECULATOR.

The Enemy OF — THE CLOSED STOCK EXCHANGE. THE UNPRINCIPLED PROMOTER. THE COMPANY WRECKER. THE "GUINEA PIG." THE "BULL" THE "BEAR." THE GAMBLING OPERATOR.

7 Fitzwilliam Place, Dublin

Pictured above are the present offices of the Institute at 87-89 Pembroke Road, Dublin. The painting on the previous page is of the office occupied by the Institute from 1952 to 1984. The first issue of the Irish supplement to the *Accountant* of 12 January 1952 reported as follows: 'In the course of 120 years the house has had ten previous owners. Perhaps the most eminent of these was Mr Seton Pringle, the Dublin surgeon, who used it as his residence and consulting rooms from 1913 until his retirement in 1944, the longest tenancy recorded. Those looking for property in this district of Dublin today will read with melancholy interest that so depressed was the market in 1894, the premises changed hands in that year for the incredibly low sum of £50. The difference between this and the cost to the Institute — £7,850 plus fees, legal expenses and stamp duty — cannot wholly be attributed to the fall in the value of money in the past fifty-seven years.' The building was sold by the Institute in 1984 for £340,000, with, of course, the addition of the library which had been built in the rere.

The Institute of Chartered Accountants in Ireland

The second annual report of the above institute does not appear to be very encouraging. The total income for the year 1889 was £410 11s., out of which no less a sum than £231 was received for entrance fees. Unless there are more accountants, and accountants' clerks in Ireland eligible to be admitted under the Institute's regulations, than we are aware of, the income under this head must speedily be reduced to vanishing point. The president, Mr. Gardener, J.P., resigned his office during the year and withdrew from the Institute under circumstances our readers are already familiar with. We had hoped better things of the Irish accountants, but, although they consider professional Home Rule best for their interests, it is a pity they imitate all the worst features of the Institute of Chartered Accountants in England and Wales.

From *The Incorporated Accountants Journal*, June 1890, the very first issue of the journal which subsequently became *Accountancy*

Ireland today: fish farming

Ireland today: Waterford crystal

Ireland today: The National Stud, Co. Kildare

Editorial Introduction to 'The Irish economy: perspectives, problems and prospects'

The Irish chartered accountant is inevitably moulded by the society which uses his services, and reacts to the economic developments taking place about him. Truly to understand *his* evolution, therefore, one needs to understand what is happening in his economic environment. Dermot McAleese analyses in this essay the significant trends in the Republic of Ireland.

Ireland is one of the poorest members of the 'rich man's club'. Even with that status it is eight times better off than the average 'third world' country and 'immeasurably better off than it was a century ago'. Yet its rate of growth has been much less than that of most of the other members of the 'club'. Why is that? Professor McAleese quotes Kieran A. Kennedy: 'Small scale, though often a disadvantage, does have one great advantage if we have the resolution to grasp it, namely that a small country which is sufficiently innovative and flexible can still find adequate markets abroad even in relatively stagnant conditions.' The country, McAleese says, has a young population which is well educated and eager to work; the social infrastructure is well developed; inflation in 1987 was down to three per cent; 'membership of the European Community offers a firm basis of support for policies of adjustment'. Why then, in 1988, is the country in the doldrums with unemployment approaching twenty per cent? Why has there been 'a lack of dynamic response from indigenous firms?'

McAleese points to many factors, amongst which he refers to 'counter-productive policies in the labour market'; an assumption in the good years that growth would continue indefinitely; a consequent emphasis on spending rather than on generating wealth; a 'quixotic' endeavour to equate Irish social services with others in the 'club'; a series of weak and indecisive

---

As my father was the shrewdest of men and had provided most of the capital it was he who kept the stores, that is to say, his cellar, and kept the accounts, that is to say, a double-entry system in which he would put down only some of the receipts and a little more of the expenditures, deducting good tithes for himself here and there.

Jean Baptiste Castor Fabre (1727-83), *Jean-L'Ont-Pris*

governments; failure to plan for a foreseeable population growth; unrest in Northern Ireland; formidable tax levels; and by implication, the failure of indigenous industry to be innovative, flexible and dynamic.

Of the future, McAleese asks, can the private sector lead a recovery while the public sector of the economy is held in check? There are, he thinks, three pillars on which growth may be built: one, manufacturing industry will have to resume the momentum of previous decades; two, agriculture will become more diversified, with an increased emphasis on quality products; and three, quality services will need development — for example in specialised tourism, and export-oriented financial services. 'Flexibility of response to changes in the international environment is recognised as a key desideratum of successful performance'. He does not suggest that the transformation of the Irish economy will be an easy task, but he certainly offers hope that it can be done.

Despite recession Irish accountancy has remained a buoyant profession. To hold that position in the future, the profession, perhaps more than any other, would need to heed that note — flexibility of response.

Dermot McAleese, B.Comm., M.Econ.Sc., M.A., Ph.D.

Dermot McAleese is Whately Professor of Political Economy at Trinity College, Dublin.

He has written extensively on Irish economic policy and has published articles on foreign investment, industrial policy and international trade.

He is a director of the Central Bank of Ireland, a member of the council of the Statistical and Social Inquiry Society of Ireland, a member of the executive and council of the Economic and Social Research Institute and he has served on numerous government advisory groups and committees.

The Irish economy: perspectives, problems and prospects

by Dermot McAleese

THE Irish economy is classified by the World Bank as a member of the exclusive group of industrial market economies, which includes, among others, the US, Japan, Germany and Switzerland. This reflects the fact that Irish living standards bear comparison with the standards of the world's strongest economies. True, average income per head in Ireland is the lowest (except for Spain) of all the industrial market economies. In 1987, average Irish income per head was IR£4,700, equivalent then to $6,800. This represented a standard of living equal to one-third of the US level, one-half of the Japanese level and over sixty per cent of the UK level. Even this lowly position in the rich man's club, however, still leaves Ireland eight times better off than the average third world economy and over forty-five times better off than Ethiopia.[1]

In terms of absolute living standards, Irish people are immeasurably better-off than they were a century ago. The major economic breakthrough occurred after the second world war, particularly in the period from the late 1950s to the early 1970s which in retrospect appears more and more like a golden age. The result is that the Irish are better fed and better housed, enjoy better health and are better clothed than at any time in their history.

Despite all this, the present mood of the country is anything but complacent. Historians such as Professor Joseph Lee remind us that while Ireland grew in prosperity, its West European neighbours were doing likewise — and at a much more rapid pace:

> no other economy in the whole of Europe appears to have experienced remotely so slow a growth of its total gross national product in the twentieth century.... Our standard of living has, of course, risen since independence. But it has risen far less than that of any other European country, except Britain.[2]

Only in the 1960s did Ireland's economic growth approach that of continental Europe for any sustained period and the 1980s have once again been years of relative decline.

Economic performance during the 1980s has been disappointing in both relative and absolute terms. Future historians will find this performance elegantly and comprehensively documented in a report by the National Economic and Social Council, *Strategy for Development 1986-1990,* published in

1986. This report identifies many weaknesses in the economy — unemployment at about twenty per cent of the workforce, renewal of emigration, weakening of industrial investment, sluggish agricultural growth, a creaking tax system. Dominating the discussion, part-cause and part-consequence of our economic ills, is the problem of public finances. Exchequer borrowing and the domestic and external debt of the public sector have reached record heights. Relative to GNP, Ireland has a higher external debt than many of the more spectacular cases of debt-ridden third world countries.

One consequence of this concern with public finances has been to elevate familiar maxims such as 'balancing the books' and 'making ends meet' to an unexpectedly high position on the nation's political agenda. Members of the accountancy profession reading over Dáil debates will be surprised to find not themselves but the government criticised for being 'obsessed with book-keeping', transforming what might be seen as a virtuous reflection of professional over-eagerness into a term of political abuse! Economists, accountants, numbers-men in general, have become rather unpopular in the Ireland of the 1980s as the grim implications of their emphasis on the need to bring government expenditure into line with government revenue have been revealed. The messengers are being blamed for the bad news.

An essay such as this must try to take a broad and a long-term view. This means that we must not be overly influenced by present problems. There has been throughout Irish history a tendency to alternate between the belief that the country is going to the dogs and that it has a wonderful future. Just as the country's problems have their root in history, so do the country's possibilities. There is much that is good and hopeful about contemporary Ireland which the justifiable concern about dismal macroeconomic indicators must not be allowed to obscure.

Deployment of resources

The main yardstick of an economy's increase in prosperity is its gross national product (GNP). This will increase over time as a result of increases in productivity, or of more workers being employed, or of some combination of these two. In Ireland, productivity has increased dramatically, so that even with exactly the same work force as in 1961, national output would have been 2.36 times as great by 1985. In actual fact, output in 1985 was 2.49 times that of 1961, the extra margin coming from the small increase in the number employed over the period. By and large, therefore, the increase in output has been accounted for by productivity gains. The labour force has not increased, mainly because emigration has siphoned off the annual net additions to the population.

These developments have been associated with marked changes in the structure of the labour force.

TABLE 1   *Labour force 1961-85*

Employment in ...	1961	1981	1985
		Percentages	
AGRICULTURE	35	19	13
INDUSTRY	22	29	24
SERVICES	37	44	46
OUT OF WORK	6	8	17
TOTAL	100	100	100

Source: *National Income and Expenditure,* Central Statistics Office, Dublin

The most striking feature is the decline in the agricultural sector. Over one-third of the labour force was absorbed by this sector in 1961 compared with only thirteen per cent in 1985. As the Irish have become better-off they have become more urbanised. Those remaining on the land have also changed. They have become vastly more productive through use of up-to-date capital equipment, more efficient allocation of material inputs and better farm management techniques. The thatched cottage, the horse-and-trap and days of haymaking have given way to the less evocative but more utilitarian two-storeyed houses, tractors and silage.

The falling share of the workforce in agriculture has been associated with a rising proportion in industry (at least until 1981) and services. Ireland has become more industrialised as well as more urbanised. Until the shake-out of industry during the recent past, it was possible to refer to a significant rise in manufacturing employment. Industrial output growth was particularly rapid, much of it related to the establishment of new export-oriented industries. Both the absolute level of productivity and its rate of growth were very high in industry. Thus, the quarter of the workforce in this sector in 1985 produced no less than thirty-five per cent of GNP.

Services have increased steadily both as a share of output in the economy and as a percentage of employment. Some sections of the services industry are part of the traded sector, tourism being the obvious example. Other sections, such as accountancy, banking and insurance, provide direct services to the consumer and also play an important role as inputs into the traded goods sector (agriculture, industry and directly traded services).

The growth in the accountancy profession is an excellent example of the increased demand caused by the growth in traded activities. Other examples in private sector services would include everything from contract cleaners to management consultants. A high proportion of total employment growth in services was attributable to the expansion of public sector activity, notably in the fields of health, education, social welfare and security. Productivity in the services sector is notoriously difficult to measure. National income data indicate that it is higher on average than that in agriculture but lower than industry. However, clearly the range of variation around this average is very wide.

While the redeployment of labour has so far been analysed in terms of its contribution to higher living standards, a major development since 1981 has been the huge increase in the numbers of the labour force categorised as 'out-of-work'. The proportion of unemployed rose from eight per cent in 1981 to seventeen per cent in 1985 and by 1987 it was approaching twenty per cent of the labour force. Officially, these people's productivity is zero. The growth in unemployment has appeared as a searing symbol of failure, as emigration did in the 1950s. Then we had books such as Fr O'Brien's *The Vanishing Irish,* predicting the eventual disappearance of the Irish race due to emigration. In 1987, there is Raymond Crotty's *Ireland in Crisis,* in a second edition, forecasting the collapse of the Irish economy as a result of massive unemployment and crushing debt. The actual degree of suffering of the emigrants or the unemployed is not the point at issue. Clearly it differs between different groups. Ireland, in any event, in the 1980s experienced large increments both in numbers unemployed *and* in numbers emigrating. To some, the apparent inability to provide more productive employment for larger numbers is seen as a symptom of deep-seated, long-running problems of the Irish economy which were papered over but not resolved by the post war growth. Others see Ireland's unemployment and slow growth as simply more severe manifestations of the European disease. They point to the high levels of unemployment prevailing in Britain, France and Germany, to the mismanagement of public sector finances in Ireland and to the adoption of inappropriate labour policies during the last fifteen years, the effects of which are only now being felt.[3].

Openness – the key to productivity growth

For a country of Ireland's small size, events in the international economy and the country's reaction to them are of critical importance. Hence, one obvious reason why Ireland prospered in the sixties is that world economic growth was unprecedentedly high. This meant that export markets were growing and that internationally oriented companies were looking actively for suitable locations for investment. When the western economies descended into an orbit of slower growth after 1973, the Irish economy followed, which again *prima facie* supports the thesis that external factors play a powerful role in determining Ireland's economic fortunes.

Of course, some trading partners are more important to Ireland than others. For long, the UK had been the dominant influence. In 1960, for example, three-quarters of Irish exports were sold to the UK and about half of Irish imports originated there. Over time, the degree of dependence on Britain has diminished sharply. By 1986, two-thirds of Irish exports were destined for markets outside the UK (Table 2). The diversification of Irish exports has clearly made the Irish economy more sensitive to global trends but the extent of decoupling between the British and Irish economies has been exaggerated.

TABLE 2

Composition of merchandise exports by area, 1960 and 1985

	(Percentages)	
AREA	*1960*	*1985*
UK	75	34
Continental EEC	6	38
Others	19	28

Source: *Trade Statistics of Ireland,* Central Statistics Office, Dublin.

British subsidiaries employed some fifteen per cent of the Irish manufacturing workforce in 1980. The two labour markets continue to be tightly interwoven and trade links, though diminished, are still very strong. The trade statistics on their own failed to capture the full dimension of inter-dependence of the two economies. For this reason, there was a serious under-estimation of the implications for Ireland of Mrs Thatcher's economic policies.[4]

Events outside the country, therefore, do matter for Ireland. But they do not explain everything. The Irish economy by and large responded very slowly to the upsurge in OECD growth in the 1950s and, during the 1980s, its growth performance also fell well behind the European average. At other times, for instance during the late 1970s, the Irish economy grew faster than average. Clearly domestic policies and national dispositions determine how the economy responds to external stimuli. Many would argue that domestic factors are the more important. As Professor Kennedy noted in his 1985 Busteed lecture:

> Small scale, though often a disadvantage, does have one great advantage if we have the resolution to grasp it, namely that a small country which is suf-ficiently innovative and flexible can still find adequate markets abroad even in relatively stagnant conditions.[5]

The importance of overseas markets was the major concern of Irish economic policy during the post-war period. Access to foreign markets was seen as the key to higher productivity and growth for the Irish economy. Foreign access to the Irish market was viewed as a means of ensuring that Irish industry and agriculture raised their standards of efficiency and kept up to date with modern technology. Market access was seen as an avenue of escape from the constraints of small size.

The major landmarks in the evolution of Irish external economic policy were, in chronological order, (a) the application for membership of the EEC in 1961, (b) the Anglo-Irish Free Trade Area Agreement (AIFTA) 1966, (c) accession to the EEC in 1973 and (d) the passing of the Single European Act referendum in May 1987. Each of these steps involved improved and more secure access for Irish exports. At first, the main emphasis was on food products which in 1961 accounted for almost two-thirds of Irish exports. The Common Agricultural Policy led to the virtual exclusion of Irish agricultural exports to the EEC market from 1964 until Ireland's accession, the conditions of entry into the UK market were unfavourable both in terms of price and uncertainty of access, and exports to the US and other countries were similarly hazardous. Getting behind the import restrictions was therefore seen as a strategic prerequisite for the development of Irish agriculture. In this regard, the really significant breakthrough did not occur until membership of the European Community was achieved. Then, and only then, was Ireland entitled as a matter of right — and not as part of a negotiated concession — to avail of the markets (and the higher prices) of the EEC member states. Moreover, instead of being a passive reactor to changes in agricultural policy determined elsewhere, the Irish government was henceforth able to participate actively in the formulation of the Common Agricultural Policy.

Irish agriculture did not, however, take off into any self-sustaining upsurge of growth as a result of membership. The share of agricultural goods in Irish exports fell steeply from sixty-one per cent in 1961 to twenty-three per cent in 1986. True, there was a pronounced shift in the type of goods exported, from live animals to processed foods, and in the geographical composition of export markets, from almost total reliance on the UK to greater penetration of continental EC. The prices earned on these exports were also substantially in excess of those which would have been obtainable on world markets. But the type of products which Irish farmers specialised in, mainly standardised dairy and beef products, were in excess supply within the Community and demand was growing very slowly. Hence freer trade in these products did not lead to a significant and sustained growth impulse. In retrospect, the effects of membership for agriculture can be seen as defensive rather than offensive. It saved the Irish farmer from being wiped out — as would certainly have occurred in a community which excluded Ireland but included the UK. But, by the nature of things, the CAP could not provide systematically improving long-term prospects for traditional Irish agriculture.

Market access was also seen as a vital element in the strategy for industrial development. Industrial tariffs have been declining steadily in the western world since the war and membership of GATT (in 1967) would probably alone have been sufficient to have enabled Ireland to benefit from these GATT round

The medieval court of Exchequer, late fourteenth century

reductions. The significance of AIFTA and the EEC related more to the security such agreements provided against the arbitrary imposition of non-tariff barriers. The security involved was not absolute — as the need for the Single European Act and completion of the internal market testifies — but it represented a considerable improvement relative to a position outside the Community. In contrast with the position in agriculture, market integration in the case of manufacturing industry resulted in the release of a new dynamic and the achievement of a sustained increase in growth. Manufactured exports rose from eighteen per cent of total Irish exports in 1961 to sixty-five per cent in 1986. This new dynamic was spearheaded not by indigenous Irish companies but mostly by manufacturing subsidiaries of overseas firms. Direct foreign investment played an exceptionally important role in Irish industrial development. Overseas subsidiaries employed some forty per cent of Ireland's total workforce in manufacturing and they accounted for most of the increase in Irish industrial exports during the past two decades. They were the powerhouse behind the huge increases in industrial productivity per worker to which we referred earlier. Ireland's experience shows that openness not only means access to foreign markets for indigenous producers of traded goods and services. It also enhances the ability of a country to attract scarce factors of production — such as technical expertise and marketing know-how — and put them to more productive use side-by-side with domestic resources.

Irish industrial policy had developed along coherent and consistent lines since the late fifties. As Eoin O'Malley noted:

> The most striking feature is the degree of continuity with the general direction of policy . . . This is not to say that no significant developments or elaborations have occurred. But once the intention was formed to join the wider free trade area that was expected to emerge in Europe, and the principle of priority for export-orientated industry had been accepted together with a willingness to encourage foreign investment to this end, most of the policies of the last two decades followed these decisions.[6]

The policies, of course, involved more than the pursuit of better market access. To encourage export industry, a package of fixed asset grants and tax incentives was devised. Grants of up to sixty per cent of fixed assets were available on certain projects and virtually all new exporters were able to avail of the export profit tax relief (EPTR) which exempted profits earned on manufactured exports from Irish corporate and personal tax. As from 1981, this has been revised to a concessionary ten per cent corporation profits tax on all profits earned by manufacturing companies irrespective of the destination of sales.

A disappointing feature of the development of Irish industry was the lack of dynamic response from indigenous firms. Indeed, the high casualty rate of these firms and the tendency of the survivors to maintain profits by shedding labour rather than by more rapid expansion of sales led to a searching debate about the underlying philosophy of industrial policy. A review of the position was commissioned by the National Economic and Social Council which led to the publication in 1982 of the Telesis report. While this report concluded that: 'the philosophy, approach, institutions and policies associated with Ireland's industrial development are fundamentally sound', it also recommended significant changes in emphasis 'designed to improve an otherwise excellent effort' (p. 35).[7] These included a substantial increase in funds devoted to the development of indigenous export business with a corresponding reduction in average grant payments to foreign firms. The recommended objective of giving priority to the promotion of strong internationally competitive firms integrated into the Irish economy has been accepted by the Irish authorities. This decision, however, was not a difficult one since slower growth of the world economy has diminished the number of firms seeking greenfield locations while competition between countries for the reduced supply of projects has increased. In other words, active encouragement of indigenous industry did not really entail showing prospective foreign investors to the door.

What went wrong?

A BBC programme on the Irish economy some years ago ended with the rhetorical question: have the Irish blown it? Certainly, it is remarkable how a country which was highly regarded as sensibly-run and successful in economic terms a decade ago could so swiftly decline in its own and others' estimation. Criticism of the economy reached a crescendo prior to the February 1987 general election with the *Sunday Times* picturing Ireland's plight as a third world country and the *Economist* pronouncing a devastating critique of Irish economic affairs and predicting further ruin if a Fianna Fáil government was elected to power.[8] The fact that the articles were exaggerated in tone, incorrect on many points of detail and, at the time of writing five months after the election, mistaken about the consequences of a Fianna Fáil victory, helps to put matters in perspective. But there is no denying the very real sense that problems of the utmost gravity have been allowed to develop and remain unresolved.

It is easy to overlook how quickly these problems overtook us. At end 1981, the National Debt was a tolerable £10 billion and unemployment 'only' eight per cent. Within the space of five years, debt had doubled and unemployment had risen to eighteen per cent. Specific external influences played an important part in accentuating the difficulties. High real and nominal interest rates transformed the cheap borrowing of the 1970s into an extremely expensive debt overhang in the early 1980s. Matters were not helped by the strength of the dollar (in which much of Irish debt was denominated) in those years. By the same token, the upsurge in Ireland's unemployment cannot be divorced from parallel experience in Britain. This lessened the effectiveness of the traditional safety valve of emigration.

The problems have not originated in Ireland's policy towards the external world. The arguments in favour of close integration with Europe remain as convincing now as they did thirty years ago. The Single European Act referendum sparked off a vigorous debate on the economic merits of completing the internal market (and a debate about other largely irrelevant matters such as Irish neutrality). The electorate voted two to one in favour of the SEA indicating their conviction that this strategic position is correct.

As far as industrial policy is concerned, there is general appreciation of the need to encourage Irish exporters and of the dangers of erosion of market access through non-tariff barriers. The principle of promoting direct foreign investment in Ireland has also received widespread endorsement, although questions have been raised as to possibilities of 'overkill' via the award of excessive grants to new enterprises and the proliferation of government support agencies. It is also possible to argue that greater priority should have been given earlier to the development of indigenous companies. Kennedy, for example, drew on the familiar fable to make the point:

> We staked our money on the hare of foreign enterprise rather than on the tortoise of native industry. The hare ran well for a time and impressive gains in output were achieved, with even more impressive gains in exports.... Yet the race is not always to the swiftest. The approach produced quick but no lasting results.... The industrial programme failed to dynamise the largest section of manufacturing — the domestic industries.... The foundations of the industrial superstructure therefore lacked depth.[9]

Nevertheless, Kennedy acknowledges that support for indigenous industry would have been more costly to implement as well as slower to yield results. Assistance was available to Irish firms, had they been in a position and willing to avail of it, on equivalent terms to the overseas subsidiary. Besides, Kennedy's verdict that foreign investment produced 'no lasting results' is surely too pessimistic. There have been significant improvements in labour and managerial capacity and in the general industrial infrastructure as a result of the influx of overseas subsidiaries.

All this points to the conclusion that the main sources of Ireland's problems lay in the non-traded rather than the traded sectors of the economy. The government being a major actor in the non-traded sectors must therefore fall under suspicion. But the problem went deeper than that, involving not alone excessive government expenditure but also inappropriate — even counterproductive — policies of government in the labour market which prevented increases in output from being translated into increases in employment. From these failings emerged the two major problems of contemporary Ireland — too much debt and too few jobs.

Turning to domestic factors, the sustained period of growth up to 1973 led Irish governments, and the Irish people, into the classical error of taking success for granted. It was assumed that growth would continue indefinitely. Successive governments concentrated on how to spend income rather than on how to generate it. According to Whitaker, the decision in 1972 to relax the convention of balancing the current budget — i.e. borrowing only for capital expenditure — marked a definite turning point.[10] Another candidate might be the 1973 coalition government's quixotic commitment to bringing about equality between the level of social services in the Republic and in Northern Ireland. This commitment was based on the premise that Ireland's *per capita* growth would continue to outpace the UK. In the heady optimism of the EEC entry debate and the pre-oil-crisis boom, it seemed not at all implausible but it ignored the inconvenient fact that, as of 1973, Irish GNP *per capita* was less than seventy per cent of the UK's. The 1977 election campaign with its extravagant promises and the subsequent abolition of rates on domestic dwellings and reduction in car taxes set the economy on an unsustainable course. A succession of weak and indecisive governments vacillated in dealing with the growing financial problems. They found it impossible to resist public sector unions and public expenditure lobbies, difficult to find sources of the revenue with which to finance increased expenditure — but all too easy to locate foreign banks willing to lend money at keen rates and without conditions.

Ireland's difficulties were compounded by the changing demographic features of the country. On the one side, there was the fall-off in emigration. Indeed this was followed by immigration for part of the seventies as workers returned from Britain to take up jobs in new factories. There was also some small net immigration from Northern Ireland. The changing immigration pattern was supplemented by the well-known tendency of the Irish to have large families. Although family size has tended to fall steeply, Ireland's total fertility rate is fifty per cent higher than the average for industrial economies. The net result was a population growth rate of 1.4 per cent *per annum* over the entire period 1965-80.

The population boom was foreseen but there was little by way of policy response. The NESC published a series of papers in the 1970s pinpointing the strains which the steep rise in the younger age groups would entail. The trouble was that few would accept that larger families might imply lower standards of living, and certainly lower standards of state-provided social services, than those pertaining in neighbouring countries. The consequence was that pressure for increased government expenditure on health, education and welfare built up both because of demographic pressure and because of a desire to emulate the social standards of Western Europe. The gap between the cost of provision of these social services and our national capacity to pay for them was made up by foreign borrowing. Through a process of incremental neglect, we reached a point where the combined tax/social welfare system discouraged the work ethic, self-reliance and innovation to an unprecedented extent, in a society where these qualities were never more urgently needed.

The tax system has been a sensitive and controversial issue in Ireland during the eighties. Although tax revenue fell persistently short of government expenditure, prevailing levels of taxation were generally felt to be intolerably high. In an effort to close the deficit, tax rates were increased during the early eighties and the tax revenues/GNP ratio rose rapidly. Income tax rates were not themselves so much the trouble as the fact that, in order to generate revenue, high rates appropriate to the rich and the very rich were applied at comparatively low income levels. For example single people with incomes of £10,000, not much in excess of the average industrial wage, paid a fifty-eight per cent marginal tax rate in 1987 and could have been paying much more than that a few years previously. A comparatively large percentage of Irish taxpayers paid above the standard rate. Furthermore, indirect taxes on alcohol, cigarettes, cars and certain white goods were also extremely high. General dissatisfaction was expressed through mass marches and constant lobbying of politicians by interested groups. This led to the establishment of a Commission on Taxation which, in a series of comprehensive and insightful reports, recommended: (a) a drastic reduction in income tax rates and their replacement by a single uniform rate combined with an expenditure tax, (b) simplification of the tax system by removal of tax credits and by reducing the number of different VAT rates, and (c) improved methods of collecting taxes. Some of the Commission's recommendations were accepted by the government, but by no means all.

Those who wish to change a system have a choice between staying in it and protesting vigorously (*voice*) or they can leave the system and exert pressure that way (*exit*). The Irish people used both forms of protest. We have already referred to the tax marches (significantly, there were no unemployment marches and no budget deficit marches) as expressions of voice. Exit was also evident in the form of (1) growth of the black economy, (2) escalation of smuggling and cross border trade, and (3) emigration. Exit was indeed a factor forcing change but it has been an undesirable phenomenon from an economic point of view. Old habits die hard. Once in the black economy, it is hard to return to the 'white' sector. Shopping in the North continues even though some of the more conspicuous opportunities for profit have been eliminated. And those who have emigrated because of high taxes are difficult to entice back. In these ways, the tax base is weakened and the burden on those who remain at home in the white economy grows heavier.

The tax system presents Ireland with a serious dilemma. The worldwide trend is towards lower taxes. Even Ireland's tax incentives to industry, diminished somewhat by the replacement of the export profits tax exemption by a ten per cent corporate profits tax in 1981, looks less enticing in the context of lower UK and US corporation profits taxes than they did a few years ago. As taxes are reduced abroad, *voice* and *exit* will combine to force similar measures on the Irish authorities. Yet the overall government financial position makes tax concessions hard to reconcile with fiscal responsibility. The only way out of the problem is by exerting even more downward pressure on government expenditure and by careful step-by-step 'costless' reform of the tax system. How these objectives will be achieved is no easy matter to judge.

An additional factor casting a dark shadow over the country has been the unrest in Northern Ireland. The continued activity of the IRA has involved the Republic in heavy additional security costs in patrolling the border, estimated at up to £200 million per annum. Additionally, the disrespect for the rule of law has spread southwards, causing an increase in violent crimes and a general deterioration in the quality of life in the Republic. A large proportion of those imprisoned in the Republic's jails for major crimes, ranging from bank robberies to possession of arms and kidnappings, are from Northern Ireland. The unrest in the North has also been costly in terms of lost tourist revenue and has damaged Ireland's reputation as a safe location in which to do business. The Irish government, of course, does all it can to distance itself from the North in relation to terrorism, a stance which rests rather uneasily with article 2 of the constitution claiming that 'they' are part of 'us'. In truth, it has proved impossible to insulate the Republic from the infection. In economic terms, the Republic has suffered more from the disturbances in the North than the North itself. The latter's costs are covered by grants from the UK exchequer whereas the Republic must meet the extra expenses out of taxation and borrowing.

Prospects for the future

Post-war Ireland adjusted successfully to the opportunities opened up by a faster growing world economy and a liberalised world trading system. In retrospect, it is clear that we were right to put resources into export promotion, right to dismantle protection, right to join the European Community and right to launch a full-blooded campaign for foreign investment. In recent times, we have failed dismally in two respects. First, we made minimal adjustment to the harsher international economic climate. Irish governments kept spending as if the world economy were experiencing a minor hiccup instead of a profound structural change. Second, the predictable, and fully predicted, rise in population met with no systematic policy response. At a time when every effort should have been made to make it possible for the huge influx of young people to find jobs, we were busy introducing legislation to make it more difficult for them. Married women were encouraged to stay in employment. Employers were burdened with more paper work and higher social security costs. Unfair dismissals legislation led to a plethora of tribunal cases brought against employers which discouraged hiring. Trade union immunities were added to by being extended to the public service at a time when we should have been curbing them.

The first step in solving problems is to identify them correctly. This has, I think, been done in contemporary Ireland. The spirit of the nation is a humbled and chastened version of that of a decade ago. A people not over-enamoured of change have come to realise that change must take place. As so often in our history, this realisation has come belatedly. The transformed economic climate in Britain has affected perceptions just as much, if not more, than the bleak reality of the domestic economy. Adjustment is necessary. The key question for the future is whether adjustment can be accompanied by growth. This boils down to asking if the private sector can lead a recovery while the public sector of the economy is held in check.

Growth in the private sector will be built around three pillars. First, *manufacturing industry* will have to grow faster — or rather resume the momentum of previous decades. There is ample scope for growth in terms of labour supply. A young well-educated population is more motivated towards business and more eager to work than at any time in Ireland's history. Marketing skills are improving, although competence in languages other than English is still a constraint. There are examples of outstanding business successes to serve as models; Smurfits, Cement-Roadstone, Baileys Irish Cream and Ballygowan. Foreign investment will continue to play an important role but domestic firms must play the leading part in the next development phase.

Second, *agriculture,* despite hard times for traditional products, will remain important as an earner of foreign exchange and an indirect provider of employment. With time, we can expect Irish farm output to become more diversified (increased emphasis on quality products such as venison, lamb and more acreage under forestry). Irish farmers will be forced to become more sensitive to environmental and health issues. The damage caused to the countryside by the land drainage schemes, yielding very low marginal returns to boot, is unlikely to be repeated.

The third pillar is *services.* This includes not only tourism but also other traded and non-traded services operated by the private sector. The Irish climate is such as to close off the possibility of the country becoming a mass-tourist resource. But sensible steps are already being taken to improve the attractiveness of Ireland as a place to visit. Air fares are down following the government's decision to permit competition on the Dublin-London route. Farmhouses offer a uniquely pleasant way of seeing the Irish countryside. Inland fishing is still an underdeveloped resource. The large western lakes offer free and largely unpoliced fishing and camping facilities to all comers. This situation cannot last. There is an urgent need to tighten up control of these valuable resources so that they can be properly maintained, cater for more people and generate more revenue and employment than is possible in their present uncontrolled state. Irish tourism could also benefit from the provision of more organised facilities for children.

Trade in services other than tourism is small in volume but shows much promise. Exciting developments have taken place in recent years. The Irish have been involved in setting up and managing hospitals in the third world. The construction industry has also gone multinational with companies like McInerneys and Rohans having interests in a number of foreign countries. Irish banks have performed successfully abroad and plans are being laid for the development of an export-oriented financial services sector. Consultancy firms are tapping Ireland's qualified labour force in areas such as computing, accountancy and economics to generate earnings abroad.

The above avenues of development offer hope for the future. The precise products which will lead the way are impossible to determine. For decades, it was thought that the food processing industry was the key to open the possibilities of sustained growth. It seemed so 'rational' and so logical, given that Ireland had the cattle and the dairy products to hand. Who could have foreseen the rise of a major electronics sector (surely 'unnatural' and illogical in a country of Ireland's size, position and level of development!)? Thirty years ago Ireland was thought to have no natural resources. Then for a brief period it seemed to be abundantly endowed with minerals, leading to the discovery of the largest lead/zinc mine in Europe. We had successively no oil, prospects of a major oil find, a small oil well leading to a debate on the need to tax the oil-barons, seminars on how we would spend the oil money, disappointing drillings and now a reversion to the no oil position. Predictions for the economy can all too easily be blown off course.

What does seem clear is that these developments will be stopped in their tracks unless the Irish economy becomes more cost-competitive and its finances get into better shape. For those of us at work in the public sector, it means a leaner and tougher existence during the period of adjustment. For those in the private sector dependent on the public sector, it means the need to diversify sources of income! The welfare state will not of course be dismantled but it will have to become a great deal more effective and more cost-conscious. The burden of Ireland's debt is so great, so unprecedentedly heavy, with interest payments alone amounting to almost £2,000 million per annum, that the adjustment process is likely to be especially painful. Although no Irish political party which went to the Irish polls with an explicitly socialist programme succeeded in capturing more than a small fraction of the nation's votes, Irish governments have, nonetheless, provided us with socialism in practice. The Irish public sector expenditure GNP ratio is well up to the standard of the avowedly socialist countries of Western Europe and just as these countries are changing, so must Ireland.

Conclusion

Ireland's economic problems are similar in kind, although graver in extent, to those of many other western countries. High unemployment is endemic throughout most of Europe. Even within the US, the average six per cent unemployment rate masks huge variations. The unemployment rate was thirteen per cent in Louisiana in 1986, twelve per cent in West Virginia and ten per cent in Houston, Texas, figures not that different from Ireland. Furthermore, most western countries have had to wrestle with the problem of over-extended public-sector expenditure and excessive borrowing. Effective tackling of these imbalances can be a painful experience. To put public finances right may often worsen the short-term prospects for employment. Nevertheless, the experience of some small countries not entirely dissimilar to Ireland such as Belgium, Denmark and New Zealand provides some encouragement. With consistent and determined governments, adjustment can successfully be achieved.

A country of Ireland's size must be prepared to live on its wits. In the words of the Irish proverb, 'he who is not strong must be clever!' Flexibility of response to changes in the international environment is recognised as a key desideratum of successful performance. An example of such flexibility was the government's response to the rise of the multinationals over the past twenty years. Incentives were put in place to ensure that Ireland obtained a disproportionate share of such investment and the Industrial Development Authority went out and marketed these incentives with internationally-recognised skill. An example of the lack of flexibility is the complete failure to make provision for the influx of young people into the labour market. Instead of allowing this new component to price itself into the Irish labour market, the government pursued policies which raised youth earnings relative to the average, emphasised policies designed to keep women in the labour force for a longer period on secure terms, reintroduced trade union privileges, made both hiring and firing labour more difficult and more bureaucratic than ever and developed a tax/social welfare system which was the one in the world most likely to discourage the will to work.

Ireland does, of course, have the capacity for a much superior economic performance. Its young population is well-educated and eager to work. The social infrastructure — telecommunications, roads, schools and hospitals — is well developed. Clearly some of the borrowing was put to good use. Inflation, which averaged almost twice the level of industrial market economies for many years, has now been reduced to three per cent. Membership of the European Community offers a firm basis of support for policies of adjustment. The 1987 Fianna Fáil government is under no illusion about what needs to be done and is showing some capacity to put ideas into action. All these considerations suggest not that the transformation of the Irish economy will be an easy task but rather that the chances of a successful transformation are much greater than would otherwise be the case.

Footnotes

The author is indebted to Finbar McDonnell for research assistance and helpful suggestions.

1. Data taken from *World Development Report*, Washington DC: The World Bank, 1987.
2. Joseph Lee, 'Whither Ireland? The Next Twenty-Five Years', in K.A. Kennedy (ed.), *Ireland in Transition*, Dublin: Mercier Press, 1986.
3, The second school would correspond to what hostile critics would term the conventional wisdom or the New Right school of thought.
4. Dermot McAleese, 'Anglo-Irish Economic Interdependence', in *Irish Banking Review*, March 1986.
5. Kieran A. Kennedy, *The Unemployment Crisis: 1985 Busteed Memorial Lecture*, Cork University Press 1985, 9.
6. Eoin O'Malley, *Industrial Policy and Development: A Survey of Literature from the early 1960s*, Dublin: National Economic and Social Council, 1980, 14.
7. Telesis report, *A Review of Industrial Policy*, Dublin: National Economic and Social Council, 1982, 35.
8. *The Sunday Times*, 8 February 1987; *The Economist*, 24 January 1987 'Ireland: How the Government spent the people into a slump'. The *Economist's* analysis, annoyingly flip to many Irish readers, focused on government expenditure as the main culprit with the political system also receiving dishonourable mention ('the nature of their politics dug the Irish into their economic hole'). The following quotation gives the flavour of the tone and content of the article:

> Their main economic problem is embarrassingly simple and self-inflicted. Their government has borrowed vast sums and spent them on welfare services that can be sustained only by more borrowing ... since their country is tiny and vaguely lovable, and they pay lip-smacking rates of interest, their creditors have for several years allowed them to carry on borrowing. Now enough is enough (47).

9. Kieran A. Kennedy, 'Industry: the Unfinished Revolution', in *Ireland in Transition, op..cit.*
10. T.K. Whitaker, *Interests*, Dublin; Institute of Public Administration 1986.

Carving of the *Ouzel Galley* on the Chamber of Commerce building, Dame Street, Dublin. The merchant ship *Ouzel Galley* set sail from Ringsend in 1695 and was eventually presumed lost. She reappeared in 1700 laden with pirate loot. The city merchants set up an independent arbitration committee to resolve the conflicting claims. This successful organisation was the precursor of Dublin's Chamber of Commerce.

Editorial Introduction to 'A centenarian renders his account'

The following essay is a personal account of the chartered accountant in Ireland today, and the 'centenarian' who has rendered this account is Timothy Quin, a Belfast practitioner. Timothy's grandfather was, in 1893, one of the first to be admitted by examination to Institute membership, and his father, who qualified in 1913, continued in active practice until his death in 1968. As Institute members, the three generations of his family have spanned ninety-five of the Institute's first 100 years.

We gave him a difficult task, willingly undertaken, to write the definitive statement on the chartered accountant in Ireland in 1988. The result is a remarkable product, tightly and economically written, in which every sentence contains food for thought. I suggest that it should be mandatory reading for anybody interested in the future of the profession!

To begin with, Timothy gives a brief historical background to the Institute, dominance in which has moved over the years from the North to the South. Why should this be so? 'Whereas Belfast remains a provincial city, Dublin has become a capital city and financial centre of some standing in Europe.' 'The larger practices in Northern Ireland would tend to see themselves operating on a Belfast-London axis.' In the South the relationship has shifted towards the USA and Europe. However, the actual contribution of the North to Institute affairs is disproportionately strong in relation to total membership.

Timothy talks of the threats to the concept of a profession: 'government has attacked as restrictive those practices and rules of conduct which are intended to distinguish and defend professional independence and objectivity against the self-seeking of skilled opportunists'; 'consumer pressure is pushing towards payment by results'; 'apart from the commercial pressures, the profession's role in society is being questioned.'

The arrival of the megafirm is a recent phenomenon, responding to the demands of megabusiness. The future of these large firms seems reasonably assured. So too the small firm relating to the smaller businessman. It is those in the middle rank who may find themselves threatened.

Inevitably there is a shifting towards Europe, a subject dealt with at greater length in Margaret Downes' essay; but whereas auditing in Europe has been government-led, here it is market-led, and therefore has been closely linked to the development of other services. In this connection Timothy talks about opportunities seized and opportunities missed, and the new opportunities to be taken.

Competition is in the air. Only recently have 'self-promotion and advertising come to be regarded as acceptable professional conduct.' The competitors are not only those in the profession, but those outside who purport to provide related services. Undoubtedly the opening-up of competition will mean the invasion of areas traditionally the stamping ground of the profession to others, and the contrary movement of the profession outside its traditional field.

But 'the broader the scope of professional activities undertaken by practising firms, the greater their risk of litigation'. Professional indemnity insurance is becoming formidably expensive. 'If government does not provide a statutory limit to liability, the alternative is to practise through the medium of a limited liability company.' Claims capable of annihilating even major firms are conceivable. Could that be in the public interest?

Practices, says Timothy, are moving towards a multi-discipline structure, a move responding to demands of larger companies. There seems to be no reason why this should not take place, though the problems of controlling professional standards are undoubtedly increased thereby.

Timothy then discusses self-regulation, which he regards as in many respects weak at the moment. 'Public expectation and government policy, however, favour more effective self-regulation, and the Department of Trade and Industry in London has stressed that it views "active monitoring of professional competence" as an important feature of the new regulatory framework required by the eighth directive. Effective enforcement of standards is thus the main challenge facing the Institute.'

Timothy then touches on training (which is dealt with in greater depth in Anthony Walsh's essay), and urges that 'it is most important that our future training covers the basic personal skills that are essential to good management.'

He feels that post-qualification specialisation should be promoted, probably linked to the awarding of fellowships by examination in specialist subjects, 'The ICAI, in common with its sister institutes, has for too long put off detailed consideration' of this matter.

He discusses 'integration or cohesion'. The integration horse has never succeeded in jumping the fence. But it is becoming very clear that the accounting bodies should speak with one voice on many matters, and that there ought to be a structure ensuring that they do so.

Finally, Timothy desires an enormous strengthening of the policy-making function of the Institute. 'There are now only twelve years to the twenty-first century. Now, more than ever, we need to plan ahead, and we need policies that are both imaginative and sufficiently flexible to deal with fast-changing circumstances.'

No editorial selection of high points could do justice to Timothy's intricate and stimulating essay. The foregoing is therefore intended only to whet the appetite, and to encourage a reading of the essay by all, and a detailed study by those who are guiding our Institute.

Balance sheet of Harland & Wolff, the Belfast shipbuilders, at 30 June 1863 and 31 December 1863. On the left-hand side the liabilities include the partners' capital. It is interesting to note that some of the ship valuations are negative!

The busy accounts department of Harland & Wolff in the main counting house at Queen's Island around 1912

Centenary Essays 1888-1988

Timothy Quin, B.A., LL.B., F.C.A.

Timothy Quin is a partner in the Northern Ireland practice of Touche Ross & Co. In 1983-4 he was chairman of the Ulster Society of Chartered Accountants, and he served on the council of the Institute until 1986. Currently he is an Irish representative on the Auditing Practices Committee of the Consultative Committee of the Accountancy Bodies. He was joint secretary of the Irish Institute from 1980 to 1982.

Timothy's original ambition was to be a barrister, and after graduating from the Arts faculty of Queen's University in 1963 he worked on to take his LL.B. degree. Following a change in his choice of career at that time he entered articles in his father's firm in Belfast, Stewart Blacker Quin, Knox & Co., chartered accountants. After qualifying in 1969, and with three years' experience gained in a leading Manchester practice, Timothy returned to Belfast in 1970. In 1972 he was admitted to partnership in Atkinson & Boyd, which has recently become part of Touche Ross International.

Timothy is forty-five years of age, married, with three children. His relaxation is to get away to his cottage on the north coast of Antrim.

A centenarian renders his account

by Timothy Quin

1988 entitles us to celebrate 100 successful years since the granting of a charter to the premier professional body of accountants in Ireland. More significantly, this is the start of our second century. It is a time to ask if the Irish chartered accountant is set to meet the challenges facing his profession.

A pattern of growth

The progress of chartered accountancy in Ireland has been ably chronicled by Howard Robinson, Institute president in 1965-6. His *History of Accountants in Ireland,* which is a fascinating record of personalities and achievements in our profession, reflects the changing pattern of economic and commercial structures in this island. In the 100 years of our history, it has been the economic and commercial developments in the last quarter of our century that have given most impetus to the growth of our Institute. From a level of 750 members in 1950 the numbers leapt to over 1,650 in 1960. Chart I shows that after a further forty per cent increase in the decade to 1970, our membership has continued to grow by approximately one-third in every five years.

CHART I
ICAI Membership Totals

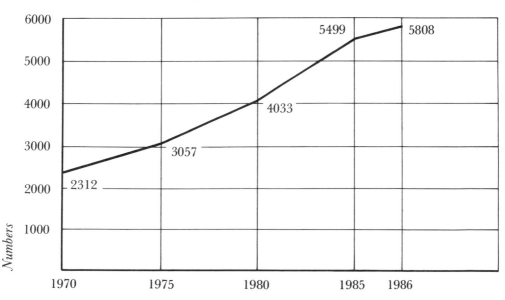

CHART II

Student intake

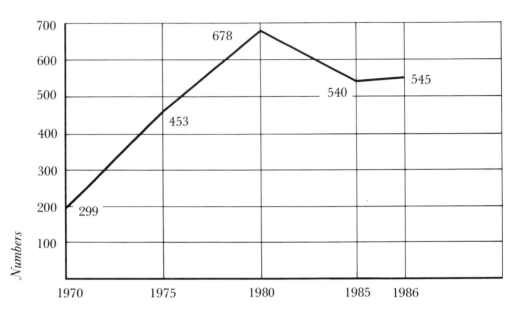

The pattern of growth looks likely to continue. The annual intake of students registering in these years is shown in Chart II. The drop in the student intake as between 1980 and 1985 reflects differing degrees of confidence in the economy. Nevertheless current levels of student intake are fairly constant and indicate that there will be little or no reduction in the numbers qualifying as chartered accountants over the next five years. Furthermore the increase in new entrants in the 1970s is unlikely to be reflected in our retiral rate until after the year 2000.

For the present, because of the increase in numbers of new members, a younger generation predominates in our profession. Within the younger generation there is a higher proportion of university graduates and a higher proportion of lady members. Indeed, thirteen per cent of ACAs are lady members, whereas amongst the FCAs (the senior members of the Institute) the ladies represent only one per cent. With these changes in the style of its membership, our Institute cannot remain staid and conservative. Its younger membership will influence the Institute to be progressive, rather than merely reactive to external pressures.

Although the Irish Institute is subject to the changes that are currently having their impact on the profession in Britain and elsewhere, some of the external factors affecting the ICAI are peculiar to Ireland.

The Irish situation

The petitioners for the charter in 1888 were drawn from Belfast as well as from Dublin and Cork. At that time the whole of Ireland was part of the United Kingdom. Belfast had developed from a small town into an industrial city, and in the period up to the first world war the north east of Ireland underwent an economic boom based on its principal manufacturing industries of linen, ship-building, rope-making, and tobacco. The importance of Belfast as a commercial centre, and the strength of the accountancy profession in the North of Ireland was a predominant feature of the ICAI in its first fifty years.

After the granting of the charter, more than thirty years elapsed before our Institute became what Enoch Powell prefers to call an 'international' body. The separation of the six counties of Northern Ireland, as part of the United Kingdom, from the twenty-six county Republic of Ireland has been an under-lying factor in the structures and activities of the Institute during the major part of its 100 year existence. With the bitterness of political sentiment that exists between the unionist and nationalist traditions in Ireland it is always a surprise for outside observers to witness the natural and unforced friendship and the pro-fessional co-operation that exists between chartered accountants of all political persuasions and from all parts of Ireland. The ICAI is notable among pro-fessional bodies in Ireland by virtue of its successful spanning of the divisions between Northern Ireland and the Republic of Ireland.

Since the late 1960s Northern Ireland has suffered from political unrest and violence. The prorogation of the provincial parliament at Stormont in March 1972 overturned political structures in Northern Ireland, and also marked the end of established patterns in commercial and social life. The symptoms of with-drawal could be sensed within the profession in the North. When Westminster removed the structures that had provided an outlet for political passions, those tensions spilled out onto the streets. For some two or three years community leadership shifted from the middle classes and the middle ground to workers' committees and to paramilitary extremists.

The main concern of businessmen and professionals in Northern Ireland was to keep their heads low and to carry on business as usual, and that cautious and self-interested reaction was perhaps the best antidote to anarchy. At the same time those Ulster chartered accountants who had strong unionist inclinations began to question their own participation in an all-Ireland Institute. Many southern members, concerned about the security situation, showed reluctance to attend conferences and other meetings in the North. The fact that those troublesome times left no lasting impression on the Institute is a tribute to the enlightened attitudes of the leading members of the profession.

Domination by Dublin

The Institute is now dominated by Dublin. Prior to the second world war the Republic of Ireland, with roughly twice the population of Northern Ireland, had fewer chartered accountants than the North. Since then the numbers in the Republic have grown at a much faster pace. Coming into its seventy-fifth year, in December 1962, the total ICAI membership of 1,770 was analysed as 50.5 per cent in the Republic of Ireland, 29.8 per cent in Northern Ireland, and 19.7 per cent in Great Britain and elsewhere. By December 1975 the proportion of Northern Ireland members had fallen to twenty-two per cent and Chart III shows that the pattern has continued.

Geographical Analysis of ICAI Membership
at 31 December 1986

CHART III

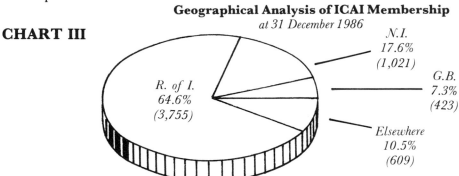

N.I.
17.6%
(1,021)

R. of I.
64.6%
(3,755)

G.B.
7.3%
(423)

Elsewhere
10.5%
(609)

It is interesting to speculate why there has been such growth of membership in the Republic of Ireland. The development of the Republic as a manufacturing base for American, European and Japanese investors attracted by the Industrial Development Authority has been relevant. Inter-related with this has been the growing importance of Ireland in Europe since the 1960s and in particular since Ireland's accession to the EEC in 1973. Whereas Belfast remains a provincial city, Dublin has become a capital city and financial centre of some standing in Europe. Since the 1960s the economic and demographic pattern in the Republic of Ireland has been one of depopulation of rural areas and of correspondingly rapid urban growth, more particularly in the Dublin area. Industrialisation and urbanisation have required financial management. There has thus been unprecedented demand for the skills of the chartered accountant.

A perhaps less positive factor is that, by comparison with Northern Ireland where higher education is almost wholly grant-aided by government, university education is more expensive for the individual in the Republic of Ireland. Particularly for school-leavers in those areas more remote from the centres of third-level education, the remunerated training and the qualification of the chartered accountant are an attractive alternative to a university degree. Where almost all new entrants in Northern Ireland are university graduates, about one-third of the intake in the Republic is non-graduate. In Northern Ireland, on the other hand, the potential intake of both graduate and non-graduate students since the early 1970s has been dissipated by the number of school-leavers going to Britain and elsewhere for their further education and qualification.

The North well represented

Despite their less significant numbers, northern members have been afforded a disproportionately high level of representation in Institute affairs over the last thirty or more years. In 1987-8, of the twenty-four members of council not currently holding any presidential office, eight are from Northern Ireland and one from Great Britain. It is not entirely accidental that the president entering the centenary year is a Belfast member whom one expects, in the normal course of events, to be succeeded in May 1988 by his Dublin-based vice-president. Until 1975 the conventional pattern was that the presidency alternated between the Republic and the United Kingdom, and since 1975 there has been a president from Northern Ireland or Great Britain at least once every three years.

There is sensitivity at council and executive levels of the Institute to the need for broad representation of all significant interests. There is a constant awareness of the demographic dominance of Dublin and the danger of overlooking the needs not only of the North but also of Cork and the other commercial centres in Ireland. Apart from that sensitivity, the other reason for disproportionate involvement of northern members on the council and committees of the Institute is the strength that the northern member can give to the Institute in operating within two jurisdictions, the Republic of Ireland and the United Kingdom.

The prominent part played by the ICAI in CCAB (the Consultative Committee of Accountancy Bodies), and in other arrangements with government and accountancy bodies in the United Kingdom, derives largely from the direct experience of our northern members in UK legal, Inland Revenue, and commercial, processes.

Belfast-London axis

The larger practices in Northern Ireland would tend to see themselves operating on a Belfast-London axis. Northern Ireland exists wholly within the fiscal system of the UK and its companies legislation has followed word for word the Companies Acts introduced in recent years in Great Britain. At least two of the Big Eight firms have Belfast offices that are wholly integrated within their UK partnerships. Others are independent Northern Ireland partnerships linking in with their Great Britain counterparts. In the last ten years, however, the Dublin firm of Stokes Kennedy Crowley & Co., which is the Irish arm of KPMG, has pioneered an all-Ireland practice with the rapid development of its Belfast office. World-wide economic and commercial pressures are making political boundaries less important for accounting firms. EEC influence and closer correlation of the Irish and UK economies may well make the Dublin-Belfast axis a more meaningful mode of operation in the future.

Republic of Ireland – a fettered economy

In the Republic of Ireland there was a failure to capitalise fully on the economic growth of the 1970s. There thus remained a need for reinvestment in order to modernise the economic and commercial infra-structure. To the casual observer the Republic's economy seems in retrospect merely to have enjoyed a delay in facing the economic upheaval through which the UK had been struggling. The Republic of Ireland overcame more quickly the crisis of runaway inflation, but it is now facing the purgative period that Thatcherite theory deems a prerequisite for economic recovery.

The chartered accountant in the Republic of Ireland faces an economy that is fettered for the immediately foreseeable future. He is the unwilling instrument of an almost punitive tax system. In little more than five years, owing to the deadlines for implementation by the Republic of EEC directives, he is having to cope with changes in company law that both follow and go beyond the legislation introduced earlier and more gradually in the UK. Although he can be forgiven for feeling defensive, the many pressures placed now on the established professions require from him the most positive response.

The professions pilloried

Prior to the 1970s, the practitioner in any profession led a stolid and secure existence. Now government has attacked as restrictive those practices and rules of conduct which are intended to distinguish and defend professional independence and objectivity against the self-seeking of skilled opportunists. The sale of spectacles by opticians and the provision of dentures by dentists have ceased to be protected monopolies. Conveyancing will no longer be confined to solicitors. Rules in restraint of advertising and self-promotion are being removed. The emphasis is on competitiveness, marketing, and commercial motivation. Consumer pressure is pushing towards payment by results. Commission-based fees are supplanting time-based charges. As price-cutting causes cost-cutting, quality is becoming secondary.

Surveyors are selling their shares on the Stock Exchange or being bought over by building societies. With other professions becoming investment targets for banks and insurance companies, profit targets will override professional ethics. In these circumstances, does the traditional concept of the professions have any place in the future?

The problem is partly that the principal offices of most of the leading accountancy and other professional firms in Britain and Ireland are London-based and, following the flurry of Big Bang activity in the City, they are too committed to the present to be concerned about the future. Despite persistent unemployment there is a shortage of skilled professionals, and a premium on staff salary costs, that is spreading from the south east throughout Britain and ultimately into Ireland. High taxation levels in the Republic of Ireland encourage emigration of skilled people, which exacerbates the problem. In London and the south east the increased salary costs can more readily be recouped from the user of professional services, but in Ireland there are constraints on cost recovery.

Apart from the commercial pressures, the professions' role in society is being questioned. The professions are perceived as middle-class in their origins and in their values. Their purpose of promoting private wealth and protecting property ownership is seen as conflicting with the public interest and the requirements of the public purse.

The strength of practising firms

If any profession is well-placed to withstand the increase in external pressures, it is the accountancy profession. Its strength lies in the dominance and importance of the larger accountancy practices.

The megafirm is a modern phenomenon. In Howard Robinson's history of the profession he notes that in 1962 there were 116 firms of chartered accountants in Dublin. 'Of these, no fewer than sixty-three were sole practitioners and thirty more were partnerships comprising two partners. Only twenty-three firms had more than two partners: Craig Gardner & Co. had ten Dublin partners; another firm had seven partners; a third firm had six partners; there were five firms with five partners; three with four partners, and twelve with three partners.' A quarter of a century later, even Craig Gardner's total complement of over 600 partners and staff (including between forty and fifty partners) is exceeded by the 700 or so partners and staff in Stokes Kennedy Crowley & Co. In the United Kingdom, the Big Eight firms between them have a total complement of approximately 35,000 staff and partners. These figures of course include students and administrative and professional staff other than chartered accountants, but they do underline the importance of the accountancy practices as major employers of persons with financial and managerial skills. As a fast-growing element of the financial services industry the accountancy firms undeniably carry clout.

Within the ICAI the increasing commitment of qualified chartered accountants to public practice is illustrated in Chart IV.

Chart IV

Occupational Analysis of ICAI Membership at 31 December

	1970	%	1986	%
In practice	624	27.0	1,592	27.4
Staff in practising offices	326	14.1	1,457	25.1
	950	41.1	3,049	52.5
Wholly outside practice	1,362	58.9	2,759	47.5
	2,312	100.0	5.808	100.0

The structure of the firms has altered to accommodate changes in the nature of their services. Specialisation in those services has led to a large increase in the employment of qualified staff in practising offices. Correspondingly those ICAI members employed outside private practice have become a minority.

The future of the accountancy profession, in Ireland as in Great Britain, is dependent on the leadership of the largest practices and on the prospects for practising firms.

Prospects for practice

It is customary to speak of the 'Big Eight' firms. There is nothing magical about the number eight, and there have been changes over the years in the particular firms making up this top division of the league. What has remained surprisingly constant is that, regardless of mergers among the larger firms, the audits of the vast majority of public companies quoted on the London Stock Exchange have been monopolised for the last two or three decades by about eight major firms. The second division of the league of UK national firms has been more closely identified with smaller public companies and with privately financed businesses. More efficient world-wide trade and communications are encouraging international corporate clients to grow larger and more numerous. This, together with privatisation of nationalised industries in the UK, and the opportunities presented by the development of the EEC, is fostering growth in the larger accountancy practices. The Big Eight will thrive in this expanding market. It is always possible that two or more of the larger firms, in Ireland as in Great Britain, may merge in order to provide new financial services on a broader base. This will only widen the gap between the first and second division firms. Even smaller PLC clients now expect from their auditors an international presence and service capability. To compete with the Big Eight, in operating a closely-controlled and credible world-wide organisation, and in providing the

PLC market with not only audit but a more extensive range of services, requires resources beyond the reach of the average second division firm.

Traditionally for practices in the UK and Ireland the important link has been transatlantic. Accounting standards and audit procedures here have followed developments in the USA and Canada, where the SEC has been the predominant influence. The success of a UK firm is still dependent on the strength of its counterpart in the USA and the impact of Arthur Andersen & Co. in Britain and Ireland reflects directly the muscle-power of the American profession.

Contrast in styles: Europe and Ireland

For the future, however, some shift in emphasis should be expected. European influence is being felt, and this difference in focus is explored fully elsewhere in this publication by Margaret Downes, under the title *Europe – big brother, best friend*. Although the third major financial market after London and Wall Street is Tokyo, and this perhaps points to another major area of potential development for the profession, the more immediate prospect is of closer contacts with accountants in Europe.

The parameters of the profession in mainland Europe are largely laid down by governments whose priority is to preserve auditing as a purely independent function. The contrast with our own pattern is clear. Accountancy in Britain and Ireland is market-led. Although the audit is the foremost function of our accountancy firms, our style of auditing differs from that in many of the other European countries. The object of our audit has moved from being a narrow checking of the accuracy of records and of the extraction of accounts from those records. We concentrate more on confirming that presentation of the annual accounts is comprehensive, comprehensible and consistent with acceptable accounting policies. In adopting this broader approach, our auditors have seen the advantage of counselling management as the accounts are being prepared rather than acting as critics when the accounts have been completed. There is thus a closeness to management and the reporting process that does not wholly reconcile with an independent role for the auditor.

Also, although our Companies Acts provide for the appointment of the auditor by the shareholders to whom he reports, in reality management selects the audit firm and negotiates its fee. The commercial pressure on a partner in an audit firm is to strengthen his relationship with management rather than to adopt an overtly independent stance. Even with smaller audit clients, where the management and the membership of the company may be identical, the independence of our audit firms is compromised to some degree by their common involvement as tax agents for the client. The preferred accounting presentation for reporting to shareholders may not be best for returns to the Revenue.

By-product of audit? Commercial opportunities

In marketing their audit services accountancy firms in Britain and Ireland place emphasis on advice and assistance to management as an element or by-product of the audit. Internal control recommendations, improvements in management information systems and tax planning points are being proffered. With this welter of add-on benefits the danger is that we will lose sight of the essence of the audit.

Because of the close contact between auditor and client the accountancy firm can gain a special insight into the problems and the opportunities of its client's business and is well-placed to promote professional services other than the audit. Practitioners in Ireland have commonly offered accountancy, taxation, and company secretarial and registration services. Very many have developed the specialism of dealing with insolvencies. In the last ten years, however, the main growth area for the larger accountancy practice has been management consultancy. The leaders in this field have included Coopers & Lybrand who, in both Britain and Ireland, have developed management consultancy to the point where it has become an important element of their fee-earning capacity. Much of the growth in Arthur Andersen's practice has come from concentration on information technology as a consultancy specialism. Other Big Eight firms have developed consultancies with perhaps a different emphasis, but with no less enthusiasm.

Self-promotion

Only in the last few years of our century have self-promotion and advertising come to be regarded as acceptable professional conduct. The mood in favour of more overt commercialism in now enabling accountancy firms to compete with outsiders. In retrospect, one can say that the profession missed its opportunity thirty years ago to extend its range of financial services. Bankers, particularly the merchant banks, seized the opportunity to act as corporate financial advisers, a role for which the chartered accountant's training and experience make him specially suited.

Our clients are offered and accept investment and insurance advice from insurance salesmen with no depth of knowledge and no professional ethic. Only now has our profession awoken to the opportunity it has overlooked for so long, and personal financial planning is being developed by all the major firms as a separate field of specialist advice. The more avant garde accountant has asked himself, who is better placed to handle portfolio management? In the fields of both investment advice and portfolio management, accountancy practices have a captive market in their clients' pension funds.

Undeniably, the opportunity we should never have missed was to be at the forefront of computerisation and information technology. The core of our professional expertise, the design and implementation of accounting systems, passed to computer salesmen through our own neglect. Even now it is unusual to find systems analysis and programming skills in any but the larger accountancy practices.

Problems of objectivity

These developing areas do present their own problems for the profession. The objectivity and independence that are the hallmarks of any profession are called into question by our accepting commissions on insurance and investment products and by the profits we stand to make on retailing computer hardware and software packages. More and more of the staff employed in accountancy practices to extend our range of services have had no previous professional training or background, and are uninfluenced by our Institute and its ethical standards. We are also having to cope with a new regime of control by government over investment business, heralded in 1986 by the UK Financial Services Act. Even those firms standing back from investment management and from conscious promotion of personal financial planning are caught by the Act's very broad definition of investment business. The Institute itself has become a regulatory agent of government under this legislation. Last year's president warned ICAI members of the likelihood that 'such a regime will entail investment business rules dealing with such matters as client money accounts etc., the establishment of a compensation fund, the regular return to the Institute by authorised firms of information on investment business undertaken, and a system of inspection visits to check compliance with regulations and accuracy of information returned'.

Following acceptance by the Institute of responsibility for the regulation of its members in this area, not only may it be necessary to operate a compensation fund to protect the public against mishandling by members of clients' money, but there is a risk that mismanagement of investments or negligent advice given by members will expose the Institute to litigation on the argument that the Institute carries legal responsibility for the standards of service of its members.

Risk of litigation

The broader the scope of professional activities undertaken by practising firms, the greater their risk of litigation. In the last few years all firms faced escalating premiums for professional indemnity insurance. Certain levels and types of indemnity insurance cover are simply unobtainable in today's market. Paradoxically the Department of Trade and Industry in London is including in its plans for implementation of the eighth directive a compulsory PII requirement for audit firms. As sources of business finance become more extensive and financial relationships become more complex the impact of any slip in our professional work has a much more widespread effect, so that the sums at which lawsuits will be settled may become astronomical.

With full PII cover unavailable, practising firms are strongly urging some form of limitation of their potential liability. If government does not provide a statutory limit to such liability, the alternative is to practise through the medium of a limited liability company. Even adopting the limited liability company format will still leave the larger firms facing the difficulty and horrendous cost of obtaining professional indemnity insurance cover. In theory limited liability should provide a shield against catastrophe if a claim were to exceed the available PII cover, but there are other means of self-protection (such as transfer of private assets into trust), and it is highly unlikely that any Big Eight firm would be bankrupted. One expects the major claims to come from governments, banks (or receivers acting on their behalf), or institutional investors. In the catastrophe situation, with a claim significantly exceeding cover, it seems inconceivable that some compromise would not be reached in the public interest to avoid the annihilation of a major professional firm. In reality it is much more than the limitation of liability that makes incorporation of accountancy firms attractive.

Multi-discipline practices

The major accountancy practices are moving towards a multi-discipline structure. Clients' problems cannot neatly be compartmentalised. When they seek our advice their enquiries range beyond our traditional accountancy and tax expertise and can cover company law, contract and employment law, stamp duty, property and investment management, insurance and pension arrangements, office administration and myriad management disciplines including marketing, personnel and production methods. We cannot fail to provide service to our clients in all these areas. Market demand will force our professional practices to acquire skills in fields beyond the central disciplines of accountancy and finance. Accountancy firms have already begun to employ staff from other disciplines, including solicitors, engineers, personnel managers and marketing specialists. If involvement in these areas is to meet appropriate professional standards it will be necessary to attract the ablest people in these other disciplines and to provide them with the standing that they warrant in the more broadly based practices of the future.

This does not imply a complete merging of the professions. One does not see accountancy practices seeking to provide criminal law or conveyancing services, but our work is so closely inter-related with company and contract law and with stamp duty that there is logic in linking corporate lawyers with the corporate financial specialists of our own profession in one professional practice. The structure of accountancy practices will need to change in order to accommodate this, and incorporation is an obvious choice.

Incorporation?

The development of multi-discipline practices imposes a greater demand on financial resources, and a corporate structure will make it easier for practices to obtain additional working capital. It should also give principals the opportunity to realise value from the equity in their firms if they can sell part of that equity to banks, insurance companies or other financial institutions.

A corporate structure, or more precisely a group company structure, should be able to meet the requirements of the eighth directive, both for audit services to be controlled by approved individual auditors (such as chartered accountants) and for the audit service to have some degree of independence from the commercial provision of other services. One can envisage the accountancy practice of the future operating its main financial services through a broadly-controlled multi-discipline company, related to which there would be an associated company providing purely audit service and controlled by chartered accountants or other approved auditors.

How big should a practice be?

The question of incorporation is a concern mainly of the larger firms. Ireland is still very dependent on the small company and the family business, however, and the accountancy profession here reflects this. Particularly in the Republic of Ireland, there is still a large number of sole practitioners and two or three partner firms. Less usual today is the independent firm with say fifty staff and four or five partners. Twenty years ago firms of this size were the leading practices in Ireland. Today it is hard to see a secure role in the future for such firms. Their best hope is merger into larger entities, rather than a continuing sad decline. Medium-sized accountancy firms are too firmly set in their pattern and too awkwardly sized to adapt as the providers of specialist services for the future. They cannot compete with smaller practices whose lower overheads give a cost advantage, and they do not have the resources to win work from the larger national and international firms.

The small firm, on the other hand, can be more flexible in its approach. In Ireland smaller practices carry relatively little audit work. Their main activity is the preparation of annual accounts and acting for their clients in the entire range of Inland Revenue compliance work. The small practitioner acts as a friend, advisor and confidant to the small businessman.

Although the need for this service is not lessening, our members in smaller practices feel threatened by competition from practitioners who are not chartered accountants and who are prepared to cut corners in order to obtain a cost advantage. The more able of our members in smaller practices can find a niche in the market for themselves, providing a more specialised service. For those in more routine aspects of practice involvement the constant question is: 'How can I compete with the cowboys down the street?'

Outshining the others

The Office of Fair Trading in Britain and consumer interests generally in Ireland have favoured opening up the profession to competition by the removal of advertising and other restrictions from our ethical guidelines and by-laws. The removal of these constraints on competition between chartered accountants has for some caused soul-searching or dissent. What has been overlooked in all this is that the real competition we face is from outside the profession. Larger accountancy practices face competition from non-professionals in the wider financial services market. Our members in smaller practices face competition from accountants who are unqualified and often unprofessional. At all levels our members feel strongly that a major role for the Institute, as our professional body, is to sell the concept of the chartered accountant as a professional in whose skills and integrity the business public should place their trust and who is good value for money by virtue of those very qualities.

In today's marketing jargon our Institute needs to carry out a SWOT analysis (for the uninitiated — an analysis of our strengths, weaknesses, opportunities and threats). It should research and identify how the public we serve perceives its own needs. What differentiates ICAI members from other suppliers of services in the same market? How can we promote the features that differentiate us?

Our Institute council is under pressure from members to initiate some form of promotional campaign. Features that must be marketable are the strength of our Institute's system of self-regulation and its insistence on impeccable professional standards.

Self-regulation

Our profession operates against a background of privilege and mystique. We hold a privileged position under companies' legislation to act where others cannot do so, and we are given a special status in our relationship with the Inland Revenue, the banks, and the business world in general. We must conduct ourselves in such a way as to deserve that special status. For our profession to have achieved its present recognition and reputation and for it to continue successfully in the future, the members of our Institute cannot afford to take short-cuts on technical standards or compromise on their code of conduct. It was this awareness that standards of conduct and a sense of public duty are essential to any profession that inspired those thirty-one public accountants to petition for the charter in 1888. In petitioning for that charter, they proposed that the Institute should compel 'the observance of strict rules of conduct as a condition of membership'. In fact, the Institute is not as strictly regulated as the charter might imply.

Until now, the only really strict rule governing the general professional conduct of members has been that contained in Bye-law 71 which renders a member liable to disciplinary action 'if in the course of carrying out his professional duties or otherwise, he has been guilty of misconduct. For this purpose, misconduct includes any act or default likely to bring discredit on the Institute or the accountancy profession'. Before a member can be disciplined it has to be proved that his conduct is likely to bring discredit on the Institute or the profession, which is very much a matter for subjective judgment. Rather than spell out in detail what a member ought or ought not to do, the Institute has until now deliberately avoided the rule book approach and has offered instead merely guidance on matters of professional ethics or conduct. Failure to follow the guidance does not of itself constitute misconduct, although it may have indicative effect. The basic principles are laid down, and it is left to the individual member to exercise his own judgment as to how those principles should be applied in particular situations.

This same looseness in our system of self-regulation spills over into accounting standards, which are frequently subjected to questionable interpretation. To be more effective, both technical and ethical standards need to be enforceable.

The more innovative any standard-setting body becomes, the less prospect there is of enforcing its standards — this was the dilemma that stalled the progress of inflation accounting. To be effective and enforceable, professional standards must be explicit and incontrovertible. To strengthen our self-regulatory system our Institute must spurn the over-complex and abstruse, and it must define the essential principles in strict rules of professional conduct whose breach is *de facto* a disciplinary matter. The ICAI membership has recently endorsed the adoption of such rules of professional conduct by their council. Not only will the publication of precise and simple rules give credibility to the Institute — it will give each member a clear and well-adjusted measure against which to judge his own professional conduct.

It is easy to establish the rules, but much harder to enforce them. The problems of enforcement are exacerbated by the prospect of the multi-discipline practice where our members will be acting jointly with others outside our profession. Also, the introduction of corporate status for practising firms could cause control problems for the Institute. Even with safeguards limiting the influence of shareholders from outside our own profession, the company structure will impose a barrier between the Institute and its individual members in practice whose responsibility for the activities of their firms will be no longer that of prin-

A conference of the Institute

Continuing professional education

Ann O'Driscoll, the Institute's 5,000th member, receiving her certificate from the president, Alan Ridley

FISC (the voluntary service giving free financial advice to the less well-off) at work

cipals but that of employees. If the larger firms, which have hitherto led the Institute's progress, should cease to be partnerships whose principals are individual members and become companies by which those members are employed, the direct and constructive relationship between the larger firms and the Institute will be affected.

Public expectation and government policy, however, favour more effective self-regulation, and the Department of Trade and Industry in London has stressed that it views 'active monitoring of professional competence' as an important feature of the new regulatory framework required by the eighth directive. Effective enforcement of standards is thus the main challenge facing the Institute.

Training for the future

What is it that makes the chartered accountant's qualification so keenly sought after? It cannot alone be the effectiveness of our education and examination system. Only over the last ten or fifteen years has the Institute really taken control of the education of its own students. Previously student education had been the preserve of correspondence colleges. Now the Institute is getting involved directly in either running or monitoring the wide variety of educational courses open to students today.

The quality in our qualification comes historically from the practice-based training which distinguishes the chartered accountancy Institutes from other accountancy bodies. If in the future European Community requirements were to result in audit firms being limited in the range of services they could provide to clients, an incidental but important point would be the impact that such limitation would have on the breadth of experience a student gains during the period of his training contract. Training in a practising office provides the student with experience of a whole range of financial disciplines and an overview of how management operates in the many different types of business that make up the client portfolio of each practising firm. This breadth of experience is complemented by the practical and multi-disciplinary nature of papers set as part of the ICAI Final Admitting Examination.

Because of the breadth of training and the high examination standards of the Institute the recently qualified chartered accountant has available to him an exciting range of opportunities both in Ireland and abroad. Qualification as an Irish chartered accountant carries with it recognition of one's skills and experience anywhere in the world. It is because we are keen to protect that success that leading members of the Institute have lately expressed concern that the chartered accountant seeking employment outside practice may not enjoy so marked an advantage over accountants from other bodies as was the case in the past. This has posed the question of whether our training programme could be made even more relevant to the student intending to make his career in industry or commerce.

Training outside the practising offices

In 1983, the council decided to implement a pilot scheme under which some Institute students might undertake their practical training in organisations in industry, commerce and the public sector. Those students coming through the pilot scheme have had a high success rate, and it has been a feature of the scheme that the Institute does not simply look for places to be offered in industry or commerce for its students but ensures that the student's progress will be monitored by a member in industry, acting as the student's principal, in a professional environment and with a properly planned and experience-based training programme.

The importance traditionally attached to practical training as a prerequisite to qualification as a chartered accountant has been carried over into the industrial training route. Training in industry within the ICAI is a process which must be distinguished from the less stringent training arrangements made by those other accountancy bodies that have always left it open to their students to take employment in industry rather than train in a practising office. It would be a mistake, however, to overstate the success of the ICAI scheme for training in industry. In each of the first four years of the scheme only half a dozen to a dozen students have registered for training in industry because of the difficulty in finding them employment with principals who can provide the right training environment. When these figures are compared with the overall student intake of five or six hundred per year it can be seen that the impact of training in industry must be relatively insignificant.

Management skills

Ireland, as a recently industrialised state, does not have a long tradition of management skills and has increasingly turned to the accountancy profession to provide individuals with those skills. Even in Britain, with its longer history of industrialisation, it has been suggested that the absence for so long of business schools and M.B.A. qualifications on the American pattern has been owing to reliance on our profession to provide to industry and commerce a major training contribution. Whether or not that is so, business schools are beginning to proliferate within the United Kingdom and the M.B.A. degree is being seen not so much as an alternative to the chartered accountancy training and qualification but even as a desirable post-qualification specialisation for chartered accountants. For the Institute to maintain its standing as a training institution producing not merely accountants but also financial managers, we need to borrow from the syllabus of the typical M.B.A. course and cover in our examinations such subjects as market research and marketing, operations management (including work study, and product and systems design), and human resources management (personnel management and industrial relations) and related subjects.

It is most important that our future training covers the basic personal skills that are essential to good management. Currently the prospective chartered accountant may learn to manage work but not the skill of managing people. We must recognise in our training that effective management of people eases the problems of managing work.

If we are successful in the training and education of future chartered accountants, have we also a responsibility to ensure that the potential demand matches the increasing number of young people passing the examinations and qualifying each year? The problem of course is that one can only predict future demand if one makes the assumption that chartered accountants will continue to fill only those roles on which they have concentrated in the past. It is impossible to predict the extent to which chartered accountants will in future transfer into areas of general management. Furthermore, it is a perfectly acceptable and indeed worthy function of our Institute that it should train young people and provide them with a qualification that will prove of value to them and to other communities beyond our own shores. For the future the number of available training contracts will and should be the only factor determining the number of prospective chartered accountants.

Accountancy technicians

The status of the ICAI as a training institution has been greatly enhanced by its sponsorship of the Institute of Accounting Technicians in Ireland (IATI). The IATI was founded as recently as April 1983 following discussions initiated by the ICAI with the Irish Institute of Accounting Technicians. The prospectus of the new institute points out that the accounting technician is not a qualified accountant and does not claim to be such. 'Young men or women who qualify as accounting technicians should be seen as persons who have acquired training, experience and knowledge that will enable them to provide support services for management in their organisations.' Nevertheless the ICAI has agreed that persons qualifying as members of the IATI who achieve high standards in its examination, may be entitled to register as ICAI students, with certain exemptions from the ICAI examinations, with a view to ultimate qualification as chartered accountants.

IATI has been highly successful in attracting its own students during the short period to date. Its mentors have hopes that the practising profession will provide a greater number of places for student accounting technicians. The services provided by practitioners, however, increasingly require staff with special skills, and the more routine accounting tasks in the practising office, to the extent that they have not been overtaken by information technology, are more cost-effectively carried by clients themselves. Furthermore, if the more mechanical aspects of audit and accountancy were passed by practitioners to members and students of the technicians' institute, there would be less scope for the basic training of first-year chartered accountancy students in practising offices. The IATI, unlike the ICAI, will not be practice-oriented. It will develop a different aura and philosophy from that of its sponsor, and the aim of the ICAI must be to avoid its protégé pursuing too divergent a path.

The member outside public practice

What has been said so far on protecting the standards, and standing, of the Institute, competing with others from outside our profession, and strengthening our role as a training institution, is as relevant to the member in industry, commerce or the public sector as to the member in a practising office. Despite the relevance of their Institute in these areas, it has always been disappointing that too many of our members in industry have been reluctant to involve themselves in Institute affairs. It is sad, when recently qualified chartered accountants enter employment outside practice, to see them cutting themselves off from their profession, not deliberately but by default. More needs to be done to draw this large and important part of our membership closer to their Institute.

One area in which the Institute has failed to serve adequately its non-practising members is in the provision of ethical guidance or regulation. The ethical guide incorporated in the Institute handbook, which was developed in co-operation with the other chartered accountancy institutes, was drafted with the practising accountant mainly in mind. Of the fourteen statements currently in the ethical guide, only three relate to members outside practice — statements on professional independence, confidentiality, and technical and professional standards. When the ethical guide was revised in June 1987 the statements were deliberately made more relevant to the member outside public practice. Both the statements and the explanatory notes to those statements, however, could be much more specific as to the circumstances in which non-practising members must have regard to ethical considerations. A non-practising member will clearly be under much greater pressure to comply with the wishes of his employer than is placed by clients on a practitioner. The non-practising member needs specific guidance or regulation from the Institute as a help in resisting pressure from his employer to accept or endorse unprofessional conduct. One of our leading members in the non-practising stream has summed it up: 'In order to resist a command, one does sometimes need a piece of paper'.

Even more difficult for the member employed in commerce or industry is where, rather than being asked specifically to approve or endorse unprofessional conduct, he merely becomes aware of unethical or illicit commercial practices indulged in by his employer. There is a need in such circumstances for more adequate guidance from our Institute.

To the extent that the reputation of the chartered accountant is consciously advanced by the Institute, it is primarily members in practice whose interests are promoted. More direct advancement of the interests of members in industry and commerce could be achieved by the Institute taking a public position on the requirements of good management and on the legal and financial respon-sibilities of company directors. For example, the Institute could campaign for a legal requirement that every public company board should include a member of a recognised accountancy body. Together with the other leading accountancy bodies it could produce, on the same lines as Auditing Standards and Guide-lines, a series of guidelines encapsulating the principles of good management.

Whatever efforts are made by the Institute in promoting our members as managers of industry, their successes in management will depend on the skills of each individual. Members in commerce and industry need to be able to counter the charge that many of them lack creativity and innovativeness. It reflects badly on our profession if many of those chartered accountants who go into industry merely become 'number crunchers' or glorified bookkeepers, churning out accounts on a monthly basis with very little real interpretation or con-structive contribution. Hopefully some edge is given to their attitudes and abilities by the expansion in recent years of the Institute's post-qualification pro-gramme of continuing professional education.

Post-qualifying specialisation

The continuing professional education (CPE) provided by the Institute for qualified members consists of a programme of day or half-day courses on wide-ranging subjects. In general, the style of the courses is didactic rather than par-ticipative, so that their effect is somewhat superficial. Even though policy is, so far as possible, to make CPE mandatory for our members, the most that can be achieved by this method of post-qualifying education is alerting members to any gaps in their knowledge. Something more is needed.

With the prospect of multi-discipline practices, with non-practising members moving more into general management, the need for specialist skills faces us all in our professional work. Not only do we need more specialised skills, but we need to be able to show that we are qualified to act in these areas outside the common core of our accountancy training and experience. The public will increasingly demand from us specialist skills, and some formal means of recognising specialisation.

The ICAI, in common with its sister institutes, has for too long put off detailed consideration of awarding fellowships in the Institute by examination in specialist subjects. The need for the Institute to recognise specialisms outside the main field of accountancy has been a missed opportunity which, in the field of taxation, has encouraged the growth of the Institute of Taxation as an examining institution and professional body. The opportunity remains, however, to identify specialisms in which Institute members can benefit from post-qualifying education, examination and specialist qualification. The problem for a small professional body such as ours, which has a smaller membership than, for example, either the Institute of Administrative Accountants or the Society of Company and Commercial Accountants, is lack of resources. The way ahead must be through co-operation with our sister institutes in Scotland and in England and Wales, if only they can be persuaded to take a positive step forward towards the award of fellowship by examination in specialised subjects.

Information technology

One area in which there is an urgent need for post-qualifying education and specialisation is information technology (IT). The development of IT encompasses much more than conventional computer systems. Not only is the means of processing information advancing faster than our ability to react to the information processed, there are also dramatic changes taking place in the modes of transmission of information. As one of our more visionary members has remarked, in 1888 the speed and cost of transacting business between Dublin and London was equal to that of the mail boat and train; in 1988 we can be in instantaneous communication with Tokyo at modest cost. This has reduced any geographical disadvantage that we have in Ireland, and Irish chartered accountants should be ready to capitalise on this change in our comparative position.

The traditional function of the chartered accountant was previously to process information. By the mid-1970s the processing function diminished in importance with the rapid advance of micro-computer technology. The chartered accountant is now more concerned with the information output by computers and with how to manage information. He must determine what information is needed for management purposes, ensure that the technology will produce it, and then interpret it for management. The skills he requires for this enhanced function are analytical, interpretative, and managerial.

While there is no need for chartered accountants to be able to write software, there is a need for the member in practice to be able to cope with fraud prevention and audit verification in the context of computerised systems. The member working in commerce or industry must be aware of the capabilities of the IT system operating within his own organisation, and be able to control the final output from any computer installation. The training and education of our students should therefore cover at least the essence of systems analysis and the design of computer-based systems, and the ICAI is again setting an example for other accountancy bodies by the implementation of a programme providing students with practical computer experience which is a mandatory training requirement with effect from September 1988. For those with particular aptitude, there must be the opportunity for more in-depth specialisation after qualification.

Government and the public sector

Concern has often been voiced that if the Institute should ignore the need to make self-regulation more demonstrably effective government intervention may result. The opportunity for direct registration and regulation of our profession has presented itself now to government with the impulse provided by the EEC eighth directive. The Department of Trade and Industry in Great Britain has indicated that its preferred route is not one of direct intervention but of ensuring that the profession is operating self-regulation effectively. In the Republic of Ireland there has been even less indication to date of any desire by government to involve itself in the registration and regulation of the accountancy profession. Nevertheless our relationship with government and the public sector has been a comparatively weak area. Although we have some representation in the semi-public bodies and there is a recent tendency for the public sector to employ practising firms for audit purposes (in Great Britain) and for specific consultancy assignments, very few of our members are in direct government employment. Despite frequent submissions made on behalf of the Institute, government has remained largely uninfluenced by us in tax and economic matters.

Generally, in the Republic of Ireland, politicians, government departments and the Inland Revenue show little sympathy for us. To make any inroads into the public sector, we need to direct some of our training effort into that area. Furthermore, there must be a continuing public relations effort to establish public sector confidence in our profession and in our Institute.

In Northern Ireland relations between the Institute and the Inland Revenue and other government departments have been more friendly and constructive. In the training field relationships have been strengthened by secondments from the practising firms to the Department of Economic Development and the Industrial Development Board. There has been a watchfulness lest any submissions made to government should be dismissed as politically motivated or representing vested interests. In this latter respect there has been perhaps a contrast between the approach of northern members to UK government departments and that of southern members to government in the Republic. There is a conflict between the wish, often expressed by grass-roots members in Dublin, for the Institute to represent the interests of private enterprise by taking a stand on the levels of state spending and taxation, and the wish to win the respect and sympathy of the Inland Revenue and other civil servants.

Integration or cohesion?

The issue of whether or not the accountancy bodies should integrate used to be straightforward, but it has become clouded by the novel concept that we should instead aim for greater 'cohesion' within the profession. A regret often expressed by leading members of the ICAI is that two attempts in the last twenty years to integrate structurally the principal professional bodies have not succeeded in merging even the three institutes of chartered accountants, let alone the certified accountants, the cost and management accountants, and CIPFA (the body representing public sector accountants). Because of the failure to integrate, considerable importance has attached to the Consultative Committee of Accountancy Bodies, which represents the six main bodies of accountants, and its subsidiary committees, the Accounting Standards Committee and the Auditing Practices Committee. When it comes to responding to government initiatives, however, each of the six bodies almost always makes its own independent submission. We thus lack the strength of unity, and we fail to project a coherent public image.

With the need for government to take some responsibility for the auditing function, the Department of Trade and Industry in Great Britain has stated publicly that: 'The Secretary of State might be able to discharge his responsibilities more effectively if the Department could talk to the professional bodies and representatives of audit consumers collectively, rather than on an individual basis.' The Department thus favours for ease of implementation of the eighth directive what it describes as 'greater cohesion within the profession'.

The concept of cohesion is now being cultivated both by those within our profession who favour structural integration, and who see cohesion as a coming together for that purpose, and by those who would prefer to see cohesion as much less formal co-operation between the separate professional bodies.

At the very least, much more co-operation is needed between the accountancy bodies. The Department of Trade and Industry in Great Britain has made the point clearly: 'Some form of co-ordination will certainly be required in relation to education and training, e.g. so as to ensure that recognised UK qualifications are, and remain, of broadly uniform standard.'

The three institutes of chartered accountants, the ICAI, the ICAEW and the ICAS, operate separate systems for examination and admission to membership. Yet the members of all three bodies call themselves 'chartered accountants' and in the the eyes of the public are indistinguishable. The public has a right to expect that all members of the same profession calling themselves 'chartered accountants' should have achieved identical examination standards and should have gone through the same process of admission to membership. From the point of view of the three institutes, and especially the ICAI with its low membership numbers and limited resources, the only cost-effective education and examination policy must be to operate systems in common with our sister chartered institutes. When it comes to progressing to fellowship by examination in specialist subjects, the only possible policy will be integration of our educational and examination processes with those of the other two bodies.

A strategy for the Institute

Even survival is perhaps uncertain for a small institute such as the ICAI when faced with so many difficulties in the foreseeable future. How can we find the resources to cope with the development of multi-discipline practising firms, the more commercial approach which is threatening our professional ethos, and the probability that outside investors will gain equity and influence in the leading accountancy practices?

At any centenary one is tempted to look back, but we must remember that there are now only twelve years to the twenty-first century. Now, more than ever, we need to plan ahead, and we need policies that are both imaginative and sufficiently flexible to deal with fast-changing circumstances.

Under Noel Stewart's presidency, in 1981-2, the ICAI council approved a medium-term plan which it began to implement in the following year under the presidency of Frank Barrett. We have almost exhausted that initiative. A Future Issues Report has been debated by the ICAI council, and the next step must be to determine the direction in which the Institute and our profession should be heading. Our council should be operating on the basis of a rolling five-year plan, identifying our objectives and setting down a comprehensive strategy.

Whatever strategy we may formulate to cope with the forces for change, we can be sure that the Institute and the profession in their present form will not exist in ten years' time, let alone in another 100 years. On the other hand the opportunities for the individual chartered accountants have never been better. To sum up our state of affairs at the start of this Institute's second century, it seems fair to say that on our current account the balance, although unsettled, stands to our credit.

It is a terrible thing for a man to find out suddenly that all his life he has been speaking nothing but the truth.

Oscar Wilde, *The Importance of Being Earnest*

Editorial introduction to 'The accountants' Big Bang'

Do accountants know what business they are in? Where their main competition is coming from now and in the near future? How vulnerable they are to acquisition? How much capital they need for acquisitions, training and technology? Michael Lafferty, editor-in-chief of *The Accountant,* in this pithy essay, doubts that they do know, and gives his views of the matter in clear and trenchant terms.

Michael Lafferty, F.C.A., I.C.A.E.W.

Michael Lafferty is chairman and chief executive of the Lafferty Group Limited, an integrated financial publishing, information and research organisation, which he founded in 1981.

With offices in London, Sydney and Atlanta, the group specialises in providing financial and business information to senior executives in the financial services industry worldwide, as well as to financial executives in industry in general.

Michael is a fellow of the Institute of Chartered Accountants in England and Wales, and the Institute of Chartered Accountants in Ireland. He was formerly a senior journalist with the *Financial Times* of London where he was both banking and accounting correspondent, and a writer on the Lex column. He received the Harold Wincott Award for 'Young Financial Journalist of the Year' in 1979.

Prior to launching the Lafferty Group, Michael Lafferty was the author and co-author of several books, including *Accounting in Europe* (1975), the *Financial Times World Survey of Annual Reports* (1980), the *Financial Times World Survey of Bank Annual Reports* and the *Survey of Accounts and Accountants* (1983).

Michael was born in Ballaghaderreen, Co. Roscommon and was educated at St Nathy's College, Ballaghaderreen.

The accountants' Big Bang

by Michael Lafferty

ON the face of it, accountants in public practice around the world are enjoying a boom period. 1986 saw fee growth of over twenty per cent from eight of the top twenty firms, and another four were up over fifteen per cent. Fee growth has been particularly strong in the area of management advisory services — most of the large UK firms showed fee growth of over forty per cent in this area in 1985, for example.

Another plus is the fact that the profession has clearly become more businesslike over the past decade. Advertising and overt marketing restrictions have gone in many countries, and are even under attack in Germany. Perhaps most important of all is the comforting thought that the profession still enjoys the great audit monopoly. Indeed it's being expanded in Europe.

There are some problems, I almost hear you say. Of course there are: increasing litigation, for one. But by and large accountants don't seem to be in the business doldrums. The profession is still one of the most popular for young people emerging from university.

Well, anyone who believes that the state of the accounting profession has never been better is, in my humble opinion, living in a dreamland. I firmly believe that many accounting firms do not yet know what business they are in, and because of this they are not even watching the right competitors. Think of the Bank of America analogy from the world of banking back in the seventies. B of A was a world player, leading the expansion of international lending and re-cycling the petrol dollars. Profits were consistently up. When I visited the bank's headquarters in San Francisco in 1981 I found an institution that confused me. Senior management did not talk about how different customer markets were performing and they were unbelievably out of touch with new technology. B of A clearly did not have adequate management accounts. In retrospect, we know that B of A lost its way — probably ten years earlier at the beginning of the seventies. It took until the early eighties for the world to be told just how serious its problems were. I fear some accountants and accounting firms are in a similar dilemma today.

My own firmly held view is that the business of public accountants is part of what we now call the financial services industry — including banking, insurance, the securities industry, and advice. Accountants provide advisory services of a business and financial nature to all economic entities — ranging from the most numerous (individuals) to elite world corporations. Unless accountants define their business in such a way they will not realise who their competitors are, let alone know what they are doing.

Let us look now at the megatrends in the financial services industry:

- A revolution is underway of unprecedented significance.
- Competition is the new name of the game.
- Cartels and restrictive practices are under fire, and rapidly disappearing.
- The barriers which have traditionally separated different types of financial institution are collapsing. More and more, we talk of a converging, integrating financial industry.
- There is a massive shift of interest towards personal consumer markets worldwide. This so-called retail financial services revolution will reshape financial institutions on customer group lines. Personal consumers are interesting because they ultimately possess all the wealth in the economy — and their financial assets and liabilities have been rising rapidly over recent decades.

  Today retail is probably the only significant source of profit for most financial institutions.
- The latest development on the retail side is towards a broad segmentation of the market — between affluent and wealthy customers and the rest. The affluent sub-sector of retail, the so-called private banking market is probably the area of greatest interest to many banks today. Some, like Deutsche Bank in West Germany reckon that eighty per cent of their retail profits come from it. It is particularly exciting because it inevitably embraces the professions, successful entrepreneurs and so forth.

  Private banking customers are interesting to banks and the financial institutions because they are not price sensitive and most of all because they want advice.
- While retail banking is booming, corporate banking is either going down the drain or becoming re-vitalised through the surge in securities market activity — as companies turn away from bank borrowing towards the securities markets for their funding requirements.
- There is a rush of new entrants to the financial industry particularly motivated by the consumer market.

  First of all there are retailers like Sears Roebuck, Marks & Spencer and Il Corte Ingles. Second, there are manufacturers like Ford and General Motors.

There are other important aspects of the financial services revolution but these are enough to illustrate the point that accountants are part of this industry, rather than something called accountancy.

The one overwhelming trend behind all these I have mentioned is that financial institutions are now dedicated to becoming the premier providers of advice to individuals — particularly the affluent — to entrepreneurs and to corporations. Accountants may think that this will not affect their profession — at least not yet. It already has.

- Financial institutions are already recruiting accounting talent in great numbers to service the different advisory markets.
- On the audit front, the financial industry is now by far the riskiest for auditors. Having lost so much credibility in their easy-going attitudes to the valuation of third world debt, auditors are now allowing banks to make their balance sheets even more misleading, because of the way so much new business is deemed to be off the balance sheet.

I have no doubt that organisations with ready access to capital are already considering the acquisition of accounting firms. A subsidiary of Scandinavian Bank has recently admitted this. And let us not forget that some accounting firms in Europe are already owned or effectively controlled by banks. Many are part of the Big Eight.

The need for capital is far greater than most accounting firms seem to realise. How else will firms finance the massive investment which is still necessary in training, in technology, let alone marketing and, most of all, acquisitions outside the profession?

But what about audit, I hear you ask? Apart from the fact that audit as a proportion of total fees is in decline — already to less than fifty per cent of the total in the case of half the Big Eight — I do not believe that a ban on outside capital is a prerequisite for independence.

Before concluding my comments about the business side of the profession let us consider another important trend.

The USA is becoming less and less dominant within the international accounting groups; in fact US fees accounted for a maximum of half of four of the Big Eight's fees in 1986. Europe and Japan are gaining ground. The balance of power is shifting. But then we should ask what the Japanese firms are up to anyhow. In my opinion Japanese accounting firms want to grow internationally and dominate their own international accountancy groups. In this the Minister for Finance is clearly playing a leading role.

> He took my father grossly, full of bread,
> With all his crimes broad blown, as flush as May;
> And how his audit stands who knows save heaven?
>
> Shakespeare, *Hamlet*

Excellence
A portrait gallery of some eminent accountants

In the next few pages we feature a small but elite group of chartered accountants who qualified as members of the Irish Institute, and who have reached the top of the ladder in careers other than professional practice. Inevitably, not all those who deserve a place have been included herein. We would have wished to include many more, had space permitted.

We are proud of these people. Many of them have brought their great abilities and professional attitudes into the service and leadership of Irish industry and commerce. But also we are proud that so many of them have reached eminence in countries all over the world. To them all we would offer the best wishes and congratulations of their mother Institute and of this Centenary volume.

The truth is rarely pure and never simple. Modern life would be very tedious if it were either, and modern literature a complete impossibility.

Oscar Wilde, *The Importance of Being Earnest*

New York skyline
London Stock Exchange

Donal S. A. Carroll, L.L.D., F.C.A.

Don was born in 1927 and was educated at Glenstal Abbey.

He qualified as a member of the Institute of Chartered Accountants in Ireland in 1952 and joined P.J. Carroll & Company, Limited, becoming chairman of that company in 1960.

He was appointed a director of the Bank of Ireland in 1956 and served terms as governor 1964-70 and 1982-5.

During his career he served on boards in industry and banking in Ireland and Britain, and on a variety of commissions and councils. Amongst those, John Jameson and Irish Distillers, Irish Ropes, Peter Kennedy Ltd, Irish Dunlop and the Irish Times, Chase and Bank of Ireland Ltd, Investment Bank of Ireland; in the UK, Dunlop Holdings plc, Lloyds and Bolsa of which he was chairman, and Rothmans International plc of which he is deputy chairman.

He has served on the councils of the Irish Management Institute and the Institute of Chartered Accountants, and was a member of the Inflation Accounting Steering Group.

He has served on the Higher Education Authority, the Public Service Advisory Council, Commission on Taxation, and was for twelve years a director of the Central Bank of Ireland.

Amongst international bodies, he has been a member of the International Institute of Banking Studies, the Atlantic Institute, and is a senior member of the Conference Board and a member of the Trilateral Commission.

He holds an honorary doctorate in Laws from Dublin University, an honorary fellowship of the International Academy of Management, is an honorary life fellow of the Irish Management Institute and an honorary life member of the Royal Dublin Society and of the Society of Designers in Ireland.

Michael J. Clancy, B.Comm., M.Econ.Sc., F.C.A.

Michael Clancy is chairman and chief executive of Exxon Energy Ltd and Esso Hong Kong Ltd, wholly owned subsidiaries of Exxon Corporation.

He is a fellow of the Institute of Chartered Accountants in Ireland and holds a masters degree in economic science. He spent many years with Esso in Europe, mainly in the UK, where he was a director of the marketing division of Esso Petroleum Company Ltd. In 1975 he was appointed chairman and chief executive of Esso in Ireland, and in 1978 was transferred to the headquarters in New York as assistant controller of Exxon Corporation. In 1980 he moved to the Far East as the finance director of Exxon's extensive exploration and production interests in Malaysia, and in 1983 took up his present position in Hong Kong.

Michael is also chairman of three power companies, in which Exxon has a sixty per cent controlling interest. These companies own four large generating stations which supply almost three-quarters of the electricity consumed in Hong Kong, Kowloon and the New Territories. He is a director of China Light and Power Company Ltd, Exxon's partner in the power business.

The fourth station is currently under construction, and when the work is completed in 1989, the combined capacity will be well in excess of 6,500 megawatts.

Esso Hong Kong Ltd is Exxon's petroleum subsidiary which operates in Hong Kong and the People's Republic of China, where the company has already established a chain of service stations, and conducts a wide range of marketing activities.

Michael and his wife Evelyn have two daughters, one of whom is a dentist in Dublin, and the other works with Price Waterhouse, Hong Kong. He greatly enjoys golf and fishing — the latter in the West of Ireland when he gets the chance.

Ronald Lewis Coppel, F.C.A., C.A.(A.)

Ronald Coppel is the executive director of Australian Stock Exchange Ltd. The Australian press asserts that he was the driving force behind the amalgamation of the six Australian Stock Exchanges into Australian Stock Exchange Ltd.

Ronald emigrated to Australia in 1963 and became a partner in the public accounting firm of Crowther Bird & Spilsbury. In 1970 he was appointed general manager of the Stock Exchange of Perth Ltd, and in February 1974 moved to Sydney to take up the executive directorship of Australian Associated Stock Exchanges, which subsequently amalgamated into the present body.

In the course of his work with the Stock Exchanges, he is responsible for relations with the federal government and with overseas Stock Exchanges.

In the accounting field he is a member of the Accounting Standards Review Board. This is a government appointment and the accounting standards which are approved by the board have the force of law.

Ronald was born in Belfast in 1933, and was educated at the Royal Belfast Academical Institution and the Belfast College of Technology. He served articles with Jackson McCann & Co., chartered accountants, in Belfast and qualified in 1955. From there he moved to take up a post with George A. Touche & Co. of London and returned to enter practice with his brother Michael Coppel in Belfast from 1956 to 1963. He then emigrated.

Ronald is married and has three grown-up children. He enjoys reading, politics, theatre and symphony music. He is a member of the West Australian Club.

Niall Crowley, F.C.A., I.C.A.E.W., C.A.(S.)

Niall is chairman of the Allied Irish Banks plc.

He was born on the 18 September 1926 and educated at Xavier School and Castleknock College. In 1953 he married Una Hegarty of Cork; they have five sons and one daughter.

In 1944 he entered his father's accounting firm of Kennedy Crowley & Co. as an articled clerk, obtaining second place in the Institute's final examination of 1949. He became a partner in 1950 and subsequently managing partner of the firm of Stokes Kennedy Crowley & Co. Until 1984 he was a consultant to that firm, which also represents KPMG in Ireland.

He took an active interest in the affairs of the Institute of Chartered Accountants in Ireland, as chairman of the Dublin District Society in 1957-8, a member of the council of the Institute from 1967 to 1973, vice-president in 1970-71, and president in 1971-2.

He became chairman of Allied Irish Banks in October 1977 having been a director since 1968, and is a director of a number of companies. He was president of the Irish Bankers Federation, and chairman of the Irish Banks' Standing Committee 1985-7, and president of the Institute of Bankers 1987-8.

He is a board member of the Fédération Bancaire of the EEC.

He is a member of the council and of the national executive of the Confederation of Irish Industry and chairman of the Financial Services Industry Association, a sector of the CII. He was president of the Dublin Chamber of Commerce for its bicentenary year in 1983-4. He is now a life member of Dublin Chamber of Commerce and of the Chambers of Commerce of Ireland, and a member of the Company of Goldsmiths of Dublin.

His hobbies are golf and bridge.

Harold Alexander Ennis, F.C.A., F.B.I.M.

Harold Ennis is group managing director of Boxmore International Ltd (BIL). BIL has three operating divisions with four separate plants, three in Northern Ireland, and one in the south. It has a number of depots in England, and trades throughout the world.

Since 1980 he has also been non-executive chairman of Tyrone Brick Ltd of Dungannon, Ireland's largest clay brick manufacturer. In 1982 he was appointed a board member of the state-owned Northern Ireland Electricity Service; and in 1984 a board member of the Industrial Development Board for Northern Ireland.

Harold was born in Co. Cavan in 1930, and educated in the Masonic School in Dublin. In 1948 he was articled to Maurice Jackson of M. Jackson & Co., chartered accountants, Belfast. He qualified in May 1953, having taken first place in all the examinations of the Institute in Ireland.

For a period he worked with Price Waterhouse & Co., chartered accountants, in London, and in 1957 joined the Dublin company, Unidare Ltd. In 1958 he was appointed divisional manager in their North of Ireland operations, and two years later he became chief executive of their recently created subsidiary, Unidare Engineering Ltd of Portadown.

In 1976 the Northern Bank Ltd approached him to become managing director of the troubled Lurgan Boxmaking Company Ltd. In 1983 the Bank's interest was bought out and the company renamed Boxmore Ltd. The holding company BIL was formed and Harold became group managing director.

In 1986 he was appointed a board member of a new government-established organisation, Technology Board for Northern Ireland.

He is also a council member of the Confederation of British Industry, Northern Ireland region, and assumed the chairmanship thereof in September 1987. Until his resignation two years ago he was a member of the Energy Policy Committee of the CBI in London. Harold has served as a council member of the Institute of Chartered Accountants in Ireland until he resigned four years ago.

Harold says that he intends to reduce some of his commitments in the near future so that he can devote more time to charitable work and to his involvement in work with the Confederation of British Industry. In the Queen's New Year Honour List in 1987 he was awarded the OBE.

Charles J. Haughey, B.Comm., B.L., F.C.A., TD

Charles Haughey has been Taoiseach (head of the government of Ireland) since 10 March 1987.

He was born in Castlebar, Co. Mayo in 1925, and educated in Dublin at Scoil Mhuire, Marino and St Joseph's CBS, Fairview. He took his commerce degree in University College Dublin, and his barrister's qualification through the King's Inns, Dublin.

In 1951 he married Maureen, eldest daughter of the late Sean F. Lemass, Taoiseach immediately following Eamon de Valera. He has one daughter, Eimear, and three sons, Conor, Ciaran and Sean.

His interests are music, reading, riding and swimming. He has always given his active support to the arts in Ireland.

He served for ten years as a commissioned officer in An Forsa Cosanta Aitiúil. During that period, from 1953 to 1955, he was a member of Dublin Corporation; thereafter his career has been political, serving as a member of Dáil Éireann continuously from 1957 to date. He acted as Parliamentary Secretary to the Minister for Justice in 1960-61; since then he has occupied a number of Ministries — Justice, 1961 to 1964; Agriculture, 1964 to 1966; Finance, 1966 to 1970; Health and Social Welfare, 1977 to 1979.

Between 1973 and 1977 he was chairman of the Joint Committee on the Secondary Legislation of the European Communities.

He was Taoiseach from December 1979 to June 1981, from March to December 1982, and from March 1987 to date. In the intervals he acted as leader of the opposition.

As an accounting student Charles Haughey won the John Mackie Memorial Prize, and later, in conjunction with his friend, Harry Boland, founded the accounting firm of Haughey, Boland & Co. He retired finally from all professional connections in 1971 to devote his life to politics.

Thomas Kenny, F.C.A.

Thomas Kenny was admitted to membership of the Irish Institute in 1941. He served for some years as a member of the council of the Institute. He practised as a partner with a London firm of chartered accountants and in later years specialised in new issues, mergers, reconstructions etc. At the behest of various banks he assisted problem companies. These activities led to his transition to the industrial scene.

For some years he has been chairman of GEI International plc, whose annual sales exceed £70 million, and of Ruberoid plc, with a turnover in excess of £137 million. In January 1985 he was appointed chairman to the largest engineering company in Sheffield, Sheffield Forgemasters plc (sales £100 million). In addition, he is chairman of Anglo Irish Bankcorp, whose gross assets exceed £100 million, and formerly of the City of Dublin Bank, apart from the two 'majors', one of the leading Irish banks. He is a director of various other companies.

His interests are fishing, horse racing and classical music. He is a member of the City of London Club, the Arts Club and the Flyfishers Club.

Howard E. Kilroy, F.C.A.

Howard was born in 1936, and is now president and chief operations director of the Jefferson Smurfit Group, which from its Irish base administers an enormous international operation, mainly in packaging.

He was articled in the firm of J. A. Kinnear & Co. In 1960 he joined CPC Ireland as financial controller, and became successively director and commercial manager of that company, planning manager of CPC UK, and European financial manager of CPC Europe, a concern with $750 million turnover in seventeen countries.

In 1973 he joined the Jefferson Smurfit Group as group financial controller.

Howard's directorships include the Jefferson Smurfit Group plc and subsidiaries, the Jefferson Smurfit Corporation, Smurfit Paribas Ltd, MacMillan Smurfit SCA Ltd, MacDonagh & Boland Ltd, Aran Energy and the Waterford Glass Group where he is non-executive deputy chairman.

He is a member of the council of the Irish Institute of Chartered Accountants, chairman of the Irish Management Institute, holding the chair in 1987, and chairman of the Irish Youth Foundation.

His interests are sailing, tennis, golf and skiing.

Sir Thomas Desmond Lorimer, F.C.A.

Sir Desmond's principal occupation is that of chairman and chief executive of Lamont Holdings plc, a group majoring in textiles, and with interests in engineering, computing and property development. He has been responsible for the Group from very small beginnings to one with an average turnover of £100 million and commensurate profits.

He was born in 1925 and was educated at Belfast Technical High School.

He practised as a chartered accountant from 1952 to 1974, becoming senior partner in Harmood Banner Smylie & Co. which later merged with Deloitte Haskins & Sells. He was appointed president of the Institute of Chartered Accountants in Ireland in 1968-9.

He was first chairman of the Northern Ireland Housing Executive, serving in that capacity from 1971 to 1975. This is a public authority created with the objective of removing housing from politics and merging the housing activities of numerous local authorities into a single professional organisation.

In 1970 he became a member of the McCrory Commission, a review body on local government in Northern Ireland.

From 1982 to 1985 he served as first chairman of the Industrial Development Board for Northern Ireland — a body charged with the task of attracting new, and developing indigenous, industry.

He was appointed chairman of Northern Bank Ltd in 1986, and his other directorships include Ruberoid plc, Irish Distillers Group plc, Old Bushmills Distillery Co. Ltd and Antrim Power Co. Ltd. In 1986 he became chairman of the latter two companies.

His recreations are gardening and golf. Sir Desmond was knighted for public service in 1976.

111

Eric W. McDowell, CBE, F.C.A.

Eric McDowell has been chairman of the Industrial Development Board for Northern Ireland since January 1986, and was a member since its inception in 1982.

Eric was born in Belfast in 1925 and educated at the Royal Belfast Academical Institution. He qualified as a chartered accountant through Wilson Hennessy & Crawford in 1948, becoming a partner in that firm in 1952. The firm merged with Deloitte Haskins & Sells in 1973, and he became senior partner in Belfast in 1980 until he retired in 1985.

He served on the committee of the students group of the Ulster Society of Chartered Accountants for four years, being chairman in 1948-9. He then served on the senior committee for nine years, and as chairman in 1963-4. From 1968 to 1977 he was a member of the council of the Institute of Chartered Accountants in Ireland, and was elected president for 1974-5.

He is a director of Spence Bryson Ltd and of TSB Northern Ireland plc. He serves the community in many ways: as governor of the Royal Belfast Academical Institution since 1958 and chairman of the Board from 1977 to 1986; member of the advisory committee of the Northern Ireland Central Investment Fund for Charities, and chairman of the committee since 1980; member of the Northern Ireland Economic Council from 1977 to 1983; and member of the Broadcasting Council for Northern Ireland from 1983 to 1986.

His recreational interests are current affairs, music, drama and foreign travel. He is married, with one son and two daughters.

The CBE was conferred upon him in 1982.

The picture opposite shows part of one of the companies which receives assistance from the Industrial Development Board.

Lochlann Gerard Quinn, B.Comm, F.C.A.

Lochlann Quinn was born and educated in Dublin. After school at Blackrock College he received a B.Comm. degree from UCD, and then took articles with a small Dublin firm, R. Stephen & Co. On qualification (1966) he joined Arthur Andersen & Co. in London. He returned to Dublin in 1969 when Arthur Andersen & Co. opened their Dublin office. He became a partner in 1976 and was in charge of the audit practice of the firm until he resigned in 1980.

In that year he took up the position of deputy chairman and finance director of Glen Dimplex, previously one of his clients while at Arthur Andersen.

Glen Dimplex, a privately owned Irish company, is today one of the largest 'small appliance' companies in the world with annual sales of some £300 million. The group, founded in 1973 by Martin Naughton — its chief executive — today employs 5,000 people with factories in Northern Ireland and the Republic (five), in England (five) and in the USA (two). The group includes companies such as Glen Electric and Dimplex Heating (UK market leaders in electric heating), Morphy-Richards (UK market leader in irons and toasters) and Hamilton Beach (US market leader in food processors and mixers).

Lochlann is married with six children and lives in Dublin. His interests include golf, food, paintings — and the West of Ireland!

Editorial Introduction to 'The American influence'

The two great sources of exterior influence on the accounting environment in these islands are North America and Europe. Of these two the American stream, at this moment, is the older and deeper. What happens over there comes to be a boon or a plague sooner or later. Partly that is because we cannot escape the might of American cultural dominance. But also the influences flow from the great American corporations to their European subsidiaries, of which there are many.

In this essay Professor Alistair Duff, of McGill University, Montreal, identifies a number of the major trends in American thought. Many authorities are of the opinion that the professions are more interested in maintaining their own position of privilege than in protecting the public. So government and para-government bodies are taking an increasing interest in imposing regulatory measures. Whilst there are many arguments to justify such action, the dangers, as illustrated by Duff, are that political rather than professional criteria may dominate; and that the (sometimes appalling) delays of bureaucracies can stymie both self-regulation and responsiveness to change.

Sometimes one could imagine that litigation was an American invention. Of course not. But 'in the US, a society more litigious than most, the payment of contingency fees to lawyers . . . and the use of juries in tort cases have led to a staggering escalation in court awards'. We can, perhaps, take some comfort that 'in most countries the legislators recognise that the current situation is intolerable', and are considering legislative action to limit personal liability.

A very interesting Canadian initiative is the comprehensive or value-for-money auditing concept, developed by that country's Auditor General.

The foregoing comments are selective, and Professor Duff's essay ranges across many other subjects.

Do but take care to express yourself in a plain, easy Manner, in well-chosen, significant and decent Terms, and to give a harmonious and pleasing Turn to your periods; study to explain your Thoughts, and set them in the truest Light, labouring as much as possible, not to leave them dark nor intricate, but clear and intelligible.

Cervantes, Preface to *Don Quixote*

How the absence of sound financial advice altered the course of American history

Alistair Duff, B.A., M.A., F.C.A.

Alistair Duff is president of the Canadian Institute
of Chartered Accountants for the year 1987-8.

Born at Coagh, Co. Tyrone, he was educated at
Campbell College, Belfast and took an honorary
degree in law at Queen's College, Cambridge.

He joined the firm of Fitzpatrick Graham &
Co. in London, and qualified as an associate of
the Institute of Chartered Accountants of England
and Wales. In 1964 he emigrated to Montreal,
and worked in public practice and industry until
1968, when he was appointed head of professional
accountancy programmes at McGill University.
He acted as director of continuing education from
1972 to 1987; served on the University Senate for
fifteen years; and on the University Board of
Governors (including its executive committee) for
three years.

For twenty years he has been active in the
profession in Canada. In 1980-81 — the year of
its centenary — he was president of the Order
(Institute) of Chartered Accountants of Quebec,
and for a while chairman of its education
committee. He has been a member of the board
of governors of the Canadian Institute of
Chartered Accountants since 1978, and was
chairman of the Council of Provincial Institutes of
Canada 1983-5. He assumed presidency of the
Institute in September 1987.

Alistair and his wife Jennifer live in Montreal
and have three daughters and one son.

The American influence

by Alistair Duff

Introduction

IF, as good accountants, we were to evaluate the influence of Ireland on North America compared to the influence of North America on Ireland, the overwhelming majority would conclude, I am sure, that the former greatly outweighs the latter. The songs and stories are merely reflections of fact. And yet the myths remain. One need only visit New York City or Atlanta on 17 March to see a St Patrick's day parade, the like of which Dublin has never seen. Everyone, and I mean everyone, is wearing green and claiming Irish ancestry — some of it can be pretty tenuous and stretch the imagination!

It is common knowledge that Ireland gave to the United States leading politicians and artists, but it is less well known that many very successful businessmen in North America had Irish roots. For example, the Mellons, who became one of the richest and most powerful families in the US through banking and other business interests, were once poor farmers near my home town in Co. Tyrone.

In large measure, however, this influence is historical. The great waves of Irish emigration to the New World have inevitably forged cultural and economic links that are extraordinarily strong. But the Second World War was indeed a turning point. What had been a flow of human resources westward became a flow of financial resources, business ideas and lifestyle eastward. The economic power of the United States spread throughout the world in the fifties and sixties, and was often referred to as the 'American influence'. These days, however, that term is used pejoratively and is associated with the Golden Arches, chewing gum, junk bonds, polyester leisure suits and pop videos. This breeds a kind of anti-Americanism 'which seeks to make the United States the scapegoat for the sins of western modernity'.

This image of the 'ugly American' persists, and yet in business and the accountancy profession in particular, the United States has had a significant influence that has largely been beneficial. While accounting may have been called 'the language of business', the real international language in business is undoubtedly English. Whether it is in aviation, computers, high-technology, science or even accountancy, the lingua franca is English. It is inevitable therefore that the largest concentration of English-speaking people, i.e. North America, coupled with the fact that it also happens to be the greatest economic power in the world (at least for the moment), should have the greatest influence in business and matters economic.

The growth of the multi-national companies, the large majority of which until recently had their head offices in the United States, has had a profound impact, in Western Europe particularly, on the way of doing business and consequently on the practice of the accountancy profession. US-imposed audit and reporting requirements, including producing information for the annual report on Form 10-K to the Securities and Exchange Commission in Washington, DC, and audit review by the parent company's auditors, have changed the practice of accountancy throughout the world. The effect on CA firms has been dramatic and far greater than the traditionally insular Americans could possibly imagine, or for that matter far greater than the British, Irish, Canadian or European accountants would care to admit.

Self-regulation and independence

It was the Scots who founded the accountancy profession as we know it today, and it was they who brought it to North America. In fact two Scotsmen — James Court and Philip Ross — organised the association of accountants in Montreal that received its charter from the Quebec Legislature on 24 July 1880. This was the first formal accountancy organisation in North America and only the second outside Scotland, the Institute of Chartered Accountants in England and Wales having been granted its charter a mere six weeks previously.

The concepts of self-regulation and independence are fundamental to the liberal professions. From the beginning, the accountancy profession has had as two of its primary objects the maintenance of professional standards and the discipline of members. By any objective measurement, the record of the accountancy profession in this regard has been second to none. Even so, the professions in North America are under increasing challenge that they are more interested in maintaining their own position of privilege than in protecting the public.

Both government and para-government bodies have moved into this arena, and in varying ways are encroaching on the rights of the profession to regulate itself and maintain its independence. In Quebec for example, in 1973 the government enacted umbrella legislation to govern all professions practising in the province. The professional code established a professions board whose responsibility it is 'to see that each professional corporation ensures the protection of the public'. The legislation requires that each professional corporation must conform to a common set of regulations covering the governance of the profession, and the system of professional inspection and discipline. The effect of this legislation on the chartered accountancy profession in Quebec has been to reduce significantly its independence, its ability to regulate itself and its responsiveness to change. Moreover, the public not only is no better protected but is in fact more poorly served. Amendments to regulations that are necessary to meet changing needs are being delayed by the bureaucracy for up to eight years.

This is one model that other governments are not likely to adopt. Nevertheless, in spite of the free market trends on both sides of the Atlantic, there is ample evidence that governments will not sit idly by if professions are seen to be derelict in their duty of maintaining professional standards and disciplining their members. In our experience in Canada, a business failure of major proportions can change the heretofore benign attitude of a government regulator overnight.

I believe that the profession in Quebec has made a significant contribution to the assurance that members maintain high standards through its system of inspection of practising offices. The Quebec Institute was the first to implement such a programme and it has been widely adopted, with or without modification, in many jurisdictions throughout the world. A similar system is expected to be adopted by Ireland in the near future. While it is an after-the-fact monitoring of professional service, it nevertheless demonstrates to the public, and to government, that the profession is serious about maintaining standards and is prepared to act where deficiencies exist. The benefit is not only in the public relations aspect, but also to the practitioner and indeed to the client.

The setting of accounting and auditing standards

The American Institute of Certified Public Accountants was the first private-sector body to promulgate accounting standards when it issued its first Accounting Research Bulletin in 1939. The Institutes in Canada, Great Britain and Ireland, have followed suit and are now well established as the standard-setters for accounting and auditing in their respective countries. Canada is unique in one respect in that the accounting standards of the Canadian Institute of Chartered Accountants are mandated by the Canadian Business Corporations Act for all federally incorporated public companies in Canada. But even this is no guarantee of compliance.

Two examples will illustrate the fragile nature of the CICA's position. In 1982 the Canadian government introduced a programme of grants to encourage oil exploration. The government, aided and abetted by some of the oil companies, for purely political purposes wanted the companies to show the grants as revenue in the year in which the grant was received rather than spread over the period of exploration as required by the CICA accounting standard. The dispute became so serious that the minister stated in a letter to the CICA president that the government would set its own accounting standard, which would have been a first, and the thin end of the wedge. Fortunately, the Securities Administrators in Canada supported the CICA and other political and economic events overtook the grant issue, so that the CICA position as standard-setter remained intact.

The second event was the financial collapse of two major banks in Western Canada in the fall of 1985. This led to considerable criticism of the accounting standards being used in the financial reporting by banks. Even though a Royal Commission gave general support to the CICA and its standards, the Inspector-General of Banks — the government regulator — is still considering imposing his own requirements.

In the United States the Financial Accounting Standards Board, although officially independent of the AICPA, is generally regarded as a creature of the profession. The Securities and Exchange Commission has affirmed on a number of occasions its intent to rely on the pronouncements of the FASB. Nevertheless, the SEC retains the final authority and has intervened in the standard-setting process several times on such issues as accounting for current costs and for oil and gas exploration.

These examples only serve to illustrate the perilous nature of the profession's right to set accounting standards. Provided the profession can respond to the needs in a timely and appropriate manner, there should be little cause for concern. But the threat of political interference exists and in Canada, ever since our experience over the Petroleum Incentive Program grants, we have been more vigilant. It would appear that in Great Britain and Ireland similar threats exist, if the editorial entitled 'Amateur Accountants' in the 11 April 1987 issue of the *Economist* is anything to go by. In a very critical piece they proclaim 'British (and Irish) accountants will have to do much better if they are to be allowed to retain their jealously-guarded autonomy'. To ignore their warning on either side of the Atlantic is to do so at our peril.

The accounting standards issued in the United States have influenced greatly the standard-setting process and the product of that process in Ireland and Britain — Canada has been influenced more than either. It has been clearly established by Stephen A. Zeff that 'the Canadian Institute committee and the Accounting Standards Committee of the CCAB have freely borrowed the subjects of many of their pronouncements from the Americans'. It is quite likely that because of the more developed securities market in the US, the aggressiveness of its financial press, and the interventionist attitude of the SEC, accounting problems will tend to arise and be addressed earlier in the US than in other countries.

Accountants' professional liability

The cost and availability of legal liability insurance has become a pressing issue to professional accountants everywhere, and it is hard to deny that this trend had its origins in the US. Over the past two years, there have been horror stories about huge increases in premiums and reductions in, and even complete withdrawal of, insurance coverage.

Insurance problems, however, are not so much the cause of the crisis as the result of it. We live and work in an increasingly litigious society in which courts favour compensation to an injured party as the absolute priority, irrespective of degree of fault or ability to compensate a successful claimant. To a large degree the 'insurance crisis' reflects the current economic and social climate as well as serious deficiencies in the tort system. In these circumstances, a 'deep pocket syndrome' has developed. A firm of auditors is often seen to have the deepest pockets of any party associated with a failed company.

In the US, a society more litigious than most, the payment of contingency fees to lawyers (hence the ambulance-chasing phenomenon) and the use of juries in tort cases have led to a staggering escalation in court awards. Suppliers of goods and services are now exposed to unacceptable risks — particularly public accountants whose personal assets are at risk operating, as they must, in a partnership or as a sole practitioner.

A medium-sized firm in the US has recently been sued for US \$1 billion — an amount many times in excess of its insurance coverage — for alleged deficiencies in the audit of ESM Government Securities, a securities dealer that collapsed in 1985. Probably the most shocking case took place in Australia, where damages equivalent to Aus \$145 million were awarded against a twenty-nine-partner firm (Fell & Starkey) which audited Cambridge Credit Corporation, a company that collapsed in the mid-1970s. If the award is upheld on appeal, each of the partners will undoubtedly be personally bankrupt, irrespective of his or her personal involvement in or knowledge of events that precipitated the suit. This is clearly unjust. No wonder then that professional accountants, faced with such unlimited personal liabilities for the sins of omissions of all partners, are having second thoughts about the once-hallowed joys of partnership.*

In a way, auditors are the victims of their own reputations. Surveys, such as the one conducted by the leading US pollster Lou Harris in 1986, indicate that the public has an extremely high regard for the auditing professionals — notwithstanding current scandals and allegations. At their 1986 annual meeting in Kansas City, members of the AICPA were warned by Mr Harris that this reputation represented a goldmine of good opinion — and at the same time a serious trap when it comes to public expectations. Because auditors are regarded so highly, their failure or inability to detect fraud, predict business failure or even guarantee investments may be regarded as dereliction of duty.

It is encouraging to note, however, that in most countries the legislators recognise that the current situation is intolerable. In the US legal reform has begun in such areas as joint and several liability, the 'privity' rule (a rule that

---

*It was reported in July 1987 that the award was not upheld on appeal. (Editor)

limits the class of third parties who can sue), and an overall capping or limitation of liability. The Undersecretary of State for Corporate and Commercial Affairs in the United Kingdom has acknowledged the liability crisis and has conceded that there exists 'a case for reexamining the current state of the laws of tort' and in particular, 'the principle of joint and several liability in the concept of contribution in negligence'.

Practice mergers and oligopolistic tendencies

As H. W. Robinson points out in his *History of Accountants in Ireland,* the economic and social changes following the second world war 'imposed heavier and more varied responsibilities on accountants. The width of knowledge required to conduct an accountancy practice, other than one of the most limited scope, became greater than the ordinary individual accountant could absorb.' The mergers that took place in Ireland during the 1960s and 1970s were in effect the second wave of associations that saw the coming together of the great accountancy firms on both sides of the Atlantic.

As the major accounting firms moved to consolidate their dominance in the profession around the world, the smaller national and regional firms moved quickly to develop alliances that would enable them to compete. All these firms are convinced that the increasing complexity of business, taxation and finance on an international level requires expertise that only size and the concomitant economy of scale can provide.

A major factor in this development was the introduction to the accountancy firms of the management consultancy and ancillary service side of the practice. Begun in the US and accepted with some reluctance in Great Britain and Ireland, this financially lucrative part of the practice has grown to the point where in most if not all large firms the audit represents less than fifty per cent of total fees.

Management consultants do not enjoy a very high reputation. Some twenty years ago, Peter Drucker, a leading American academic and author, condemned management consultants as those who borrow your watch to tell you what time it is — and than keep your watch! Too harsh perhaps, but nevertheless it has had some major implications. The perception that firms use their position as auditors to gain profitable consulting contracts, thereby putting themselves in a position of possible conflict of interest, has led some US congressmen and senators to suggest that firms that do the audit of a company should not perform consulting services to that same client. The fact that bidding for audit contracts has become fairly common in North America and that some firms are prepared to submit bids that are ridiculously low, only confirms this opinion.

The concentration of major audits in the hands of the biggest firms is clearly established. In Canada for instance, between 1971 and 1981, the Big

Eight CA firms moved from having forty-two per cent of the large public company audits to ninety-nine per cent of these audits. In spite of the fact that these firms are fiercely competitive, this concentration is viewed by many outside the profession to be unhealthy, and there have been calls from different groups such as a Royal Commission in Canada and a Congressional Hearing in the US for required rotation of auditors.

In this age of entrepreneurship and deregulation, there is a natural urge to let the competition of the marketplace drive the pace of change in the accountancy profession. Public support for such a path is likely, and such enticements are attractive, even seductive. But the accountancy profession is not just another commercial enterprise, to be deregulated in a manner similar to airlines and telecommunications. We would do well to remember the admonition of Chief Justice Burger of the US Supreme Court, who in a case in 1984 stated 'the independent auditor assumes a public responsibility transcending any employment relationship with the client'.

The international perspective

As business has increasingly crossed national borders and taken on a global dimension, so too, of necessity, has the accountancy profession. The development of the Irish Institute parallels the Canadian experience. Both Ireland and Canada are relatively small countries, but with world class accountancy professions. Economically they are similar in that they are highly dependent on world trade, and they are both next to and dominated by large, economically powerful neighbours. For these reasons they have strong commitments to the international harmonisation of the accountancy profession.

The Irish and Canadian Institutes are active members of and contributors to the International Federation of Accountants and the International Accounting Standards Committee. It is interesting to note that the United States is not so committed. In a 1986 publication of the Organisation for Economic Cooperation and Development, entitled Harmonisation of Accounting Standards, the then chairman of the FASB, Donald J. Kirk, stated: 'relatively few US companies have significant international business activities. Therefore, the majority of business enterprises are not concerned with overseas problems, and are unlikely to see the need for international accounting standards. As a result, giving special weight, or even equal weight, to overseas imperatives is just not possible in the US standard-setting process.' Nevertheless, intentionally or otherwise, the influence of the US on international standards and professional practice is great and likely to remain so.

Other trends

There are a number of recent developments in North America that could affect the practice of accountancy in Ireland in the future.

Comprehensive or value-for-money auditing involves an examination that provides an objective and constructive assessment of the extent to which financial, human and physical resources are managed with due regard to economy, efficiency and effectiveness, and accountability relationships are reasonably served. This field has grown considerably in the past ten years and has expanded from strictly the government sector to the large not-for-profit sector including hospitals and educational institutions. The methodology of comprehensive auditing was first developed by the Auditor General of Canada and from that the Canadian Comprehensive Auditing Foundation was established in 1980 as a research and training-oriented organisation. The Foundation has promoted the concept of value for money auditing in Canada and throughout the world, where it has been well received and implemented in many countries. Although initially a field restricted primarily to legislative auditors, the Canadian experience has been that a large number of CA practitioners have gained an expertise in the area and are developing it into an important part of their practice.

The board of governors of the Canadian Institute decided in June 1987 to implement a number of recommendations contained in the report of its Long Range Strategic Planning Committee. The most far-reaching of these is the move towards the formal recognition of specialisation within the profession and the effect that it will have on the programme of pre- and post-qualification education. There is a consensus in Canada that the body of knowledge expected of a chartered accountant has expanded to such an extent that it is not reasonably achievable at the initial qualification level. It is proposed to have two distinct areas of knowledge — core and elective. Core knowledge would be required of all members and would equate to the current syllabus. Elective refers to specialist knowledge in recognised areas of the profession that would be acquired by members at a later stage in their professional careers and on an elective basis.

Meanwhile in the United States, the council of the AICPA in May 1987 approved the 'Plan to Restructure Professional Standards', which calls for, among other recommendations, a practice-monitoring programme, a 120-hour continuing professional education requirement over a three-year period for members in public practice, and a post-baccalaureate education requirement beginning in the year 2000.

Another example of the changing times in which we live, is the implementation by the Securities and Exchange Commission of its Electronic Data Gathering and Retrieval System (EDGAR). In future all registrant companies will be required to file with the Commission electronically. The question is posed, whether computerised systems such as EDGAR and the central balance-sheet data service of the Banque de France will determine more than just the format of financial reporting and what role will be left for the accountancy profession?

Conclusion

Influence is a stimulus for change. In the past forty years the Institute in Ireland has been profoundly affected by events in North America, but not all of those influences have been beneficial — witness the professional liability problem. In spite of the shift in economic power to the Orient, and the growing importance of the European Economic Community, I believe that the influence of North America on the accountancy profession in Ireland and indeed throughout the world will continue as a major force for many years to come.

It is hardly conceivable that the accounting profession will ever reach a position where certain groups or individuals will be empowered with authority which will permit them to decide definitively and exclusively all matters of principle and procedure.

Brother La Salle, 'Basic Research in Accounting', *The Accounting Review*, October 1959, p. 604

Editorial Introduction to 'Interlocking with Europe'

There is nobody better than Margaret Downes, now president of the Fédération des Experts Comptables Européens, to comment on the relationship between the Irish accountants and their European colleagues. The influences are by no means one way. By virtue of the nature of the Irish accountancy structure, and the broad range of work which Irish accountants do, the membership of the profession here is greater than it is in any other country in Europe except Britain, France and Italy! So our influence is considerable, and it is interesting indeed to be told that whatever shocks we have had here on the introduction of the various company law directives, they are as nothing to the effects the directives have had on much European practice.

Margaret sketches the fundamental differences in the practices of the 'Anglo-Saxons' and most of the rest of Europe; and then assesses the major import of the company law directives. As far as auditors are concerned the regulations designed to ensure independence, when they come, may be the ones having the most far-reaching effect.

The directives, of course, are not the only source of change. Market forces are also at work to bring the two traditions together. The ultimate outcome of convergence, it is hoped, will lead to the mutual recognition of diplomas and professional qualifications, and will therefore open the doors to Europe-wide competition, and ease of movement for professionals.

How much influence we have on the meeting point of convergence depends greatly on whether our profession is a good advertisement for self-regulation. Margaret suggests that we may need to tighten our braces somewhat!

> The final cause of speech is to get an idea as exactly as possible out of one mind into another. Its formal cause therefore is such choice and disposition of words as will achieve this end most economically.
>
> G. M. Young

The European parliament

Margaret Downes, B.Comm., F.C.A.

Margaret Downes is a past president of the Institute of Chartered Accountants in Ireland and is president of the European Federation of Accountants (FEE) for 1987-8.

She is a director of the Bank of Ireland and a number of Irish public and private companies. She is chairman of the state-owned Kilkenny Design Limited. She is a director of the Douglas Hyde Gallery, Trinity College, and our Lady's Hospital, Crumlin.

She was a partner in Coopers & Lybrand for twenty years, has participated in a number of government reviews/committees and was for four years chairman of the Archbishop of Dublin's financial council. She has published articles and given talks on accounting related matters. Her interests are art, travel and tennis.

Interlocking with Europe

by Margaret Downes

O N 29 October 1986 in Lausanne the Fédération des Experts Comptables Européens (FEE) was founded to bring together in a single organisation a total of thirty-two accountancy bodies from twenty-one European countries, which between them have a membership of over 300,000 individuals. The fact that its first president and first secretary general are both members of the Institute of Chartered Accountants in Ireland is a measure of the extent to which our Institute plays a major role in the accountancy profession in Europe. One reason for this is our size: although it may come as a surprise to many, in all of Europe, only Britain, France and Italy have professional accountancy bodies which are larger than our Institute, despite the relatively small size of our population.

Our involvement with the European profession is, however, only some twenty-five years old. FEE replaced two existing organisations, the Union Européenne des Experts Comptables, Économiques et Financiers (UEC) and the Groupe d'Études des Experts Comptables de la CEE (Groupe d'Études). UEC was founded in 1951, yet the Irish Institute did not become a member until 1963; and we joined the Groupe d'Études, founded in 1961, only on Ireland's accession to the EEC in 1973.

For most of the one hundred years since our foundation, it has been easier for us to identify more closely with our fellow professionals in the Anglo-Saxon countries — England, the United States, Canada, Australia, New Zealand and so forth. To a large extent, this is because we share a common language. Of even greater importance, however, is the fact that we share a common conception of what the accountancy profession is.

Our profession was in existence long before the statutory audit requirement was introduced, and for us auditing was always only part of accountancy. Our professional bodies are old and well established, our members work both in public practice and outside of it, and the range of tasks to which we can apply our skills is very wide.

The legal systems in our countries have diverged over the years, but they are all built on the foundation of English Common Law, and governments have traditionally granted us a large degree of autonomy in the running of our own affairs. In most of the countries mentioned, the profession continues to set its own accounting and auditing standards, it decides on education and training requirements, it controls access to the profession and it administers its own disciplinary procedures. Recognition to carry out statutory audits is normally granted indirectly on the basis of membership of one of the professional bodies, rather than directly on an individual basis.

This self-regulatory autonomy has reduced the importance of state borders and has enabled a very large degree of international co-operation within the profession. Nowhere is this more obvious than in the case of our own Institute, which is unique in Europe in that it is the only one which covers two separate jurisdictions. Going slightly further afield, we can see how the six CCAB (Consultative Council of Accountancy Bodies) organisations in Britain and Ireland have been able to co-operate very effectively in the setting of joint accounting and audit standards. On a more worldwide level, the International Federation of Accountants (IFAC) — founded in 1977 — grew out of the Accountants International Study Group which, for the ten preceding years, had joined together the American, Canadian, English and Welsh, Scottish and Irish Institutes.

The European background

The background in continental Europe is very different, but not consistently so, since national differences are much more pronounced. Indeed, there is no such thing as a homogeneous European accountancy profession. Some European languages do not even have a word for accountant. In those countries, the public accountancy profession is first and foremost an auditing profession.

There, as a generalisation, the statutory audit requirement came first, and governments then set up auditing professions under very strict and detailed legislation. It is therefore not unusual for accounting standards to be set by government agencies, for education and training requirements to be laid down in law, for examinations to be run by the government, and for disciplinary actions to be taken by semi-government bodies, or even the courts. It is by virtue of licence from the state that a professional may audit, and the state can take that licence away. In many countries, accountants must resign their qualification if they leave public practice, and Belgium goes as far as to say that they must derive all but a small percentage of their fee income from audit work.

This has led, in many European countries, to highly specialised and highly qualified professions, but ones with very little by way of public profile. Germany, the most developed and most prosperous country in Western Europe with a population of some sixty-two million, has less than 4,500 Wirtschaftsprüfer, whilst we in Ireland have some 6,000 chartered accountants. There are explanations for this: to be a Wirtschaftsprüfer you must be in public practice and a German resident — whereas over fifty per cent of our members work in industry and many members work abroad. In Germany, tax advisers are a separate profession, insolvency work is done by lawyers, very few management consultants are members of the profession and banks are major advisers to small businesses. And, last but not least, it is a truly exceptional Wirtschaftsprüfer who qualifies before the age of thirty-five.

It is therefore easy to see how much the image of the accountant in many European countries differs from that of the Irish chartered accountant, and from accountants in the Anglo-Saxon areas with which we are more familiar. However, given Ireland's membership of the European Communities, the differences are important and the factors giving rise to them will have an increasing influence on our Institute and its members in the future.

The Treaty of Rome

In 1957, the Treaty of Rome set as one of the major objectives of the EEC the establishment of a single European market in which there would be free movement of goods, capital, people and services — hence the expression 'Common Market'. Progress towards achieving this target has been slow, which recently prompted the commission to publish a crash programme of 300 steps which must be taken to complete the internal market by 1992. It is not certain that this deadline will be met, but it is indicative of the new sense of urgency underlying the legislative programme of the community.

Directives on company law

Of greatest importance to us in the accountancy profession is the series of directives on company law. The directives aim, inter alia, at achieving a greater harmonisation of financial reporting throughout the twelve member states, and address such areas as accounting principles, disclosure and publication require-ments, consolidation and so forth. Recognising the importance of the external audit function to the financial reporting process, they also lay down a statutory audit requirement and deal with the independence, training and qualification of auditors.

This is a welcome recognition of the significant contribution our profession can make. However, and this is what is important to us in Ireland, the approach and philosophy underlying the directives are based on the continental image of the accountant. They deal only with accountants in public practice and concen-trate on the accountant's role as auditor. The concept of the accountant as friend and adviser to his/her client is not one with which the Commission is com-fortable. We are perceived to be bloodhounds, not watchdogs — policemen and women acting for the public, not business advisers acting for our clients.

The development of the company law directives can be divided into a number of different categories:

- The first category covers those directives aimed at companies, with little or no impact on the profession. Coming under this heading are the first, second, third and sixth directives which deal, respectively, with publicity requirements, ultra vires and nullity; the formation of companies and capital and dividend requirements; mergers of public limited companies; and splitting of public limited companies. These directives were largely non-controversial and have been implemented in Ireland and most other member states without much bother. Still outstanding in this area are the draft ninth directive on the law on groups of companies and the proposed tenth directive on cross-border mergers of group companies, neither of which is likely to be adopted in the near future as these issues are not perceived as being particularly urgent.

- The second category is made up of those directives which have a major impact on the work we do but do not really affect the way the profession organises itself. So far, these are the fourth and seventh directives which deal with company and consolidated accountants, respectively. Ireland implemented the fourth directive in 1986 (only Italy, Spain and Portugal remain outstanding) and its influence is one of form rather than substance. Standard formats have been introduced for accounts and private companies must file a copy of their accounts with the registration authorities for the first time, but we have not had to change our accounting principles or throw away our Statement of Standard Account Practices (SSAPs). The same promises to be true for the seventh directive, which is supposed to come into force in 1990. So far, only France and Germany have passed the necessary implementing legislation and it is only realistic to expect delays elsewhere similar to those with the fourth. The fourth and seventh directives excluded banks and insurance companies because of the special considerations involved, but in December 1986 the directive on bank accounts was adopted, whilst the proposed directive on insurance accounts was released in January 1987. Subject matters still outstanding include deferred tax and foreign currency translation, but progress is being made.

- It's only when we reach the third stage that our present comfortable world begins to be threatened. This is the stage at which Brussels, having determined what work we should do, starts to tell us how to do it and how to run our profession. The first element in this is the eighth directive which lays down requirements for the education, training and qualification of auditors. The directive was adopted in 1984 and is due, barring the inevitable delays, to become effective in all member states in 1990. Reading through the text, we in Ireland would seem to have little to worry about, since our education and training system easily meets the requirements of the directive. Only at the end do we come to the sting in the tail, when the directive requires that auditors be independent.

Independence is not actually defined in the text, but one need only look at the consultative paper issued by the Department of Trade and Industry in the UK in the autumn of 1986 to see what wide interpretations can be put on it. Our colleagues in our two sister Institutes are resigned to greater governmental regulation and the most realistic strategy, which they have adopted, is to keep it to a minimum. But some regulation there will be.

And that's not the end of it. The eighth directive does not actually define independence and many of the proposals in the DTI paper were taken from the draft fifth directive. Most of this draft directive deals with the structure of public limited companies and has been stuck in the machinery in Brussels for years. Having begun life when most European governments were left of centre, the fifth directive now finds itself in a right of centre environment, and many of its proposals, increased worker participation for example, are the subject of criticism. The directive is unlikely to be finalised before the end of the decade. Untouched by all of this controversy have been the sections of auditors' independence. These propose maximum length audit appointments (three to six years), significantly extended audit reporting requirements, and severe limitations on the movements of personnel between audit firms and clients. Fixed fees, compulsory rotation and a prohibition of providing non-audit services are also possible.

For a while it appeared as if the implementation of these proposals would be subject to the same considerable delays as the rest of the fifth directive, but the Commission is now considering whether to take the audit-related sections out and include them instead in a separate directive devoted entirely to auditing, or possibly add them on as an amendment to the eighth directive. This would place the spotlight squarely on our profession, and there is no telling what might happen to us when we are subject to the undivided attentions of the Commission, the European Parliament and the Council of Ministers.

Shocks and adjustments

FEE, through its EC committee, is recognised by the Commission as being the sole consultative voice for the European accountancy profession and, as a result, we are closely involved in the drafting of directives from the earliest stages. FEE does its utmost to protect our profession's interests but, as we have already seen, the accepted tradition in Europe is that the profession should be tightly regulated by government, and not self-regulating, as we in Ireland take for granted.

Some would say that it is time the profession here got a shock. We have already seen how the directives adopted so far had little effect on us, but their impact elsewhere in Europe has sometimes been little less than shattering. Until the implementation of the fourth directive, French and German financial statements didn't have any notes, just a balance sheet and profit and loss account.

Normally, only the very largest companies were subject to audit. Until the seventh directive was implemented, German consolidated financial statements did not include foreign subsidiaries. The eighth directive, which requires that accountancy firms be controlled by accountants, will lead to significant changes in ownership in many countries, where firms were subsidiaries of banks and insurance companies. Why should we be let off lightly?

Why indeed? Only if we can demonstrate beyond doubt that our way of running our profession is clearly better, do we stand any chance of retaining the freedom and flexibility which we now take for granted. Although difficult, this is not an impossible task. Even though the Commission's image of the profession has been conditioned by the continental environment, they do acknowledge that the profession in Ireland and the UK is different. In size alone, the difference is enormous. Well over a third of the accountants who, through their Institutes, are members of FEE, are Irish or English. This is out of all proportion to the populations of these countries and, to be blunt, gives us a degree of political clout which some of our continental colleagues don't have. The strength of this can be judged by the extent of the changes made to the fourth directive, then in draft form, after Ireland and England joined the EEC in 1973. By insisting that a true and fair view be incorporated in the directive, we introduced a concept unheard of in any other European country except the Netherlands, causing untold difficulty for everybody else, and put back adoption of the directive by five years.

The fact that the concept of a true and fair view is now enshrined in Community law is extremely important because it is an admission, unique in the context of codified law, that the law cannot be expected to cover everything. The extension of this is that the auditor knows best, and therefore must be left with some room for manoeuvre or self-regulation. This is only a small chink in the armour, but one which we must exploit to the full, and quickly. We believe we know the difference between substance and form, but for many brought up in the continental tradition, legal form is the only substance which financial reporting has. If, as in Germany, the overriding concept is prudence, so as to keep distributable profits and dividends low, thereby protecting creditors, it is very difficult to speak in terms of economic reality. The French have come to grips very well with the concept of a true and fair view, as is demonstrated by their translation 'image fidèle'. But when one considers the distinctly un-snappy German version 'ein den tatsächlichen Verhältnissen entsprechendes Bild' one begins to appreciate the problem.

Therein lies the challenge to our profession in Ireland. The directives represent a force for convergence between the Anglo-Saxon and continental approaches within the accountancy profession in Europe, but it is not yet clear where the two will meet. If all goes according to the Commission's timetable, the die will have been cast by 1992, so if we wish to influence events it is essential that we become fully involved as a matter of urgency.

Market forces

But the directives are not the only source of change. Market forces are also at work to bring the two traditions closer together. At the same time, for example, as German auditing firms — which are normally limited liability companies — are having to reduce the influence of outside shareholders, many firms in England and Ireland are considering the benefits of incorporation as a means of attracting outside capital. Faced with the problems of increased litigation, and the associated difficulty and expense of obtaining adequate professional indemnity insurance cover, many of us might envy our colleagues on the continent, where suits for damages are much less frequent, and the amounts involved are much smaller. Germany, for example, places a legal ceiling of DM 500,000 on the damages which can be awarded against a statutory auditor. The disadvantage, though, is that greater use is made of the criminal law.

Also of importance have been recent developments in the financial services sector throughout Europe. Recently, most attention has been given to Big Bang in London, but this doesn't mean that nothing is happening elsewhere. London is by far the largest capital market in Europe, and will remain so for the foreseeable future but the other centres are nonetheless important.

In Germany, there was no need for a Big Bang to change the structure of the financial markets. There, the large so-called universal banks have always been allowed to engage in the full range of banking and investment activities, without any apparent agonising over Chinese Walls. Traditionally, however, German companies have been highly geared and equity finance has been relatively unimportant. Now that is changing and the addition of companies such as Nixdorf, Porsche and Flick to the stock exchange has added life to previously sleepy markets. More, and smaller, companies are going public and the several regional exchanges are linking up in a process which will probably lead to Frankfurt, or possibly Düsseldorf — now on the fast track — being the centre of most trading.

In France, equities have also become more popular and this, combined with inflows of capital from abroad following the abolition of exchange controls, has led to a dramatic rise in the market. This has speeded the privatisation of many government owned companies, including banks and insurance companies. At the same time, the government has reduced its interventionist role and allowed market forces to have more impact, while the stock exchange has permitted outside companies, mainly banks, to buy into stockbroking firms.

In Italy, financial markets have become freer, share ownership has expanded and the small group of families who traditionally controlled most of

Italian industry has been loosening its grip. The Milan stock exchange has been one of the most bullish in Europe in recent years, helped by an increase in the number of merchant banks. Successful Italian companies such as Fiat have taken advantage of this, and have been in the forefront of introducing new financial instruments.

Financial reporting

Apart from the tremendous amount of work for our profession which flows from companies going public or state-owned enterprises becoming privatised, there is another equally positive, long-term trend. As accountants, we are in the business of financial reporting, as preparers, auditors or even users. As a rule, financial reporting is less important where the user of financial statements is closely associated with the preparer, or where other means of obtaining information are available. Conversely, financial reporting becomes very important when financial statements are the only source of information available to the user.

The role of financial reporting becomes increasingly important in the light of privatisations; of the trend for companies to go public and replace debt finance with equity; of banks attempting to reduce the amount of lending on their balance sheets by securitising loans and selling them on the securities markets; and of the growth in the offshore and Euromarkets where companies seek capital outside their own countries. For with all of these developments, the distance between preparers and users of financial statements becomes greater and the risks borne by investors broaden.

This has had an impact on the way in which the profession in many continental countries has organised itself commercially. When, after the war, there was a vast amount of foreign — mainly US — investment in Europe, some governments took steps to ensure that the work accruing from this would be handled by local accountants rather than by the large international accountancy practices which had followed their clients. Since then, and taking advantage of the protection offered, standards in several countries improved dramatically and local firms now are confident of their ability to compete on equal terms. At the same time, the economics of scale which operate throughout the world have led to inter-firm mergers, and the emergence of several European-based groupings. Thanks to the fourth and seventh directives, the audit market in Europe is still an expanding one, and the decline in the value of the dollar has made European-sourced revenues even more valuable. The importance of the continental profession is underlined by the fact that, for the first time, the current chairman of the International Accounting Standards Committee is not from an English speaking country, but is a Frenchman.

These developments highlight the trend towards convergence. On a personal, individual basis it will be strengthened by the implementation of proposals put forward by the EC Commission for the mutual recognition of diplomas and professional qualifications. This will make it easier for accountants to move from one member state to another, and will allow an Irish chartered accountant to practise anywhere within the Community with the same ease as he or she now has in England. The only requirement is to have sufficient language fluency and adequate knowledge of local law. It is rather disappointing to note that, as of 1 January 1987, out of a total Irish Institute membership of approximately 6,000, only ninety-three worked in continental Europe. Let us hope that this will change.

Self-regulation

In the meantime, the major contribution we can make is to the debate on the nature of our profession, on deciding where exactly the two converging European traditions will meet. To take advantage of the opportunities presented by the changes and developments which are currently taking place in Europe, our profession must be flexible and fast moving, responding in a timely fashion to changes in the marketplace. Legislation, particularly at a Community level, is very slow moving, which makes self-regulation so important. We should do all we can to defend it.

The fundamental question we must ask ourselves is whether our profession is a good advertisement for self-regulation. As auditors, we are paid by our clients but act in the interests of the public, who don't pay us, so the question is an especially tricky one. It is never easy to answer convincingly — George Bernard Shaw spoke for many when he said that every profession was a conspiracy against the layman.

How well, for example, does our record on standard-setting speak for us? What about inflation accounting? Putting aside for one moment what each of us might have thought about the Statement of Standard Account Practice No. 16 (SSAP 16), the fact of the matter is that it went through the established standard setting process, not to mention the Sandilands and Hyde reports, Exposure Drafts (ED) 18 and 24, and SSAP 7. Despite that, it was never fully accepted or supported, the subsequent ED 35 was unceremoniously dropped and the chairman of the Accounting Standards Committee was driven to wish that the law would make his members obey standards: hardly a good advertisement for self-regulation. Similar developments in the US led to the profession, in the form of the American Institute of Certified Public Accountants' Accounting Practices Board (APB), losing its standard-setting authority in the area of accounting to the Financial Accounting Standards Board, and there are now moves to take away APB's powers to set auditing standards.

As our Institute now celebrates its centenary, members should remember that the Institute, and through it the Accounting Standards Committee and the Auditing Practices Committee, is not something working against them, but for them. When any organisation grows to be the size of the Irish Institute it becomes difficult to keep open the lines of communication which remind members of the common interests involved. Self-regulation, and Institute membership, involve sacrifices in return for privileges. There is a price for everything. We can only defend self-regulation for the profession as long as accountants are prepared to accept small burdens voluntarily, rather than have greater ones imposed on them by government. This entails a commitment to adhering to professional standards, both technical and ethical, keeping our competence up to date and taking an active interest in our Institute affairs.

Entering our second century, it is clear that the nature and extent of the challenges facing us are changing. Our focus will increasingly be on Europe, as we both shape and react to the developments unfolding there. The basis of our response, however, remains the same — a commitment to professional excellence.

Lines from the opening of a long philosophic poem by *Robert Bridges,* written about the time that Per Jacobsson was starting on his career —

Our stability is but balance, and conduct lies
in masterful administration of the unforeseen.

That gives you, with poetic compression, the essence of the matter. The assertion that stability in human affairs is not standing on immovable rock but achieving a balance, a trade-off, an equilibrium, is as true in business as it is in economic and political management. And there is a balance in the second phrase, too. The unforeseen will happen — shocks, crises, turning-points in cycles, shifts in trends — and when it happens we are not to be defeated by it or just ride with it but to manage it, and manage it masterfully. That word implies technical competence, but it also implies a sense of direction. So the balance is between sense of direction and adaptability, avoiding the extremes of overplanning on the one hand and opportunism and crisis management on the other. This again applies equaliy to running a business and to running a mixed economy whether at the national or international level. We must be ready for anything, but we ought to know where we are going.

Sir Jeremy Morse, *The 1985 Per Jacobsson lecture,* Lloyd's Bank

A very small accountant

Editorial Introduction to 'The changing world of the smaller firm'

The case study which follows, based on the firm of V. F. Nathan & Co. of Cork, and compiled from interviews primarily with Vivian Nathan, the founder and senior partner, gives insights into the attitudes and outlooks of a progressive and innovative 'smaller firm'.

But what is a 'smaller firm'? Is it a distinctive entity, fulfilling a useful function in Irish commercial life, and having clearly defined characteristics? And has it a long term future; or will it disappear eventually, becoming absorbed in the 'larger firms'?

The following table gives some indication of the numbers involved in the larger and smaller leagues:

	Number of firms	Number of partners	Number of C A staff employed
Firms with four partners or less	796	1,051	155
Firms with five partners or more	32	381	627
Total	828	1,432	782

The division is a crude one, since the criterion of number of partners alone may not have any useful significance. Despite that defect the figures do indicate that a very large slice of the accountancy and accountancy-related services in the country is rendered by the 'smaller' firms, however they are defined.

This group has probably less say in the affairs of the Institute and of the accounting world than has the big league, though indeed in recent years the contribution of the smaller firms has been growing, both in committees and on the council itself, where, at time of writing, out of a membership of twenty-four, nine represent the larger firms, six the smaller firms, and the remainder are outside professional practice. There are factors which make it more difficult for the smaller firms to give a commensurate contribution: (a) it is not easy for, say, one man running his own practice, to devote the time necessary to contribute in any major way to technical or institutional affairs; (b) there is a very widespread dispersion of the firms through the country which renders joint and effective action rather difficult; and (c) most of the major technical matters dealt with by the Institute refer to the accounts of public companies where the exposure to public scrutiny is high.

It is probably appropriate at this point to attempt to identify the characteristics of the 'smaller firm' which distinguish it from the 'larger' concern. That there is a distinction is, I think, generally accepted, even if many of the larger firms incorporate in their structures small business departments. However, the words 'larger' and 'smaller' are not adequate, since, as pointed out by Nathan in the case study, the distinctive features do not refer to numbers of partners, sizes of staff, or overall amount of gross fees. The distinction rather refers to the nature of the work being carried out, and the manner in which it is conducted. There are a few firms with very small numbers which are rendering a specialised service to large companies, and it is possible that the converse also applies — certain firms with fairly large numbers, whose business is essentially 'small'. However, for want of better I shall continue to use the terms 'larger' and 'smaller'.

Tentatively I identify the following as being characteristic of the 'smaller' professional practices:

●   The availability of a very personalised service to the smaller business. The relationship between many accountants and their clients approximates to that of common membership of a management team, with the attendant risk of loss of independence. The larger firms also give a personalised service, but in many cases by virtue of the nature of the skills offered, and of the limitations of time available, the service to smaller clients is delegated to senior or medium staff.

●   The smaller practitioner provides a generalist service at a certain level. There is occasionally some temptation to offer services in excess of available skills where clients seek such services, but in most cases the generalist skills provided by a one-partner or two-partner firm are adequate for the needs of the smaller clients.

●   Dependence on specialist input. At all levels and in all firms there is a dependence on specialist input. Clearly in the case of the smaller firm the input on, for example, complex taxation problems, is not available within the firm and must be sought outside.

●   The work undertaken has a far greater emphasis on providing services which in the larger client company would be catered for internally. Primarily this involves bookkeeping and financial accounting, and sometimes management accounting and financial management. Auditing tends to be less system-based than in the larger situation, with assurance often accrued partially through involvement of the practitioner in preparation of the figures themselves.

●   Staff in the smaller firm is often motivated by a preference for giving service in the smaller and more containable commercial units. Motivation in the larger firm is frequently that of obtaining qualifications for managerial posts in larger companies in Ireland and abroad.

Many smaller businessmen and farmers would find the general atmosphere of the smaller office, where at least everybody is known and recognisable, to be more acceptable and less threatening than the atmosphere of relatively impersonal efficiency of the larger office.

If this analysis is correct, then, despite the enormous pressures towards mergers and the establishment of international connections, there will be a continuing place for the smaller firm in Ireland, even though advancing technology and the increasing complexity of the commercial environment may require the smaller firm to seek specialist inputs from outside to an increasing extent. There also may be some move towards specialisation — for example, the provision of computerised farm accounting services. A lead has been given by a firm in Scotland which pays monthly visits to a group of farms with a van equipped with computers, typing facilities, and the appropriate client files, for the purpose of updating their accounting and statistical records, and providing such other services as they may require.

The Nathan case study highlights a number of these points, and illustrates the fact that a firm can grow to a considerable size in terms of staff and gross fees (it has at present a staff of fifty with five partners) without losing the characteristics of the smaller firm mentioned above. It further illustrates two primary features which have general application, but are here set in the context of the smaller firm. These are:

● The commercial decision of the firm to identify the market demand and specifically to gear itself to meet that demand; and
● The decision to ensure technical relevance by taking on an educational role, thus upholding the long tradition in the profession of passing on to succeeding generations the skills and ethical attitudes which are its hallmark.

One day a tax collector called at Wilde's house in Tite Street.
  'Taxes! Why should I pay taxes?' says Wilde.
  'But, sir, you are the householder here, are you not? You live here, you sleep here.'
  'Ah, yes; but then I sleep so badly!'

Oscar Wilde, *In Conversation*

Nathan's office

The changing world of the smaller firm

(compiled from an interview with Vivian F. Nathan)

The case

A quiet evolution is transforming the image of the Irish accountancy profession as it enters its second century.

Hi-tech developments are playing an ever increasing role in hundreds of practices throughout the country, highlighting the need to provide improved services for clients and also to place greater emphasis on more effective education and training for the future.

This case-study charts the progress of an Irish practice which has grown over the past decade, establishing new offices at a rate of one a year, and playing a quiet but significant role on the education front as the profession faces the twenty-first century.

Seventeen years ago a new accountancy practice — Nathans — was established in Cork, the first to be set up in the city in over a decade.

Like many Irish firms, it began as a sole practitioner business. Indeed, it could be said that Vivian Nathan was fortunate in having access to a premises beside the old family wholesale business on Lavitt's Quay where he established an office directly across the Lee from Shandon Steeple and the old Butter Exchange, once the heart of Cork's commercial life.

As a young boy he had worked behind the counter of the family drapery shop near the Coal Quay and Cornmarket Street, getting an early but first-hand experience of business later to prove invaluable in dealing with clients.

From those small beginnings, Nathans has grown to a level where gross fees now exceed £1 million and the practice today employs fifty people in ten offices.

The firm has reversed a recent trend which has seen Dublin companies moving increasingly outwards to take over firms in cities and towns throughout Ireland. Nathans has taken on one practice in the capital and is presently negotiating the takeover of another there.

Given Vivian Nathan's background, the move into accountancy came more or less naturally. Having put in the customary four year stint at University College Cork, he became apprenticed to a firm (Kirby & Kirby) with a good auditing profile, and qualified in the late sixties at a time when only three or four qualified as chartered accountants each year in Cork.

Within twelve months he decided to seek a more immediate experience of large scale business and joined Galtee Foods, a division of Mitchelstown Creameries, as financial controller.

He quickly realised, however, that his interest was to be a practising accountant in main-stream accountancy and decided to set up in business on his own.

Early days

What may seem like a straightforward move today was nonetheless daunting seventeen years ago. It was the first new accountancy practice to be established in Cork in twelve years, a sharp contrast with the intervening period in which up to sixty new firms have arrived on the local scene.

Financially helped by a lectureship in accountancy at UCC, his first priority was to build up an office and to develop the practice.

The young company's expansion can be attributed to a number of factors:
1. A great many existing offices had too much work on their books;
2. Changes in fiscal policies such as the introduction of VAT and other taxes stimulated new work;
3. The expanding practice dealt with the work acquired in an efficient, professional manner.

From the start the firm's policy was to establish the closest and most purposeful relations with clients. Professionally remote and distant attitudes of the past they felt were old-fashioned, unnecessary and counterproductive.

Steadily, as the business came in, the company began to develop a working portfolio, gradually building up the local reputation.

The seventies

The structure of the practice was strengthened in the seventies, with new staff joining, as the firm reacted quickly to new developments technically and commercially.

These were good times in Cork for both the industrial and commercial sectors. In a world of growing competitiveness, the financial institutions began to look at company performances in terms of figures and the bottom line rather than at the pedigree of prospective borrowers.

Realising that the region's healthy economic situation presented an ideal prospect for expansion, Nathans began to look for fresh opportunities to develop new outlets for the practice. The firm calculated that the main towns of Co. Cork had been somewhat overlooked by the accountancy profession in general down the years.

It began to make contact with firms and individuals in the outlying towns and soon realised it was pushing an open door, providing an on-the-spot service for them. Prior to this, local businesses had to go into Cork for accountancy services. The firm was in a market which had been by-passed for years.

The average office scenario in those days reflected a profession run on the lines of a gentlemen's club. Clients had to travel long distances to make appointments to see their accountants in the city and expected to sit in dusty offices waiting to be ushered into the presence of their accountant.

From the mid-seventies Nathans opened new offices at the rate of one a year.

The first move was made deep in West Cork when a new office was set up in Skibbereen in 1974. Others followed in rapid succession in Bantry (1975), Mallow (1976), Fermoy (1977), Charleville (1978), Kanturk (1979), Castletownbere (1979) and Clonakilty (1980).

They carved a path into towns in the rich farming heartland of Co. Cork and it paid off. The move outwards from its main base in Cork city has been so important that to this day some of its biggest clients are associated with these county towns.

Other accountancy firms were soon to follow the opening created by Nathans and there was virtually a mini-explosion of accountancy practices across the county, the result of which can be seen today in towns like Skibbereen where as many as six firms are now doing business.

A similar growth in accountancy business was taking place in other cities and towns throughout Ireland. Many of these new firms were small practices in terms of staff size and by the nature of the work undertaken by them, having few big clients and mainly offering small client oriented services.

However, any blanket application of the term 'small' can be extremely misleading. For instance, an apparently small firm, with relatively few partners, could have a large financial turnover and command significant business, particularly in specialised fields such as insolvency or taxation. Conversely, an apparently large firm could be seen as falling into the 'small' category because of the type of clients on its books.

In a sense, the unique position of the smaller practitioner in an Irish context is based on the close personal service available to clients. That was certainly true of the seventies and early eighties. More recently, however, this special relationship between practitioner and client has been diminishing as the market demands become more complex, with companies having to adjust to changes in the economic and technological environments. Clients are demanding a broader range of services and a greater degree of sophistication in their professional advice, and this, inevitably, is straining the resources of the smaller practice.

The problems of growth

Nathans' expansion was not achieved without difficulties and problems of the kind experienced by many other growing concerns today. Invariably, as a firm expands it encounters numerous 'growing' problems. Normally these result from the actual growth in the volume of business being handled by the firm.

It can, for example, encounter administrative problems affecting the proper recording of work and the billing of clients. Obviously without an efficient billing system young firms will run into cashflow difficulties. These are often compounded by the traditional problems experienced by firms dealing mainly with individual clients who tend to put payments to professional advisers on the long finger. Delays of up to a year could sometimes be experienced, imposing great strain on the resources of a young firm building up a business.

In its early years Nathans was in no way exempted from this problem, particularly as its workload was rapidly expanding, hence the capital requirements for work-in-progress and debtors. It was believed that to handle the situation too rigidly and with too great emphasis on early cash collection might well risk the loss of newly acquired clients.

So Nathans took the only course that seemed possible: it concentrated on keeping the firm's running costs as low as possible, and drawing from it as little as possible. The UCC lectureship fees helped greatly at this time by providing a regular cash inflow.

Problems can also arise for young firms if they overlook the need to maintain the level of administrative staff necessary to handle a growing volume of work. Too often they neglect this vital aspect of their business in favour of concentrating on rapidly expanding a work portfolio of clients and assignments. Ultimately, this can prove a costly error, often culminating in high work-in-progress balances which are hard to bill, and high debtor levels, with many debts either bad or uncollectable, mounting cashflow problems, and invariably a loss of confidence and morale as more and more effort is expended by fee earners in shoring up administrative holes.

Undoubtedly, a thoughtful, energetic and innovative practitioner will find it extremely difficult to resist growth. Ironically, his main difficulty may be in resisting growth at too fast a pace. Indeed, some of the better companies operating in Ireland today make a conscious decision to remain small.

They deliberately carry out constant policy reviews, reassessing their client base to suit the business, secure in the knowledge that a valuable market exists for a highly skilled and adaptable sole practitioner who sets up his own firm and then gives an exceptionally good local service.

By far the greatest problems facing a small practice as it gradually evolves and grows will be in the area of policy and long-term aspirations — for example whether it decides to concentrate on individual small accounts or to seek larger assignments in industry and the public sector.

A growing practice must go through a constant process of reassessment and self-analysis as it plans its future direction. A successful accountant's strength often lies in his ability to perceive the needs of his clients and to fill these needs successfully. However, this approach involves an inherent danger for the small

firm which can sometimes find its professional objectivity under strain, in its attempts to comply with client requirements.

For this very reason it is essential for the smaller firm to monitor carefully and plan its own growth, and to pose constantly such basic questions as: 'where is the practice now?' 'where will growth arise?' 'what services should we provide to our existing base and to meet our perceived growth area?' 'is the firm capable of providing these services?' 'what must we do to ensure the capacity will be there when we need it?' 'does the firm wish to continue along this growth path or remain static?' 'what will be the consequences of these decisions and what should we be doing now to ensure that our policies and goals are achieved?'

In theory there is no doubt that a large firm, given good local partners and the right corporate ideals and policies, can compete with the small firm on its own ground. But in reality, the bigger firms tend to concentrate on larger jobs and assignments, and find it difficult to compete at grass roots level. More often than not, they have no visible interest in seeking out small local jobs and assignments. They may, indeed, only be in the local market place in the hope that a percentage of their small clients will ultimately grow sufficiently themselves so as to become more appropriate for large firm services.

This sometimes poses problems for the smaller practitioner because if he fails to grow as fast as his best clients, then there is a constant risk that they will be snapped up by the bigger operator. And if a small firm consciously decides to remain in the small league, it will inevitably face the problems of shepherding clients through their most traumatic phases of growth and then possibly losing out on the benefits of the client's success as it outgrows the practice and moves its business to a larger firm of accountants.

A growing challenge facing smaller (and indeed larger) firms in Ireland today is that of keeping up to date with accounting and auditing standards so as to reflect the greater complexity of domestic and international business operations and the financial marketplace. This challenge can pose particular problems for the small practitioner who is expected to give not only an all-round financial service, monitoring performances and analysing trends, but also advice on tax, pensions, investments and a growing range of other specialist topics.

Nathans has over the years made considerable use of the service of the Institute and in particular of the Small Practices Advisory Service in helping to deal with new developments, unusual specialist problems, and in helping to assess and raise the operating standards of the firm. Further anticipating the challenge to keep up to date, Nathans decided a few years ago to add an extra dimension to the company's policy spectrum.

New directions

In the hey-days of the seventies business was booming and the firm's fee income grew substantially every year. But at the start of the eighties when the recession began to bite hard in the Cork region, the pace of economic growth gradually tapered off and Nathans decided to become involved in education, a move which effectively kept the practice abreast of current developments.

The company established a strong in-house training and educational division. In addition, it operated seminars, conferences and courses for the Institute of Chartered Accountants, AnCO and other bodies. In this context, it remains critical of the profession's lack of foresight in assessing and tackling the crucial question of providing a real business education for young trainees, embracing finance, management and accounting.

In its view, the profession has adopted a role as examination convenors. The firm sees the major problem as a proliferation of educational bodies, universities, regional colleges, and schools of commerce all concentrating their efforts too much on a small number of topics with outdated syllabi. For example financial accounting and management accounting which occupy large sections of most courses have hardly changed over the last twenty-five years. Nathans believes the Institute should take the question of business education by the scruff of the neck, and set up a progressive business school, staffed by enlightened accountancy cum financial tutors and educators to give the young men and women joining the profession a really practical insight into business both in Ireland and internationally.

Another significant development for the firm was the decision to move to Dublin where it encountered new challenges and business opportunities. More recently it has taken over a thriving practice there and is currently looking at the possibilities of acquiring another firm.

The firm now employs fifty staff, including fifteen qualified accountants, three tax experts, five in an expanding liquidation division, ten in the administrative, secretarial and computer divisions and seventeen trainees. The practice has five partners.

Having consolidated its Irish operations, its next move will be to establish strong links internationally and negotiations for an affiliation with a large international accountancy group with offices in twenty-four countries is in prospect.

The future – views and hopes

From this perspective, looking at the future of the small accountancy firm in Ireland, Nathans believes those operating outside the sphere of influence of the dominant groups will experience difficulties and that some 'deadwood' will be weeded out over the next few years unless more firms can evolve in this era of rapid change.

The birth of the retail accountant

Computerisation and a vastly improved tele-communications system are transforming the Irish chartered accountancy scene. Among other developments, a virtual revolution is looming in the profession, bringing it increasingly into the High Street 'supermarket' category.

This will see the introduction of retail financial services in line with the kind of stores now bringing the stock exchange to the man in the street.

People are used to dealing at retail level in almost every aspect of their lives nowadays and there is no doubt they can find the kind of world associated with a chartered accountancy office both intimidating and off-putting.

Manned by perhaps one or two people with direct computer communication to the main office these 'supermarket bureaux' will be able to offer ready access to sophisticated computerised accountancy software, providing for example on-the-spot projections and other spreadsheet type options. Accounting, financial and taxation advice would be available. Computer communication with the main office would mean ultimately that one person in such an 'outlet' would be able to tap all the resources of the firm without delay.

Nathans believes professional firms in Ireland should give considerable thought to the introduction of such outlets here. To be effective, they should offer a broad spectrum of services embracing taxation, accountancy, bookkeeping, auditing, both corporate and personal financial planning, insurance and assurance, computer and new technology services.

Ultimately the chartered accountants of the future should have the ability to deal professionally with such a range of services for any client who walks into the High Street financial supermarket looking for advice.

The firm regards bookkeeping as a neglected discipline which should be brought into the twentieth century by the establishment of a modern Irish School of Bookkeeping. Nathans believes that not enough emphasis is currently placed on teaching bookkeepers the importance of their job and their responsibility within an organisation. The subject should be taught within the general context of office procedures and administration, and should be closely related to the business environment in which the bookkeepers are likely to be operating. Too often nowadays the emphasis is placed on theoretical skills which may never be utilised subsequently. A good bookkeeper, particularly one who can combine that skill with administrative abilities, is an essential part of any business and may well contribute greatly to its success. Such people are becoming a rarity, which, considering the amount of money and effort expended in training should be a cause of considerable worry.

One of my most treasured memories — you might call it auditing in the good days — is of the Irish Rabbit Skin Company. It was situated near O'Keeffes, the knackers, and the odours in that part of the city were something else! Upstairs in a long loft, the skins hung around braziers to dry out. The air was warm, heavy, malodorous, moist — an ideal breeding ground for maggots. The floorboards were rough and illfitting. Directly beneath the den was the small and dingy main office where we worked. Papers were everywhere, ancient ledgers, spike files and grubby invoices. There a little creative accounting was needed to balance the debtors control, and the 'advances to staff' was an endless delight of detection. Every now and then a maggot dropped on the working papers, and after a while we hung the newspaper over our heads for protection. Those were the circumstances where 'double entry' was truly learned and retained forever!

David Rowe

Editorial Introduction to 'The making of the chartered accountant'

Anthony Walsh, a fellow of the Chartered Institute of Management Accountants, has always taken a constructive interest in the education of the chartered accountant, and in his capacity as examiner for one of the multi-discipline papers in the Final Admitting Examination has done much to shape the concepts underlying those papers.

Anthony says that 'Irish chartered accountants undertake one of the most demanding and progressive educational programmes for professional accountants in the world' and that they 'are in great demand at home and abroad'. However, the pace of change in the environment in which accountants operate is, if anything, increasing, and the educational structure will need to be flexible and responsive to new demands upon it.

Anthony lists briefly what he perceives to be the main trends in development. It is interesting to compare his list with that of Timothy Quin, the 'centenarian' in the essay on page 61. In order to respond to these trends in coherent and effective fashion the Institute will need to 'evolve a common mission'.

Anthony Walsh, M.Sc., Ph.D., F.C.M.A.

Anthony Walsh is head of the School of Accounting and Finance at the National Institute for Higher Education, Dublin.

A native of Waterford, he lives with his wife, Christina and daughter Laura in Castleknock. He received his secondary education at Mount Sion, Waterford and holds the degrees of master of science and doctor of philosophy from the City University, London. He is a fellow of the Chartered Institute of Management Accountants. Before joining NIHE, Dublin he was group financial accountant with Waterford Glass plc.

The author teaches on NIHE Dublin's bachelors and masters degree programmes in accounting and finance. His research interests are in computer applications in accounting and capital market reaction to financial statement information.

To stay sane, he plays tennis and helps restore old cars.

The making of the chartered accountant

by Anthony Walsh

Introduction

AT the human level, one of the most tangible common bonds between individual members of the Institute is their education and training. On social occasions, it is quite common to find chartered accountants, even (or perhaps especially) those advanced in years, recounting for each other with great vividness the trials and tribulations of life as an articled clerk. At the professional level, major determinants of the standing of the Institute have been and will always be the education and training of its members. It is opportune in the centenary year of the Institute to examine and evaluate current education and training for chartered accountants in Ireland and to attempt to predict future directions.

Historical perspective

Although the Institute has a long tradition as an examining body, its role in education is of recent origin. Up to the seventies, a perceived conflict of interest between examining and educating kept the Institute from assuming any direct involvement in the provision of education. Educational activities were supported only by local societies. During the sixties, there were two developments which helped shape current education. In 1966, holders of approved university degrees were exempted from a substantial part of the Institute examinations. In the same year, the minimum entry standard to articles for non-graduates was set to that required for entry to university.

In contrast with the sixties, the early seventies saw many developments in accounting education. Four of these developments merit special mention:

- Ben Lynch was appointed to direct a new education and training department which would co-ordinate the Institute's education and training activities.
- The Derryhale report reviewed the major issues facing accounting education in Ireland. Though it did not make specific recommendations, it was a watershed in that it argued strongly that the Institute should

assume much more responsibility for education. These arguments were eventually accepted.

- Full-time commencement courses of one year's duration for non-graduates were established in four centres. These courses proved so successful that all non-graduates were soon required to undertake them.
- *Prospectus for a Profession* was published in 1974. It presented the findings of a major enquiry conducted by David Solomons, a leading American accounting academic, into the education and training of accountants in these islands. A central finding was that there should be graduate entry only to the profession with final admission being based on a test of professional competence. The Institute set up a committee to assess the implications of the Solomons Report. This led to the 1978 policy document on which current structures are based.

Current education and training

Progress in the last decade

Figure 1 shows the current major entry routes to the profession. There are three components to the preparation of the chartered accountant — first, full-time education, second, practical training under the guidance of a chartered accountant and third, part-time accounting education which is undertaken during the period of practical training. Each entry route provides flexibility with respect to the length and nature of the full-time education component.

The current approach is based on the 1978 policy document *Education and Training for Future Chartered Accountants* which grew out of the Institute's response to the Solomons Report. The objectives which the policy document set out to achieve included:

- Increasing the level of full-time education undertaken by students preparing to be chartered accountants;
- Creation of more formal structures for part-time education; and,
- Adoption of a multi-disciplinary final admitting examination.

The level of full-time education undertaken by students has been increased mainly in two ways. First, full-time post-graduate diploma programmes in professional accounting are now available to both business and non-business honours graduates entering the profession. These programmes are provided by four universities in Dublin and Belfast. The post-graduate diploma routes for graduates currently represent over twenty-five per cent of the annual intake of students. Second, an optional second year of full-time education is available on commencement courses in five centres. Ninety per cent of students entering training contracts in 1986 had completed at least two years of full-time third level education (see table 1).

Figure 1: **Major entry routes to the profession***

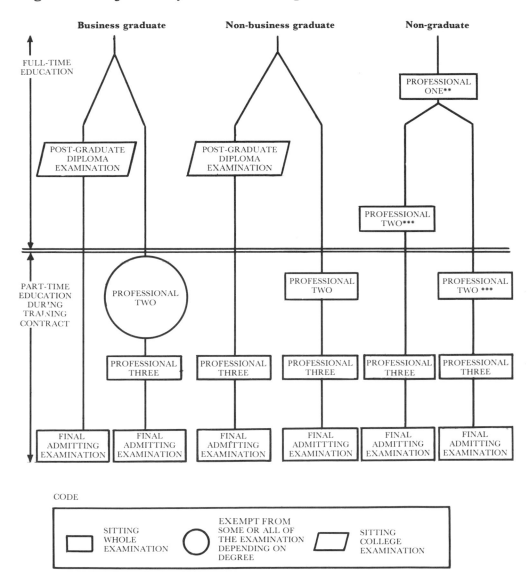

Table 1: Analysis of entrants to the profession by educational background

	1978	%	1981	%	1985	%	1986	%
Graduates								
Business	234	52	258	41	219	41	204	37
Non-business	88	20	118	18	45	8	59	11
Post-graduate diplomates								
Business	—	—	56	9	86	16	117	21
Non-business	—	—	5	1	39	7	30	5
Non-graduates								
1-year commencement programmes	117	26	149	23	61	11	41	7
2-year commencement programmes	—	—	39	6	73	14	87	16
Other	10	2	13	2	17	3	18	3
TOTAL	449	100%	638	100%	540	100%	556	100%

A major step towards formalisation of part-time education took place in the summer of 1978 when the Institute established the Centre of Accounting Studies. The centre now has five full-time staff and draws on the services of over fifty lecturers on a part-time basis. The centre provides block-release, evening and weekend educational courses for students who have completed their full-time education and are undertaking practical training while preparing for Institute examinations. Though based in Dublin, the centre provides courses throughout Ireland.

A revised syllabus to implement the third objective was phased in during the early 1980s and has now completed three full cycles. An overview of the syllabus is given in table 2. The implementation of the current syllabus which includes a multi-disciplinary, open-book final admitting examination was possible only in the context of greater levels of full-time education and more formal structures for part-time education. For example, rigorous screening, aptitude testing, interim assessment, extended study release, 'hands-on' computing and, in the Final Admitting Examination, case-study-based learning are now integral parts of preparation for Institute examinations. For this reason a student must obtain a Certificate of Due Participation (in an educational course) before being allowed to sit for an Institute examination. It should be recognised that the introduction of multi-disciplinarity represented a considerable innovation on the part of the Institute. This was the first time any institute of professional accountants in Europe had adopted such an approach although the work of the accountant is recognised as containing a significant element of multi-disciplinarity.

Table 2: Subjects contained in current syllabus of the Institute
Professional One
> Financial accounting I
> Law I (general principles of law and mercantile law)
> Statistics
> Organisation and management control systems
> Economics

Professional Two
> Financial accounting II
> Law II (company and partnership law)
> Data processing and management information systems
> Taxation I

Professional Three
> Financial accounting III
> Auditing I
> Taxation II
> Management accounting

Final Admitting Examination
> Auditing and the general duties of professional accountants
> Financial management
> Multi-discipline paper I
> Multi-discipline paper II

At work on a case study

In 1986, the Institute introduced a course on microcomputer applications in accounting which is available throughout Ireland. It offers a flexible, 'hands-on' approach to gaining a working knowledge of the uses of microcomputers in accounting. All those being admitted to membership of the Institute from 1988 onwards must have completed the course.

The Irish Accountancy Education Trust Fund established by the Institute as an independent charitable trust in 1981 has provided funding to help support some of the recent educational developments described above. For example, the Trust provided partial funding for the provision of educational materials for the Final Admitting Examination and for the establishment of the microcomputer applications course. A proportion of all fees paid by students undertaking educational courses for Institute examinations is contributed to the Trust and this represents the Trust's major source of income. The objective of the Trust is to support the development of accounting education and research in Ireland.

The importance of practical training

The role of training in public practice has always been a key component of the preparation of the chartered accountant. The high standard and relative homogeneity of that training is regarded by many as a factor in the prominence of chartered accountants in so many commercial fields in Ireland and abroad. Under the current training guideline, issued in 1982, the desirability of some diversity in training is recognised but the need for all students to receive adequate experience in at least two of three core areas is stressed. The three core areas are accounting, auditing and taxation. Training in public practice is aimed at reinforcing students' education by providing an opportunity to apply that education in a practical, yet controlled setting. Many firms of chartered accountants also provide in-house courses for students covering a wide spectrum of topics ranging from firm-oriented issues (for example, the firm's auditing procedures) to broader issues (for example, taxed-based financing). Students must maintain a record of their training and experience and submit it to the Institute when applying for membership.

In 1983, on a pilot basis, the Institute introduced a scheme for training students in industry. This was (and still is) the only scheme in operation anywhere in the world for training chartered accountants outside public practice. A small number of students have already qualified as chartered accountants under this scheme. The progress of the scheme is still being monitored but early indications are very positive.

Continuing professional education

Education and training does not cease on entry to the profession. The Institute (mainly through a continuing professional education department) and many firms of chartered accountants devote considerable time, attention and resources to ensuring that chartered accountants keep up to date with developments in the profession. The Institute recommends that all chartered accountants undertake at least minimum levels of continuing professional education. Currently, the minimum recommended levels are ninety hours per three years for chartered accountants in practice and sixty hours per three years for those not in practice. However, such education is not mandatory.

Comparison with other countries

Sister institutes in Scotland, England and Wales
As might be expected given their reciprocity of recognition, there is broad similarity between the approach of the Institute to education and training and that of its sister Institutes in Scotland and in England and Wales. As in Ireland, the current syllabi of these Institutes emphasise accounting, auditing and taxation with attention to supporting subjects such as law and economics. While the Scottish Institute introduced multi-disciplinarity in its final examination in 1986, the examinations of the Institute of Chartered Accountants in England and Wales are based exclusively on single subject papers. The entry paths to the three Institutes and required periods of practical training are also broadly similar.

Canada and the USA
If we look further afield, we find equivalent institutes abroad adopt different approaches to education and training. For example, both the Canadian Institute of Chartered Accountants and the American Institute of Certified Public Accountants restrict membership to graduates. Each of these bodies administers only one national (or uniform) examination. To sit for this examination, a student must satisfy educational requirements (which are predominantly met by completion of university and college programmes) and/or experience requirements. The Institutes maintain quality control by accrediting university courses and administering their own entry examination and training requirements. In Canada, the 'Uniform Final Examination' consists of four papers. Approximately seventy per cent of the examination is multi-disciplinary and the material examined is mainly accounting, auditing, taxation and planning/control. In the USA, the 'Uniform CPA Examination' has five single-subject papers — three accounting papers, one auditing and one law paper. Sixty per cent of the marks are for multiple-choice questions.

• •

[Continental Europe

Given the number of countries involved, it is not intended to give a comprehensive outline of each individual national system in this section. Although there are certain similarities between countries, the differences can be quite considerable, and these extend to the nature of the profession itself.

As a generalisation, the main feature of the accountancy profession to continental Europe is that its primary emphasis is on statutory auditing, and in many countries membership is confined to those in public practice. Accountants moving to industry or commerce must often resign their professional qualification. This means that the number of professional accountants on the Continent is relatively small in comparison to Ireland or Great Britain.

In most cases, as is to be expected with countries having a codified system of law, the accountancy profession was established and is regulated by law. Therefore, admission to the profession is controlled by governments or government agencies, which set syllabi and administer examinations. Licences to practise are granted by the state, which is normally responsible for policing ethical requirements. Membership of professional bodies equivalent to our Institute is voluntary and is open to those already licensed to practise, which is the opposite of our system, where membership of the Institute gives the right to audit.

As a consequence, professional bodies often have only an indirect influence on the requirements for entering the profession.

Most countries require candidates to have a university degree, often in a relevant discipline; to have completed a minimum period of practical training;

and to pass an examination before admission to the profession. Standards vary from country to country and use is made of theses and oral examinations. The relatively small size of the profession in many countries makes the administration of such a system possible. The subjects covered, however, are much the same as those in Ireland.

Owing to a number of factors (higher school leaving ages, military service obligations, longer university courses and different periods of required practical experience) entry to the profession in most continental countries occurs at a much older age than in Ireland. Many German candidates, for example, do not qualify until they are thirty-five.

In European Community member states, a certain degree of convergence can be expected with the implementation of the eighth directive which governs the qualifications required of statutory auditors. Furthermore, the proposed directive on the mutual recognition of professional qualifications should lead market forces to cause a harmonisation of systems in each member state. (Material supplied by John Hegarty of the FEE, Brussels.)]

• •

Evaluation of current education and training

Irish chartered accountants undertake one of the most demanding and progressive educational programmes for professional accountants in the world. Complementing and reinforcing that education, this period of training exposes them to a variety of accounting and business experience. Irish chartered accountants are in great demand at home and abroad. In fact, the remarkable increase in recent years in the efforts of foreign firms to recruit Irish chartered accountants might well be regarded as a testimony to their international standing and as a validation of their preparation.

The process of education and training of chartered accountants is not without its critics. However, the level of criticism is low and stems largely from critical self-evaluation. Criticism centres on the adequacy of the preparation of the chartered accountants for their role outside public practice. Forty-eight per cent of chartered accountants currently work outside practice though this proportion has at times been as high as fifty-seven per cent during the past twenty years (see table 3). As a result of training as independent auditors, newly qualified chartered accountants are sometimes perceived as lacking commercial awareness, having difficulty becoming part of a management team and communicating effectively with non-accountants. By some colleagues they are seen as risk-averse and lacking creativity, entrepreneurship and the strategic vision. Chartered accountants have also been accused of pre-occupation with accounting rather than with developing the diversity of quantitive and qualitative measures needed by management. While these criticisms should not be dismissed lightly, some are rooted in unrealistic expectations of young chartered accountants who are just beginning their professional careers. Others may be related as much to the characteristics of individuals as to the education and training process.

Table 3: Analysis of the membership of the Institute by professional stream

	1965	%	1970	%	1975	%	1980	%	1985	%
In practice	503	32.1	579	30.1	861	28.2	1,151	28.5	1,544	28.1
Employed by public practices	186	11.9	250	13.0	507	16.6	821	20.4	1,325	24.1
	689	44.0	829	43.1	1,368	44.8	1,972	48.9	2,869	52.2
Industry, commerce and the public sector	879	56.0	1,092	56.9	1,689	55.2	2,061	51.1	2,630	47.8
	1,568	100.0	1,921	100.0	3,057	100.0	4,033	100.0	5,499	100.0

Towards the twenty-first century

Introduction

The Institute can be proud of its achievements in education and training, particularly in the last decade. However, the last thing the Institute should consider is basking in the glory of its achievements. The professions, including accountants, are entering a period that, for them, can accurately be described as revolutionary. Like all revolutions, it will present both great threats and great opportunities. The role of some professions and professional institutes will decline while the role of others will grow. The professions will be far from helpless during this revolution. Indeed their own actions as much as external forces will determine their future. Education and training will be vital components of the strategic planning of the profession and major determinants of their future role. Many professional bodies including accounting institutes have recognised that we are entering a period of great change and have begun to plan accordingly. The fruits of those planning efforts have been varied. Some have evolved far-reaching, imaginative and, in some cases, dramatic proposals. Others have made proposals that are little more than minor adjustments to established patterns and which ignore the scale of impending change.

The remainder of this chapter will focus on: first, the forces that will shape the future accounting profession; second, the characteristics of the profession which will emerge; and third, the resultant issues arising for future education and training.

Knowledge

There are two fundamental forces at work as we approach the twenty-first century which will bring major change to the accounting profession — first, trends in the structure and application of knowledge and second, change in society. Traditionally, professionals could be characterised by competence in a specialised body of knowledge such as the law, medicine or accounting. Once a professional had acquired that knowledge, it could be applied virtually unchanged for a lifetime. We are already learning to live with continuous change in the body of knowledge. But, this is only the first phase of the knowledge revolution. There are others impending. The next phase will arise from the increasing capacity of computers to manipulate less structured information to find new insights to less structured problems. These 'expert systems' will accelerate the rate of growth of knowledge (the stock in trade of the professional) to unprecedented levels. Expert systems will have many applications within the professions. By cloning the knowledge and intelligence of individuals for use by thousands, the professions' control of bodies of technical knowledge will be greatly reduced.

(left) Sean Quigley, first place in the 1985 Admission Examination of the Institute of Accounting Technicians in Ireland

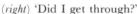

(right) 'Did I get through?'

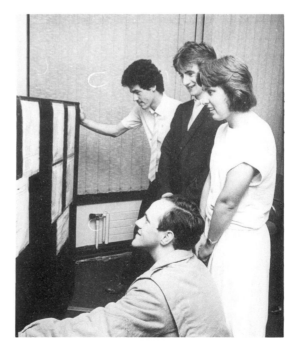

Change in society

As the pace of acquisition of new knowledge quickens, the structures, institutions, values and expectations of society will change. A changing society presents a more complex environment for the work of the professional. However, more realistic and wide-ranging models of social and economic relationships will be developed to give us a more complete understanding of the social context of business. This will result in demands for new measurement methods, analytical techniques and bases of business accountability. In the final analysis, this will lead to a broadening in the scope of the work of those concerned with information for decision-making and accountability.

The profession of the future

Under the influence of these two fundamental forces, certain characteristics of the future profession which are relevant to assessing future directions in education can be predicted:

- More specialisation: Firms of chartered accountants are already expected to provide expertise in an array of specialised fields. As society changes, the information required to plan and control will become more diverse and complex leading to even greater levels of specialisation. Continued growth of government regulation of business activity will accentuate this trend.

- Broad perspective: In the more complex society of the future, while more specialisation is inevitable, business advisors including accountants will continue to need a broad perspective to give sound business advice. For example, as well as assessing their technical elegance, the accountant will need to evaluate the management consequences of alternative computerised information systems.

- Information technology: Computers will assume a wider range of clerical and middle management roles both in accounting and in other fields. The impetus will include growth of expert systems (which will be particularly suited to performing middle management tasks), improved communication between humans and computers and pervasive use of computer-controlled manufacturing.

- Future of the audit: Society will demand more and more accountability of business entities. Chartered accountants will have a significant, though not an exclusive, new role in attestation of non-financial and non-historic information. However, the audit of historic accounting information (what I call the traditional audit) must be regarded as a mature service with little scope for growth.

- Competition: The range of services offered by chartered accountants will expand far beyond traditional boundaries as the relative importance of the traditional audit declines. Chartered accountants will not be the only professionals to expand their range of services dramatically as each profession's control of a specialised body of information weakens. There will be increased competition between accountants and other professionals such as bankers, stock brokers, solicitors, software houses and management consultants. Ultimately, the distinction between the services provided by many professions may become quite blurred.

- Regulation: The accounting profession in Ireland enjoys a large measure of self-regulation. This is unlikely to continue. Admittedly, the prevalent political sentiment in many developed countries is broadly towards less government involvement in business. On the other hand, first, the mainland European tradition is for more regulation of accountants. Second, accountants are likely to face many more difficult choices between ethics and earnings as competition intensifies. Governments have already shown interest in regulating this situation, and indeed there is a significant group in the profession which would welcome the support of outside regulation. On balance, the accounting profession will probably gradually find itself the subject of greater government control.
- Emphasis on innovation: With the *relative* decline of the traditional audit and the application of expert systems, the professional who can create new solutions to the informational needs of management and to strategic financial management issues will be in even greater demand.
- Globalisation of business: Manufacturing and service companies as well as firms of chartered accountants will continue to be more multi-national both in location and orientation. This is an inevitable consequence of continuing progress in communications, information technology and transportation. Globalisation of labour markets will also continue apace.

The combined impact of these new characteristics on the Institute of Chartered Accountants in Ireland should not be underestimated. If it is to remain independent, united and the pre-eminent professional accounting body in Ireland, the Institute will have to evolve from being essentially public-practice-oriented to serving the needs of a membership with immensely diverse fields of interest. It should be quite feasible for chartered accountants with heterogeneous interests to evolve a common mission (possibly based on the provision, interpretation and attestation of information). Indeed, a similar mission was proposed in a 1986 report commissioned by the Canadian Institute of Chartered Accountants. In examining the future of education and training, I assume that the Institute will adopt a similar course. Nevertheless, it should be recognised that the membership may decide to take a very different course. For example, it may decide that the Institute should concentrate on its established role in auditing and financial accounting and allow new bodies to cater for emerging specialisms or it might decide to become part of a larger European Institute.

Issues facing future education and training

Introduction
Planning the education and training of chartered accountants who will operate in the profession characterised above presents a daunting challenge. That challenge will only be met if it is part of an overall strategic plan for the Institute. Let us now examine the major issues and directions which will have to be considered by those planning education and training for future chartered accountants.

A broad base
To equip chartered accountants for a complex, changing, competitive and international environment will require an emphasis on developing fundamental capacities and abilities. Paramount among those capacities and abilities will be logical thought, critical analysis, understanding of values, synthesis and communication. Foundation education will have to be broad-ranging and should be evaluated by its contribution to the development of basic capacities and abilities rather than the coverage of specific disciplines. The Institute will have to address whether or not the continuation of non-graduate entry conflicts with the need for a broadly-based education for chartered accountants. The record of non-graduates in the profession is excellent but it is difficult to see how the necessary capacities and abilities can be developed in shorter educational programmes.

Professional education
In addition to basic capacities and abilities, chartered accountants will continue to need a specific set of knowledge, abilities and, to a lesser extent, techniques to function effectively. This set of knowledge and abilities will be acquired during a phase of 'professional accounting education'. Future professional accounting education will be concerned primarily with the development of students' understanding of accounting and related disciplines at the conceptual and applied levels in order to equip them to deal with both prevailing practice and future developments. Emphasis on technical content or techniques would not be suitable in a society characterised by change, availability of expert systems and decline in the relative importance of the traditional audit. The precise content of professional accounting education will depend on how the issues raised below with respect to specialisation are resolved. The teaching and learning approach in this phase should continue to develop students' basic capacities and abilities but in a more applied setting. Because of the increasingly competitive environment in which future chartered accountants will operate, the professional's responsibility to society and the importance of professional ethics will have to be stressed throughout professional accounting education. If international trends are indicative, future professional accounting education will be provided pre-

A chartered accountant trainee in industry

dominantly in full-time programmes in universities or specialist schools of accounting.

Specialisation

The trend, already established, towards many chartered accountants working predominantly or even exclusively in specialist fields will, as already indicated, accelerate. The Institute does not currently formally recognise, accredit or validate specialist education and training. Indeed large areas of specialisation have been relinquished already to other bodies, for example the Institute of Taxation in Ireland. This means that chartered accountants are expected to acquire specialist expertise largely outside the Institute's formal educational structures. This situation will have to change if the Institute is to continue to serve all its members. Otherwise, new bodies will continue to be established or supported by chartered accountants to serve their specialist needs. Four questions in particular will face the Institute when it addresses the recognition of specialisms:

- What range of specialisms should be recognised? This question can only be answered in the context of the future mission of the Institute. However, clear boundaries to the profession must be maintained. Specialisation is a vehicle for reinforcing excellence and not a means of extending the profession into an unreasonably wide range of activities.

- When should specialisation take place? A fundamental choice is whether specialisation should precede or follow initial qualification as a chartered accountant? The post-qualification approach has a number of advantages:

    The length of time taken to qualify as a (generalist) chartered accountant will not be unreasonably long;

    Chartered accountants will possess a strong common core of knowledge which helps reinforce the broad perspective; and,

    Specialisms can be added and deleted without structural change.

- Should all chartered accountants be qualified to audit? The Institute will have to decide if all chartered accountants should continue to be considered qualified to audit in an era of *relative* decline in this activity. Auditing might be treated as a post-qualification specialisation like any other with future auditors being required to complete the auditing specialism. This would facilitate provision of a broader professional educational base than at present. However, treating auditing in this way will be difficult unless sister institutes adopt a similar approach. There is considerable pressure from continental Europe to break all links between the practice of auditing and the provision of other professional services.

- How should specialists be designated? Specialists will expect a separate designation. Apart from rewarding those who complete the Institute's requirements for recognition as a specialist, this would help the public recognise those qualified to advise them in given situations. One solution would be to designate generalists and specialists by different grades of membership. Distinguishing between specialists in different fields will require particular care to avoid a confusing proliferation of designations.

A new phase of 'specialist education' will be needed to support specialisation. Specialist education will have to treat current practice, technical knowledge and immediately usable skills though it would seem sensible to do this in the context of the application of data bases and expert systems. There should also be sufficient conceptual underpinning to ensure that the specialist can predict, understand and evaluate future developments.

Diversity in training

Today's relatively standardised, largely public-practice-based training for chartered accountants will not continue as the Institute moves from a primary orientation towards public practice to greater diversity. Even those who will train in the public practices of the future can expect much greater variety of experience and training as the *relative* importance of the traditional audit declines and the range of services expands. High-quality training and experience in accounting is not dependent on standardisation. Training schemes for chartered accountants will be evolved to suit public practices, and industrial and commercial organisations to exploit diversity and to maximise experiential learning. This development will overcome some of the shortcomings at present perceived in newly qualified chartered accountants.

Continuing professional development

In an environment characterised by rapid change, continuing professional education will assume an enormous importance in ensuring that chartered accountants continue to provide the highest quality service throughout their professional lives. It will simply be unacceptable to legislators and the public for accountants (or other professionals) to license generalists or specialists solely by entry examination. At the very minimum, chartered accountants will have to undertake mandatory continuing professional education and this is likely to be linked to periodic review of professional competence as a condition of continued designation as a chartered accountant.

(right) The Leinster Society of Chartered Accountants Published Accounts Award, which is given each year to the company whose accounts have been judged the most excellent in regard to presentation, clarity and adequacy of information, technical quality and so forth

(left) The Accountancy Ireland Award, granted to the author of the best article printed in *Accountancy Ireland* in each year

A School of Accounting?

To support specialist education, certain elements of initial professional education and continuing professional education, the Institute may have to consider expanding the role of the Centre of Accounting Studies into a larger scale 'School of Accounting'. This is more likely when one considers first, that the public sector's expenditure on third level education will be under some pressure for the foreseeable future and second, that the Institute is serving 8,000 people (2,000 students and 6,000 members) which is more than the student-body of most Irish universities. Future developments in education may make it feasible for smaller, private institutions to provide a high quality learning experience to geographically dispersed locations on a cost-effective basis. For example, there will be massive expansion in the application to education of computer-assisted learning techniques and modern communication technologies such as satellite transmission. These technologies will be used both on campus and in distance learning.

Summary and conclusions

The Institute's relatively short tradition in accounting education and training culminated in the establishment, in the last decade, of a sophisticated infra-structure which supports a programme which is progressive and demanding by international standards. This has contributed to a strong demand for Irish chartered accountants at home and abroad.

Like all professional bodies, the Institute will be faced with a period of revolutionary change in the twenty-first century. Fundamental forces relating to the structure and application of knowledge and to change in society will result in the emergence of a profession with very different characteristics to that of today's. The Institute will have to dedicate a great deal of time and resources to evolving a mission and strategic plan to serve its membership in a way that consolidates the current national and international standing of Irish chartered accountants. Education and training will be critical elements of strategic planning.

The characteristics of the future profession will bring a demand for a broad educational foundation but this will have to be reconciled with a trend towards greater specialisation. Specialist education will, in itself, bring many difficult philosophical and structural issues which will only be resolved by reference to the mission of the Institute. New approaches will exploit diversity rather than homogeneity in both public practice and in industry to facilitate high quality practical accounting and business training. The increasing complexity and diversity of initial, specialist and continuing education together with future developments in teaching and learning may lead the Institute to consider establishing a reasonably large scale school of accounting under its own auspices.

Reminiscences of an articled clerk during the war, or 'emergency period' as it was known in Ireland

by C. Gordon Lambert

I served at a time when one's parents paid a lump sum for the privilege of having their offspring work as an articled clerk, out of which one was paid nothing for the first year, £2 per week and £3 per week for the second and third years, after which on qualification one was offered the princely sum of £180 per annum!

This meant that one bicycled everywhere, even to the Zoo Dance with one's partner in formal dress on the crossbar – trams were a luxury. Shortages of everything predominated – the glimmer man stalked households to prosecute the unlawful use of gas, and I remember that part of a junior clerk's duties was dampening the coal slack in order to mould it into briquettes with newspapers in the hope that some kind of fire could be lit to heat the large office rooms in Stokes Brothers & Pim in College Green under arctic conditions.

We were subjected to the strictest of disciplines which included the mandatory obligation to wear a hat when visiting clients' premises on an audit – we were trained on the theme 'if you want to get ahead get a hat!' One senior clerk insisted that I demand used tram tickets as vouchers for local petty cash travelling expenses! Perks were like gold dust – on an audit at Jameson's Bow Street distillery there was a tradition of 'a ball of malt' in the tasting room at the end of the week and although I was in training for various sports I was warned to accept such a generous gesture for fear of spoiling it for future clerks.

Player's cigarette audit was even more popular because one shared in the modest staff ration at the end of a fortnight which could easily be 'blackmarketed' within one's own family!

We were a hardy budget-conscious lot destined to suffer a lifetime of concern over irresponsible attitudes to public expenditure!

Who's who at the Institute

R.F. Hussey

R.L. Donovan

A. Hopkinson

B. Walsh

P. O'Boyle

B.J. Lynch

Name	Title	Main Functions	Reporting to
R. F. Hussey	Director	General management/policy/ external relations/international activities	Council
R. L. Donovan	Secretary/ Director of Membership Services	Professional conduct/ethics/ membership services/district society relations/smaller practitioner matters	Director
(A. Hopkinson C. Leggett)		Member professional education courses	Director, Membership Services
B. Walsh		Practice advisory service/ practice review development	Director, Membership Services
E. Jenkins		Library services	Director, Membership Services
D. Bourke	Technical Director	Technical matters/accounting standards/taxation (Republic)	Director
J. Bowen-Walsh		Auditing standards/insolvency matters/parliamentary and law taxation (Northern Ireland)	Technical Director
B. J. Lynch	Director of Education	General education/examination/ student matters	Director
D. Byrne		Institute/IATI examinations	Director of Education
(K. Cronin J. Conway)		Centre of Accounting Studies/ student education	Director of Education
M. Murray		Institute of Accounting Technicians in Ireland	Director of Education
S. Brady		*Accountancy Ireland*	Director of Education
P. O'Boyle	Industrial Members Executive	Industrial member matters/ information technology/ public relations and communications/special working parties	Director
J. Nolan	Director, Finance and Administration	Finance and administration	Director
J. Monks	Registrar	Member registration	Director — Finance
A. Bradshaw	Financial Services Executive	Financial Services Act (UK) matters	Director
J. Duncan		Belfast office and library	Director

Note: Direct executive servicing of the Leinster and Ulster Societies are provided by H. O'Loughlin and J. Duncan in the Institute's Dublin and Belfast offices respectively.

Desmond Downes, F.C.A.

Desmond Downes is the chairman of Downes
Holdings Ltd. He is a member of the Institute and a
recognised collector of Irish Art.

He has been a member of the selection committee
of the Contemporary Irish Art Society for some
fifteen years and has written and broadcast on the
importance of support for contemporary Irish artists
by individuals and corporations.

He is responsible for the discovery and the casting
in bronze of a very important piece of sculpture by
Jerome Connor and the presentation of this work of
art to the City of Dublin, sited in Merrion Square,
for the centenary of his family bakery company.

The Institute art collection

by Desmond Downes, F.C.A.

Reprinted from Accountancy Ireland *of April 1986*

WHEN the move was made from Fitzwilliam Place to Ballsbridge the
Premises Committee very wisely recommended, and the president and
council agreed, that works of visual art by young Irish artists be
acquired to adorn the new premises. It was further decided that members and
member-firms be invited to subscribe to a purchasing fund with a subscription
upper limit of £500.

I was asked to make the selection and, whereas it is my selection, I had the
valued opinion of our fellow member Gordon Lambert who is nationally and
internationally recognised as an art collector and who is chairman of the Contemporary Irish Art Society and a member of the International Board of
the famous Museum of Modern Art in New York. I also had the valued
opinion of my wife Margaret, who was chairman of the Guinness Peat Aviation
Awards for Emerging Artists.

The chief executive of GPA wrote in the catalogue to the first exhibition in
1981 and I quote: 'The art of a country is the product of all its people. In this
sense, the advancement of the arts is a national enterprise. The opportunity to
participate — for an individual or for a company — is vast. It is also immensely
rewarding.' I share this view and I was delighted to participate in this wise
decision for our Institute to acquire and hang a permanent collection of contemporary Irish Art.

Francis Tansey, *Floating Blue*

The pieces have been hung in the most public places and I hope that all members will enjoy them and, having seen this small collection, some more members and member-firms will subscribe to the fund for further acquisitions.

All the work is new. All the artists are young, mostly born in the 1950s. All are established, have exhibited widely and have received many awards. Their work has been exhibited in South America, Australia, Berlin, Paris and London, all the places that I can remember. The artists chosen have figured prominently in major Irish awards and scholarships in recent years, including the Arts Council Bursaries and the GPA Awards.

I very much enjoyed putting together the collection. There are other artists I would like to see included but whose work as yet we have not been able to acquire for such reasons as too expensive, already spoken for or not fitting in with the collection. I would very much like to see included in our collection the work of Michael Warren, Anne Carlisle, Mary Fitzgerald, Samuel Walsh and Tom Fitzgerald, to name but some.

Michael Murphy, *Tea for Two Turkeys*

Cecily Brennan, *Evergreen*

Vivienne Bogan, *Red Leaves in a Landscape*

Audrey Mullins, *World Activity Measured*

Eithne Jordan, *Head of Woman with a Young Animal*

Helen Comerford, *Shadow Rails*

Euromast, Rotterdam

A telephone in the car

Editorial Introduction to 'Accountancy and technology — a creative partnership'

The most impressive characteristic of electronic technology in recent years has been the extraordinary reduction in both cost and size of equipment combined with enormous increase in potential. Any discussion of today and tomorrow is exciting, and somewhat daunting. Crystal gazing is heady. Nothing seems to be impossible. The great genie awaits only our capacity to use him.

The electronics industry must be one of the most competitive in the world. In the early days of punched card accounting the names Hollerith and Power-Samas were prominent. Now it is Amstrad, BBC, Apple and many others, all fighting for a foothold in an immense and rapidly expanding market. Obsolescence is alarmingly rapid.

Tony Furlong views this world from his IBM desk. In this essay he describes much of what is available to the accountant today — computerised accounting, word processing, desk top publishing, facsimile transmission, personal computers, electronic telephone exchanges, and especially for the auditor, computer assisted audit techniques.

Already accountants and auditors are encumbered with far less routine than in the past, and are required to devote their time much more to acquiring knowledge of and using the equipment and software available to them, to deciding what they require of the technology, and to analysing and assessing its output. Furlong, in his twenty-first century scenario, foresees the auditor employing 'complex software tools' which ascertain that company reports 'provide a true and fair view'. He would accept that his anecdote is simplistic, perhaps, but nevertheless it does give an authentic taste of tomorrow's world.

Seductive stuff, this. One can be lured into a world of gadgetry, and forget the men and women for whom it is all created, with their illogical needs and prejudices. Typewriters and telephones transformed the social world of their day. There is no doubt that electronic technology is transforming our social world today. How far-reaching that transformation will be only history can tell.

But the age of chivalry is gone. That of the sophisters, economists and calculators has succeeded; and the glory of Europe is extinguished for ever.

Edmund Burke (1729-97), *Reflections on the revolution in France*

Anthony P. Furlong, A.C.M.A.

Tony Furlong was born in Waterford in 1934. He was educated at Mount Sion, Waterford, and following this received the ICMA qualification from the Institute of Cost and Management Accountants. His first job in 1952 was with the ESB and he remained with that organisation until he joined IBM Ireland in January 1960.

Tony worked in many areas of the company and has held several management positions. In 1967 he opened an office in Cork for IBM and was based there for seven years while he developed the business in the southern region.

In 1983 he was appointed managing director of IBM's International Software Development Centre (IBM Ireland — Information Services Limited), which was just being established in Dublin. In July 1984 he was appointed managing director of IBM Ireland Limited.

Tony is married and has five children.

Accountancy and technology — a creative partnership

by Anthony P. Furlong

HAD Ireland ever launched a space programme of its own and started to design rockets, the history of computing in this country would have been dominated by scientists and engineers. But that was not the way things happened. Looking back on the tremendous progress of computing in Ireland since I joined IBM more than twenty years ago, it is striking that accountants have played a central role in the spread of this technology.

Over those twenty years Irish industry and commerce have seized the opportunities presented by data processing and communications. The history of information technology is not, of course, limited to changes inside commercial enterprises. This technology has also had a profound influence on the education sector, where school and university students today are learning with the aid of computers just as naturally as they acquire knowledge from textbooks. Its importance has also been recognised by successive governments, which not only have encouraged others to adopt it, but are also using it to help in the task of streamlining the public service.

At the heart of Irish computing, though, is the commercial enterprise which wants to manage its finances more efficiently. Thus, ever since the sixties, the accountant has been a key partner for my industry. Together, accountants and computer manufacturers began to apply information technology in large organisations, then helped it to filter down to even the smallest enterprises. Together we explored new application concepts. Together we have trained the business community how to use the technology. And together we are helping that community prepare to tackle the challenges of the new millennium.

I believe that our partnership is stronger today than ever before.

One hundred hi-tech years

The origins of this joint adventure lie much further back than the installation of the first computers in Ireland. The accountancy profession was one of the main beneficiaries of the office technology revolution of the late nineteenth century. That was the revolution which gave us the typewriter and the telephone. Both made business communication easier. Commercial life no longer followed the rhythm of messengers conveying handwritten notes from one trader to another.

Furthermore, these new tools encouraged the spread of standard business procedures and laid the foundations for modern bookkeeping.

In the early decades of the present century, another major innovation arrived — the punch card controlled accounting machine. Bookkeepers started to adopt these tabulating and recording devices with which, incidentally, IBM first established its reputation world-wide as an office equipment manufacturer.

Another leap through history takes us into the late 1950s, the arrival in this country of the first computers, and the launch of an industrialisation wave that was to transform the Irish economy.

These were large mainframe machines that only the biggest commercial enterprises and state agencies could afford. The top priority for most of the early installations was to harness the computer for financial record-keeping, using it as a superior form of punch card tabulator.

In those stone age days of information technology there were no computer science graduates whom companies could employ to implement their applications. Nor was it possible to buy standard software that would make the machines run. Every installation had to train its own computer experts and devise its own routines. Thus is was that accountants in industry began to study programming and systems analysis, acquired the skills of data processing management and pioneered new ways of handling business information.

During the sixties there was little scope for the chartered accountancy practices to install computers. None of the offices in Ireland were big enough to justify the introduction of even the smallest mainframes. Some of their clients, though, were prepared to rent out processing time on their systems so that others could develop and run applications. This service allowed accountants in practice to discover and experiment with the new technology.

The first explorations began in 1966, when costs were still recorded in pounds, shillings, and pence, the pocket calculator had not yet been introduced, and the processing power on any one of the handful of mainframes in Ireland was a fraction of that available twenty years later on a standard desktop computer.

Craig Gardner was the first practising firm off the mark, developing a job costing system. Staff timesheets were transcribed to punch-cards monthly and the evaluated time was accumulated against the client records, providing summaries to the accountants. The system, though primitive by today's standards, provided great benefits in terms of timeliness and availability of information. By the early seventies, Craig Gardner had outgrown the initial system and had developed a replacement to run on the IBM mainframe at Aer Lingus. The development costs were shared by Kennedy Crowley & Co. and Stokes Brothers & Pim, who were by now keen to have access to such facilities. Although it seems almost quaint now, Craig Gardner handled all of the data preparation and the reports were sent from them to the other companies to distribute to users.

During the seventies the service was enhanced with management information and budgeting facilities. The processing operations were switched

Technology in a modern office

around among a number of mainframe sites, depending on where the lowest charges could be negotiated. Computer owners with machine time to sell regarded the accounting group as a prize catch. In addition to the greatly improved management information, the accountants gained valuable experience of developing and implementing systems; this experience was to form the basis on which many consultancy services were built.

By the end of the decade, though, the practices began to run part or all of these operations on computers of their own. Minicomputers like the IBM System/3 family made data processing affordable among a much wider range of organisations than before. Software also became more standardised in the seventies and first-time computer users were able to buy in proven packages and modify them to their own requirements.

These trends altered the responsibilities of thousands of accountants in industry. When small and medium-sized firms took delivery of minicomputers, it was usually under the direction of financial managers. Typically their systems ran billing applications, debtors' and creditors' ledgers and a company payroll. With products such as these, computer manufacturers became accustomed to shipping dozens of machines to customers every year.

Few suspected, though, that just a few years later our annual shipments would be counted in thousands of units.

Desktop computers and countrywide communications

The present decade will be remembered as the age of the personal computer. I recall the tremendous sense of expectation when we launched the IBM PC in Ireland at the start of 1983. All sorts of organisations expressed an interest in helping us to market the system — established minicomputer suppliers, entrepreneurs setting up shop as retail dealers, software companies, and companies which already sold specialist equipment to particular trades and professions and felt that their customers would like to buy computers as well.

We were even approached by the owner of a small grocery store who wanted to know if there was some way in which they could participate in the exciting new PC business!

Microcomputers in the late seventies were usually regarded as hobby machines rather than as serious business tools. Much of the credit for the PC wave of the eighties belongs to the developers of spreadsheet software which boosted demand for desktop machines and convinced many a company that these systems were much more than gadgets for computer enthusiasts.

Spreadsheets were designed for accountants. Working alone, independent of computer department staff, they were able to use this new resource to draw up budgets, set prices, plan and review spending, and analyse cash flow. The software allowed them to experiment with their figures, asking how changes in costs or prices or exchange rates would affect company plans. These 'what if' enquiries helped accountants to explore permutations of their budgets in ways that had never previously been possible.

Each new release of the financial planning software products increased their capacity, added more functions and accelerated their operating speeds. Today's spreadsheets can process data transmitted from mainframe computers, consolidate groups of tables into single files and exchange information with other PC software packages. It now seems strange that the accountancy profession could ever have functioned without spreadsheets!

No less important than financial planning products was the introduction of ledger, payroll and inventory control software so that applications originally designed for much larger computers could be run on personal computers. Every manufacturing, trading or professional firm, no matter how small, could now control its own accounts on a PC.

Irish accountants are not only involved with computer applications which support financial planning and recording. They have also benefitted from word processing and from desktop publishing systems. Some make use of computer graphics to prepare reports and presentations and to produce slides from the displays created on their screens.

Computer based training is increasingly important for chartered accountancy practices where young recruits can study in their own time and at their own pace with software packages containing lessons. Products are also available for non-professionals to study the basic principles of financial procedures with the aid of a PC.

Many accountants in manufacturing industry have grown accustomed to integrated sets of computer applications such as IBM's MAAPICS which not only caters for financial transactions, but also links them to shopfloor operations such as production scheduling and inventory control. Others have learned the value of database systems which store company information in electronic form and let staff examine it in various ways related to their own responsibilities.

Apart from the PC revolution, though, the most important change in the eighties has been in the area of communications — the transmission of data over telephone networks.

Since the start of the decade the Irish telephone network has been upgraded by the replacement of mechanical switches with electronic exchanges, the introduction of sophisticated network monitoring and fault finding systems, and the installation of earth stations for international transmissions via satellite. More important still, the foundations have been laid for the services of the future by installing a digital trunk network connected to fully digital exchanges throughout the country. So what we are witnessing in this decade is the transformation of the Irish network from the provision of plain telephone service to the data, text, image and voice service now required by modern business.

Already there have been exciting innovations. Since Telecom Éireann took charge of the communications infrastructure in January 1984 it has launched the Eirpac data network which provides a nationwide channel for information services and data transmission. This network has opened up new business for existing services and supported the introduction of new ones. Some relay up-to-the-minute information on subjects like exchange rates or share prices. Others allow accountants to examine transaction records on their banks' computers or to initiate complex financial modelling exercises on mainframes in other countries. IBM in Europe operates an extensive international network on which several services of interest to the progressive accountant are offered.

We have also seen the introduction of a cellular radio service for telephones installed in cars or carried around in users' pockets. Cross-country and international videoconferences have been held — business meetings where participants save travel costs by communicating across voice and video links.

The operators of network services tell us that we are still just starting to tap the possibilities of advanced communications.

Even if we ignore products and services that have not yet reached the market, there is a wealth of information technology resources available to the accountant in Ireland today. Let us look at how they are being adopted.

Technology options today

Accountants in industry are experiencing an acceleration in the pace of business brought on by information technology. Smaller batches of goods are being manufactured in factories where automation has brought a new flexibility in production. Consumers are calling for more choice in the shops and retailers want more frequent deliveries to reduce their storage costs. Service organisations like insurance companies and airlines are experimenting with ever wider choices of policy and fare categories.

It all adds up to a greater range of variables and a greater volume of information for the accountant to monitor.

Consider the challenge facing IBM's own accounts staff. Ten years ago, when we sold a typewriter, the transaction was recorded as a single exchange of product for revenue. Today, when we sell a Personal System/2 we need to itemise some twenty components in that sale — electronic modules, software packages, cables, training materials, operations manuals and so on.

As an international company we also need to coordinate our local operations with those of our colleagues overseas. Each month, for example, IBM Ireland transmits a trial balance in electronic form to our European headquarters in Paris.

Information technology enables us to sort out all the variables in time to deliver our reports. Through our company network we distribute information and applications from one country to another. Accountants, like other staff, choose which applications they intend to use and are authorised to download them from mainframe computer into their own workstations. Computer-based financial planning and analysis help to control inventory levels. All transactions are logged and tracked by computer and databases assist us to keep our customer records up to date.

As the systems become more sophisticated, it is increasingly important for accountants to involve themselves in forward planning. When a constant flow of information on an organisation's finances is processed electronically, analytical routines can quickly identify areas where money is being made or lost. The accountant in industry is therefore able to supply strategic advice to technical marketing and administration managers on a regular basis.

It will take time for many companies to develop such procedures, but even in situations where the only computer applications are tried and tested ones like ledger packages, today's systems generate data with a strategic value.

Chartered accountancy firms are also able to employ computers in ways that give them advantages over their competitors. Many firms have still to install their first system; there are many others that began to use minicomputers and PCs several years ago and are now planning to enhance their facilities with office networks and portable computers.

A feline-sounding acronym is creeping into the profession. CAAT stands for computer assisted audit techniques. Several breeds of CAAT are becoming available. One area that they now address is the interrogation of client companies' data files using the auditor's own PC. The relevant information is extracted from the client's computer, is re-formatted and then transferred to the auditor's PC. Alternatively, that data can be transmitted through Telecom Éireann's networks from the client's premises to the auditor's office.

Some accountants favour portable PCs to assist in performing statistical sampling. These systems generate random references to transactions or balances and are used to log the chosen records for subsequent examination.

As data communications improve, the physical location of the auditor will matter less and less. His or her supervisor can decide when work should be handled from the auditor's own office and when to go to the client's premises in search of information. Some suggest that the best option may be to treat the client's premises as a base camp for an audit and, using data communications, to keep in regular touch with developments back at the auditor's office. It might be worthwhile, indeed, to transmit progress reports from the client's premises every evening.

Most of the CAAT applications now in operation can be described as 'number crunchers'. They include spreadsheets which manipulate the auditors' working papers. (Sooner or later these 'papers' will have to be retitled to take account of the fact that they exist on computer screens instead of on the stuff that books are made from!) Other examples include analytical review and flow charting routines. Word processing and other software also take the drudgery out of making amendments to company statements. Now, however, a very different sort of auditing software is starting to appear — decision support tools that help with the qualitative, rather than the quantitative, aspects of the job.

One example is the audit procedure guide which helps an accountant to plan in advance the tasks which will have to be performed for an individual client. Another is a computer-based representation of tax legislation and precedents which can suggest to the auditor the optimum way for a client company to minimise its tax liabilities.

In other countries it is also possible to seek advice from accountancy database services. These store volumes of information on company law, auditing practices and on the published accounts of major companies. They can be consulted via the public networks to help professionals choose among alternative courses of action or to show them precedents from client organisations similar to their own customers.

It can only be a matter of time before Irish accountants make use of such services.

There is another service provided to businesses by chartered accountancy firms which also must be mentioned. Partners and staff in some practices have now become highly influential information technology consultants.

They set out on this path around twenty years ago. Computers were so closely associated with financial applications in those days that it seemed natural for commercial enterprises to seek the advice of the accountancy firms when they started to consider the installation of their own systems. Practices which conducted audits in organisations with computers soon developed a feel for the suitability of particular models for different categories of client. They sent staff to be trained in the intricacies of the technology by the manufacturing companies which produced it. Gradually, then, the technical consultancy role evolved, opening up a new sphere of activity for the profession.

I have been impressed, on the international level, by the way that the large accountancy firms have become innovative software developers. In the production of computer applications for their own use and for their clients, they have been pioneers in the use of sophisticated software design methods — techniques which accelerate development speeds, techniques which make it easier to integrate applications with each other, and techniques which have dramatically improved the management of software production projects.

Quite clearly, information technology has greatly expanded the range of services offered by accountancy firms and this process is bound to continue. Where might it lead? If we look at the directions of technological change, it is possible to draw up a scenario for the future of accountancy — a glimpse of things to come within the working lifetimes of most of the qualified people currently employed in industry or in the profession.

Trouble-shooting in the twenty-first century

The twenty-first century has just begun and the rain is pouring down in Dublin. A cure has been found for cancer but modern medicine still cannot stop the common cold. Claire has caught a cold and she is feeling miserable. Worse than that, there is a problem with the financial database. As chief accountant with a fast-growing firm that manufactures instruments for biotech laboratories, she is automatically alerted whenever there is a mismatch between the value of a newly produced batch of goods and the revenue received for them as soon as they are delivered to a customer.

On this wet morning the system has reported a significant discrepancy in the previous day's transactions. Thousands of European Currency Units have somehow disappeared from the computer files.

It does not take her long to establish that the missing money was payable by a well-known genetic engineering company in Kildare — a small outfit, but one which had bred three of the last four Derby winners.

Yesterday it took delivery of a customer-designed analyser. Almost every item produced by Claire's company is custom-built. Its materials acquisition system and flexible robot assemblies are able to cope with any new configuration invented by the engineering design department. She double-checks the financial database. The money was paid over yesterday, but has not been lodged in any of the firm's nineteen bank accounts. 'I guess', she says to herself, 'I will have to call Tom.'

Although Tom is an auditor, very little of his time is devoted to 'auditing' in the sense that his predecessors understood the term. Every business enterprise now runs databases of up-to-the-minute trading information, from which comprehensive financial reports may be generated at any time, while chartered accountants employ complex software tools which ascertain that these reports provide a 'true and fair view' of financial affairs. On a day-to-day basis Tom and his colleagues in accountancy practice pay more attention to other matters, like the financial and technological services they provide to clients.

Claire tries to contact him through the Integrated Services Digital Network (ISDN). But a voice synthesiser inside his office workstation tells her that he is away on business in Switzerland. Leave a message, it suggests, and he should be able to call you back within the hour. She does not bother with a text message or the voice mail facility in the ISDN. Reaching for a light pen on her workstation she scribbles two words on her screen 'HELP — CLAIRE', and the image is automatically stored for Tom's attention when he next logs-in to his system.

Back in his hotel forty minutes later Tom plugs his computer into the network and sees the message. He carries his IBM Personal System/99 everywhere. It is a slimline model and it fits very neatly into the lid of his briefcase. Earlier that day he had demonstrated his firm's expert system on European company law to a group of Swiss bankers, using this portable machine.

Making contact at last, Claire explains the situation. Tom decides that he should probe the financial database himself. Security on the system is tight, but he has been authorised to access the database by using a fingerprint identification routine to establish his credentials. His computer contains a tiny scanner which sends the image of his finger through the network for comparison with a specimen held in his client's system.

Another way that Tom could have tackled the problem would have been to refer to a trouble-shooting expert system that his firm has developed. This holds records on thousands of incidents experienced by clients and allows staff to check for precedents whenever difficulties arise.

In the end Claire's problem is resolved when her personal assistant Joe walks into her office waving a small piece of paper.

'I didn't know what to do with this, Claire,' he says, handing over the first cheque to be seen in the company for several years, 'I recorded it as a payment, but couldn't get the money into our account. Those gene geniuses in Kildare have been cut off from the ISDN by a cable fault and they weren't able to pay us through the electronic funds transfer service.'

Looking forward, looking back

In reality, the differences between accountancy today and in the year 2000 are unlikely to be so dramatic. Technological capabilities alone do not determine the shape of organisations and jobs. In the sixties, for example, some future-gazers forecast that every audit would involve the interrogation of computer-based accounts by 1970 — a prediction that was over optimistic by twenty years.

From a purely technological point of view, however, most of the elements in this account are quite plausible in an end-of-the-century timeframe.

The highly flexible, highly automated factory where Claire works will be feasible through the development of computer integrated manufacturing (CIM). This involves the interconnection of planning, design, production, distribution and accounting applications inside industrial enterprises and, through online links, between their computers and those of their suppliers and customers. CIM creates a constant information flow for all areas of the company.

Some accountants in industry feel that CIM is too much like management by formula and are sceptical about its prospects. But manufacturers and distributors are already planning to connect together their financial and non-financial computer applications in the near future (IBM manufacturing plants in Europe are already planning such online links with supplier companies.)

The ISDN is also coming. Telecom Éireann hopes to offer this facility, which transmits voice, text, data and image signals through a common line, to business customers in the early nineties. It is not yet clear exactly what services will be provided through the network or how the terminals required to use it will look. But the range of communications options available in industry and commerce by the end of the century will be infinitely richer than today.

Links between portable computers and mini and mainframe systems will become much more widespread and more powerful. We expect, indeed, that today's terminals and PCs will, in time, be replaced with intelligent workstations that provide users with the software applications and processing power most appropriate to their needs. It will become irrelevant to them whether the operation on their screen originates in a disk drive under their desk, on a host computer in the building where they work or on a networked computer thousands of miles away.

For the accountant in practice, the development of expert systems technology holds out the promise of powerful new tools in the decade ahead.

Two general categories of these knowledge-based computer applications are evolving. One will help the professional to interpret accounting standards, guiding the accountant through, for example, the financial reporting and taxation legislation in the parent countries of client companies. The other type will enable practices to build up computer files with stores of precedents based on their own working experience especially in the tax area. These will be designed with enquiry facilities to direct users to similar cases for any given situation.

The spread of expert systems in the profession is difficult to forecast. Developers are finding it difficult to progress beyond the prototype stage to applications which may be used in a routine way and there are problems to be overcome in the electronic classification of some types of specialist knowledge, such as the auditors' instincts to zero in on a particular problem area that is not immediately obvious. Nonetheless, this is an area of information technology that accountants should watch.

Another key development will be the introduction of electronic funds transfer. The major banks have already established network services for switching money electronically from one account to another and it is quite conceivable that, by the end of the century, instantaneous transfers of funds from company to company will be the norm in industry and commerce.

These services will demand a high level of network security. An awareness of the importance of data protection is only starting to emerge in this country, as organisations recognise the growing risks of computer fraud if access to sensitive information is not carefully controlled. Those risks will multiply as more data is entrusted to communications networks.

Encryption techniques can convert information into coded form before it is sent down the line. These are not the stuff of spy stories, but will become essential tools for protecting financial data in computer files. Access controls and user identification routines will also be vital, although it will probably be a long time before finger prints or voice prints replace passwords and personal identification numbers as the usual techniques for authorising people to access data.

As for the functions that are going to be available on the IBM Personal System/99, I will leave it to the reader to speculate how our products are going to look at the end of the century!

The information technology industry and the accountancy profession face a common challenge in the years ahead, sifting through all the possible products and services to implement those which provide the greatest benefits to industry and to the accountant in practice.

Looking back on the progress of our partnership so far, I have no doubts that the profession will be able to respond to that challenge. I foresee a high demand in the nineties for the multi-skilled qualified accountant who can navigate a course through financial databases and complex computer systems as expertly as from one end of a balance sheet to the other.

Information technology is a tool for Irish industry and commerce and will be as natural a part of the accountant's working day as the quill pen was to the Victorian scrivener. I am confident that the accountancy/technology partnership which has achieved so much in the past twenty years will generate many more exciting innovations in the decade ahead.

THE
DESCRIPTION
and vſe of the
SECTOR.
The Croſſe-ſtaffe and
other inſtruments.
For ſuch as are ſtudious
of Mathematicall
practiſe.
AT LONDON
Printed by Williã Iones.
and are to be ſold by:
Edmund Weauer.
1624.

L. 20
61

Computing through the ages

From September 1986 to March 1987 Trinity College, Dublin, mounted an exhibition in the Library of methods of computing through the ages. The College has kindly permitted us to publish, in the following pages, a few examples of the equipment and methods there illustrated. In these days of the sort of high technology described by Anthony Furlong in his essay on page 188, it is fascinating to dwell for a while on the remarkable thinking and inventiveness of those who helped to lay the foundation for our present intricate and wonderful machines.

The Irish contribution to the development of computing has been significant. Percy Ludgate (1883-1922), for example, who was born in Cork and worked in Dublin as an accountant, developed a strange and cumbersome method of multiplication using index numbers. But he also published a paper describing an analytical machine (which incorporated the main concepts of the digital computer), before ever he had knowledge of the work of the more famous Babbage. George Boole, another Corkman, wrote an extremely important book on mathematical logic, and was the inventor of what is now known as Boolean Algebra.

The illustrations which follow include the work of others who worked in Ireland — W.E. Lilly of Trinity College, George Fuller of Queen's College, Belfast, and Redmund Naish, who may have been an accountant also.

Napier's Bones. The famous Scottish mathematician, John Napier (1530-1617), invented a device to aid multiplication, division, and the taking of square- and cube-roots, which was known as Napier's bones. The book was published in 1617. Each bone is just a column of the multiplication table. The bones illustrated were presented to Trinity College not later than 1743 by John Lyon, a minor canon of St Patrick's Cathedral, who assisted Swift in his last illness. They are set up here to enable a number to be multiplied by 2430251.

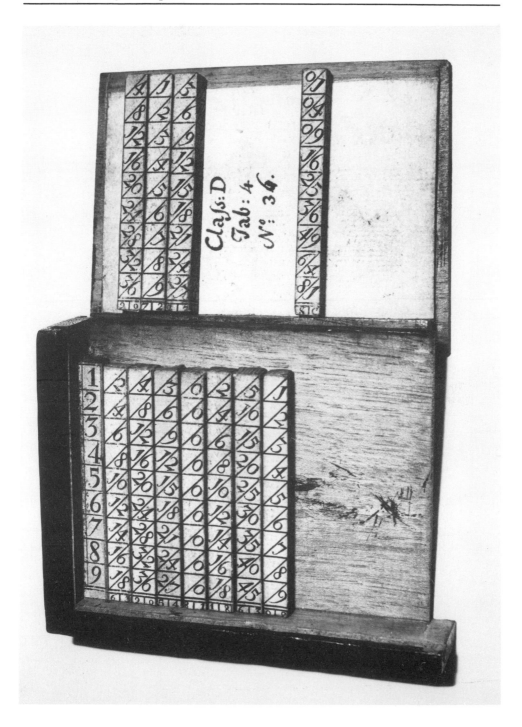

Pascal's Machine Arithmetique, 1642. In 1642, at the age of nineteen, Pascal (1623-62) designed the first calculating machine which is still extant. It could be used only for addition and subtraction. The engraving showing some of the internal features of the machine is part of Diderot's (1713-84) Encyclopaedia, the first volume of which was published in 1752. The machine can still be seen in the Musée des Techniques in Paris.

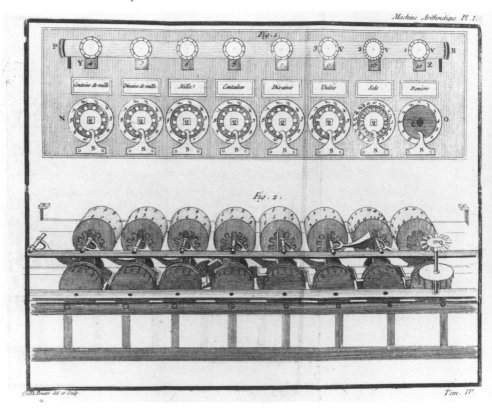

Redmund Naish's Logarithmicon. The most unusual slide rule illustrated is the Logarithmicon. It was designed by Redmund Naish in 1898 and made by Yeates of Grafton Street, Dublin. The table can be read to four significant figures. Naish used a formal notation to describe the operation of the rule, and all of the examples he gives are concerned with financial computations.

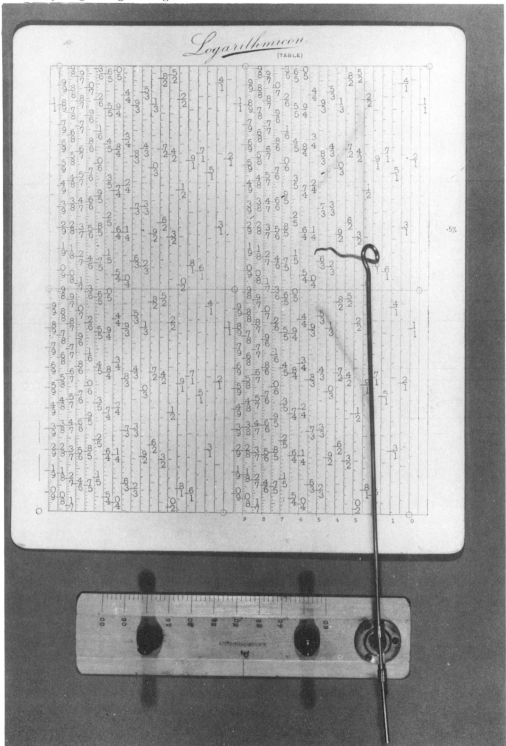

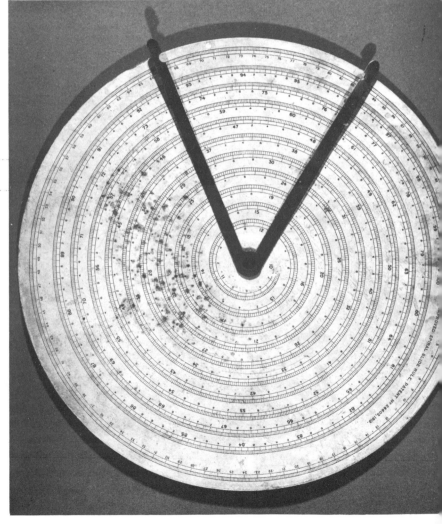

(*left*) George Fuller's Spiral Slide Rule. George Fuller was professor of civil engineering in Queen's College, Belfast, when he designed his spiral slide rule, which is equivalent in length to 83 feet 4 inches. It was extremely successful and very widely used in engineering offices in these islands.

(*below*) Lilly's Circular Rule. The large circular rule was designed by Dr W.E. Lilly, a lecturer in the Trinity College, Dublin, engineering school from 1893 to 1923. He patented his rule in 1912.

'Bankers' Audit

Bankers are now busy balancing their books for 1886, in collecting and crediting the January dividends for their customers, in preparing dividend warrants and balance-sheets for distribution to their shareholders. In the midst of this heavy work they are interrupted by what becomes a perfect nuisance, the interference of a professional auditor and his clerks. Our grandfathers knew him not; he is an invention of modern days.

The Companies Act of 1879, which was passed to enable banks to register with limited and reserve liability, made audit compulsory; and it is there stipulated that a director or officer of the company may not be an auditor of the accounts. The consequence is that an outsider must be found, the certificate of the manager or secretary, together with not less than three directors' signatures, not being deemed a sufficient guarantee of the correctness of the company's affairs. There is no doubt that the agitation brought about by chartered accountants and the sympathetic but unnecessary exertions of weak and nervous shareholders were the cause of the legislation; but with the exception of the frauds on the London and River Plate Bank, about which the chartered accountants sing such a joyous song, we do not know that the services of these auditors have consisted of much more than ticking figures which have been duly certified by managers and directors. The chartered accountants at a recent provincial meeting took unction to their souls that such a state of things as was disclosed in the disastrous failures of the City of Glasgow, West of England, Oriental and Munster Banks could scarcely have arisen or been continued 'if the certificate of a qualified auditor had been required.'

Let us see what a professional accountant is called upon to do. The Act of 1879 provides that every auditor shall have delivered to him a list of all the books kept by the company; and we should say that this preliminary is enough to upset the nerves of anyone, especially in the case of large banks, such as the National Provincial or London and County. But his peace of mind is soon assured, for he recollects that an efficient staff of inspectors and officers are ever on the watch for irregularities, and that the books are faithfully balanced and agreed daily. Having carefully examined his formidable list, he has to make a beginning; of course he has had a few polite words with the manager, for his difficulties would be increased if they were omitted. It is exceedingly rare for the accountant to find out errors in the works, but he affords fun to the clerks by the mares' nests he frequently discovers. Some auditors are, of course, more searching and efficient in their examination than others, and follow up the work with creditable zeal; but with all their ability, their ignorance of banking practice continually finds them wanting, and they pass over, year after year, the very cobwebs they are supposed to discover.

Banker's Magazine, January 1887 quoted from *Belfast Bank 1877-1970* by Noel Simpson, Blackstaff Press

Editorial Introduction to 'The true and fair sex'

Those brave females who first dared to knock on the doors of the all-male accountancy world caused the men many moments of self-conscious embarrassment and — sometimes — ribald amusement. But the females battled on, and in the last few years the proportion of female to male membership has increased enormously. There seems to be no reason why, in time, the ladies should not form half the membership, or more.

Oddly, though, the proportion of lady members in the top positions in practising offices and outside falls very much below total membership. Why should this be so? In this delightful essay, Pat Barker explores the reasons, and offers her own conclusions.

Patricia Barker, F.C.A.

Patricia Barker was educated in Dublin and served articles in Stokes Bros & Pim, qualifying in 1973. She worked in Harrods of London, Peat Marwick Mitchell in Manchester and in Manchester Polytechnic. She is currently lecturing at NIHE, Dublin. In her student days, Patricia was a member of the Dublin Society Student Committee and of ACASSI and is currently a member of the Institute's Accounting Review Committee.

She is married to Robert Barker, tax director with Stokes Kennedy Crowley & Co., and they have two children. She is a scout leader and is keen on hill walking and canoeing; she is one of the few lady helmsmen of cruiser class boats sailing out of Howth.

The true and fair sex

by Patricia Barker

I T'S a long time since the Brehon days, when it was the women in Ireland who governed the country, made all the important decisions of state and delegated the domestic chores like scrubbing the goatskin vests and cooking up the porridge to the men.

By the time the mists of Irish history had rolled on to the nineteenth century, the cutting edge of the Irishwoman's power had been somewhat blunted. Her standing in society had seriously diminished. It was, by then, as if, upon entering life's theatre, she was immediately shown to a seat behind a pillar, ensuring that she had only a restricted view of life's splendorous pageant. Families, throughout the country, expecting the imminent arrival of a baby would nearly go into mourning on the birth of a girl; and could only be consoled with the thought that as she grew up she could help to make the beds, to iron the shirts, feed the chickens, cook the food, clean the house and generally dance attendance on the men of the house. And of course, her supreme contribution to the history of the nation — the culmination of her life's efforts — the crescendo of her very being? Why, the speedy delivery of another Irishman, of course. Didn't matter if he grew up to be arrogant, ugly, cruel, dim or even alcoholic — so long as he was a man! It was always assumed that the expectant mother would bear a son unless she had transgressed in some manner during the pregnancy; like burning the Sunday joint or omitting to carry in sufficient stocks of wood to carry the household over during her time off for labour and childbirth!

It was during these post-Brehon days of cosy family bliss that the Institute of Chartered Accountants was born. A solid body of men in black and white, with precisely sculpted goatees and pince nez glasses jammed uncompromisingly against gloomy eyes which gazed suspiciously at copper plate accounts prepared by nervous sweating clerks. After a day's work with the fine quill pen and the green ink, the chartered accountant would put aside the ledgers and journals and make his way home to where his wife would await him with slippers warming by the fire, whiskey standing in the tray, supper simmering on the hob and a line of gleaming children ready for inspection before banishment to bed. A place for everything and everything in its place!

Imagine the horror with which this body of stony-faced bearded stoics received Edward Kevans' application, in 1901, for his daughter Cecily to be

6·7%

admitted as a student of the Institute. At that time, women were permitted to act as public accountants in America and even in France, although not in the United Kingdom. Edward, whose son, Patrick had served with him as an articled clerk from 1889, qualifying in 1897, was anxious that his daughter should have a similar opportunity. Patrick, having taken first place and the President's prize, subsequently entered into partnership with his father and remained there until his early death in 1910. Cecily, however, was doomed neither to hold the glorious title of 'first lady chartered accountant' nor to join her father and brother in the firm. The members of the Institute, in a bit of a tizz about this application, decided to consult the sister organisation in London. London fairly bristled! There was stiff opposition to the notion of allowing a *woman* into the profession. This probably confirmed London's belief that the Irish were just a bunch of crackpots. Faced with this formidable opposition, Kevans agreed not to pursue the matter.

Even in the USA, where there were lady CPAs, the prediction for the future of women in accounting was gloomy. A. P. Richardson, in an editorial in the Journal of Accountancy in December 1923, said of women in accounting;

> When a member of an accounting staff is engaged, it is understood that he is to hold himself in readiness to serve whenever and wherever called upon to do so. In the wide variety of modern accounting practice a staff member may be required to go from one end of the country to another, in company with groups of staff members, working at high pressure and under living conditions not suitable for what might be termed post-graduate co-education. Then, again, there are many assignments to which staff members are sent, involving working all night long in places of difficulty and inconvenience. For example, an audit of a bank must be performed between the hours of closing and opening. Large numbers of men are sent to work, but any attempt at heterogeneous personnel would hamper progress and lead to infinite embarrassment.

One wonders what exactly he had in mind. In all my years of auditing banks and other business enterprises, both in town and out of town, both during the hours of daylight and darkness, I completely missed out on the experience of being sent off with a large number of men to engage in progress-impeding, embarrassing activities of a co-educational nature. I have written a strong letter of complaint to my principal!

It was not until after the first world war — ah, that war again! It was the root cause of the ruination of the cosy domestic picture. Women never again were to realise their place in the order of things! After the war, at the thirty-first annual meeting of the Institute in May 1919, a resolution was carried (by a large majority) that women should be allowed to qualify for membership. In 1920 a new by-law was adopted providing for the admission of women to membership of the Institute on equal terms with men, so as to bring the by-laws into harmony with the Sex Disqualification (Removal) Act of 1919. The Irish Institute was the first of the chartered bodies to recognise the rustle of taffeta sweeping through the portals hitherto untrod by other than male footsteps. And due credit to those early Irish accountants! Our separated brethren across the pond, however, were unimpressed. Did the Irish not realise, they thundered, that there would be '... nothing to prevent its women members from practising in England, Scotland or Wales, and there describing themselves as ACA or FCA?' One can almost sense the smelling salts passing along the table.

It was not until 1925 that the first woman was admitted to membership of the Institute. She was Eileen Woodworth, a lady of impeccable lineage, whose grandfather was one of the signatories to the charter, and whose father was a member of the council. She married Norman McAllister in 1930, and practised in Rangoon with a break of one year in 1932. She continued to practise during the war years and remained in Burma until, sadly, she died in Madras in July 1942. She must have been a formidable feminist of her time, in the first instance to qualify as the only woman amongst almost 200 male accountants, and secondly to continue in her profession at a time when most married women were expected to devote themselves exclusively to home and family.

Eileen was very shortly followed by Miss Kathleen O'Neill. She was the daughter of John O'Neill, managing director of John O'Neill Limited, a motor company, and of Beleek Pottery Limited. He was a founder member of the Dublin Industrial Development Association, and a prominent member of several government financial committees. Although he had a large family, Mr O'Neill sent his daughter to university where she graduated with a commerce degree. She was accepted into articles with Kean & Co., qualifying in 1926. Miss O'Neill, who is now Sr M. Denis O'Neill at the Dominican Convent, Sion Hill, found no difficulty in relating to the staff of Kean & Co. and expressed her appreciation of their efforts to involve her in every type of accountancy work in the firm during her training. And whilst clients might have been a 'bit curious' at a female auditor, they all behaved like gentlemen. She was sent on country work usually in the company of married family men, although it was decided not to send her on the Maynooth College job, as it might have caused 'a bit of a sensation'! Her very first audit was of Mooneys Public Houses, and she studied by correspondence course with the Metropolitan College in London for the examinations, without the benefit of student societies or lectures. After completing her H. Dip. in Ed. Miss O'Neill entered the Dominican order and was sent to St Mary's Training College in Belfast, where she was college bursar for many years.

Miss O'Neill was soon followed by a trickle of women which included Emma Bodkin, a daughter of Judge Bodkin and a sister of the famous Dr Thomas Bodkin. Having served her articles with Craig Gardner & Co., she was admitted to membership in 1928, remaining a member until 1965. Sylvia McWilliam was admitted in 1932, and Edith McHoul and Clare O'Rourke in

1935, bringing the total of lady members to six from a total membership of 339.

Over the years, the membership records give us some clue as to how the Institute struggled with the dilemma of how to describe this new breed of member in its records. From 1925 until 1939, women members were listed under their surnames and Christian names while the men had surnames and initials. From 1940 until 1986, women were listed as the men but with Mrs or Miss in parenthesis after their names. In 1980 we see the first self-conscious use of that abomination of the feminist movement: the 'Ms'. It was the choice of only one member, a Ms Gillian O'Connell. However after a couple of years of the use of this title, the record keepers obviously thought that it would be more appropriate to describe all members, male and female, by their initials only, lest the

Sister M. Denis O'Neill, the second woman chartered accountant in Ireland, and the oldest surviving

use of this title 'Ms', should spread, and all lady members should be made to sound like some sort of swarm of eunuch wasps.

The phenomenon of a female accountant has now, in the latter half of the 1980s, become fairly commonplace; so much so, that in some instances, an entire audit team may be female. However, in the late sixties, a female auditor arriving at the client's doorstep caused something of a stir, particularly when this innovation was combined with the (then) very new practice of attending stock-takes, circularising debtors, physically checking a pay-out and verifying the physical existence of fixed assets. My very first audit assignment was a physical check on the payroll for the B and I dockers. This involved checking the payroll for mathematical accuracy and then physically ensuring that there was a different docker for each name on the payroll. I arrived early in the morning and did all the sums. Everything was grand, now all I had to do was the 'physical'. The dockers, who had been in the pub since seven in the morning, started to queue up the stairs of the pay office from 10.30, and by eleven o'clock, when the tiny sliding window was due to open for the pay clerk to hand out the buff envelopes, the stairs and passageways of the little office were heaving with swearing belligerent men, most of whom had the physical appearance of a Centurian tank! Outside on the docks, an equally vociferous queue was forming — the dockers' wives, who were hoping to collect some of the contents of the buff envelopes before they disappeared into Arthur Guinness's coffers. Francis, the pay clerk, had barricaded the door of the pay office with desks and filing cabinets as the pressure from the mountain of muscle outside increased; and, crossing himself, he opened the little wooden sliding window. The men were a bit taken aback when, instead of seeing Francis's hand emerge through the window with the first pay packet to be exchanged for a signature, they saw his face, or part of it, and heard him bawl: 'Will yiz shurrup and listen! This girl wants to make sure you are all there, physically!' There was a split second of stunned silence and then they all erupted! Modesty forbids me from tabulating the suggestions I received as I bent down to peer through the window at the big hairy hands grabbing the money from Francis and signing the tattered notebook; suffice it to say that all of the language, curses or lewd suggestions I heard from transport managers, stock clerks, foremen or even engineering labourers for the rest of my career as an auditor caused me not one second's thought after the baptism of fire I had that day!

Women, of course, do not always wear the most appropiate clothing for the job. The most acceptable form of clothing appears to be a suit of sober cut and subdued colour with smart (but not flashy) court shoes. I wore a brand new suit for the audit of Irish Distillers. It was a pale lilac number with a little flared mini skirt. I felt most professional and cosmopolitan with my two-inch platform shoes in pale pink and lilac suede with handbag to match, as I drove down to Midleton to do a physical stock check on the maturing whiskey stocks. I swept into the little office and, flourishing my list, I announced to the all-male

The 'balanced' approach: Geraldine Mullaney, B.Comm., A.C.A., of the Industrial Credit Corporation. Her 'other life' is sport.

company that I was the auditor and that I wanted to see the following barrels, kegs and firkins, and that I wanted to sample each of them to ensure that they contained whiskey! A startled looking man in a faded navy suit picked up the phone and announced, breathlessly, to the unseen superior at the other end of the line: 'Th' otter's here, an' it's a woman, an' she wants to taste the whiskey!' There was a yell of disbelief from the other end of the phone and within seconds, an inner door swung open and a manager-type in a less faded blue suit entered and asked me to state my business. A little less cocky now, I told him the story of how I wanted to satisfy myself as to the existence of these highly valuable items of inventory. After a lot of discussion with head office and the customs officer who would have to break the seal on the bonded warehouse, they agreed that maybe I could look at the whiskey, if it was the only way of getting rid of me. Paddy, the poor chap who was designated to locate the items of stock I had selected, gave my lovely new suit and shoes a decidedly querulous look. Maybe I'd like to borrow something a little more appropriate for climbing around centuries-old damp warehouses with fungus-covered mud floors and wall to wall cobwebs? I said yes, and, twenty minutes later, the entire staff lined the courtyard to watch the procession of the customs man, Paddy and me — clad in a navy blue boiler suit that would have fitted Rambo, a pair of size eleven wellies and carrying a torch which would have understudied for the RNLI searchlight and my list of inventory! We conducted ourselves in as dignified a manner as was possible under the circumstances, and, six hours later, we tottered out into the daylight with our mission completed. Paddy hesitated, glanced at my grimy face, my enormous floppy clothing and my canal barge footwear and asked: 'I suppose you'd take a drink?' We parted the best of friends some three hours later.

Position of women members in the Institute through the years

In spite of the supportive attitude of the Irish Institute towards the acceptance of lady members, the number of lady members in the Institute remained below ten until 1956, and then stayed below twenty until 1973 (see figure 1). However, there has been a dramatic increase both in the number of women and in the percentage of women members from 1980 to 1987. When viewed in perspective, however, although the increase from 1.4 per cent to 6.7 per cent is dramatic, 6.7 per cent of total membership is hardly evidence of female success in battering down the gates and storming Castle 'Accountancy'. Comparative figures for other professions can be seen in figure 2, showing that chartered accountancy is a very close contender for the title 'last bastion of male domination'!

It would seem that the men had better guard the postern, however, as the recent statistics of the number of girls choosing a degree course in commerce (including business studies and accountancy) has almost trebled since 1976. In these commerce undergraduate courses, girls now represent over one-third of the total class.

In examining the profile of the lady members who are currently registered in the Institute, one can see that by far the greatest age grouping is in the twenty-five to twenty-nine age bracket (figure 3). This, of course, reflects the recent increase in membership. However, it is not greatly out of line with the national figure for professionals with men showing a median age of 36.6, and women of 30.5. One wonders if this increasing number of women who are fast approaching that dreadful age when one becomes an 'F.C.A.', will give the council pause to consider the whole issue of fellowship. Most of us would probably agree that some post-qualification education is imperative, and that, should a member

The 'balanced' approach: Olwen Law, B.Sc., A.C.A., of Arthur Andersen & Co., chartered accountants, in London. Her 'other life' is the stage.

complete ten years of continuing professional education (CPE) as evidenced by some form of examination or assessment, it is right and proper to award a fellowship. However, it came as quite a shock to me, at a time when I could coyly pass myself off as 'late twenties', when the Institute came along with its 'F.C.A.' branding iron and, ignoring my screams of anguish, blazoned my thirty-three years for all the world to see across my forehead — and then, just to rub salt into the wound, they told me I would have to *pay* for this cruel disclosure of my age to the world! Was there ever a crueller blow dealt by man upon woman?

Geographic spread

It can be seen from figure 4 that the majority of women members are working in the Republic, with a relatively small proportion overseas. It is interesting to note that there is a higher proportion of the Ulster women married than all the rest. So, if you want to catch a husband, girls, take the next day shopper train to Belfast. Of the married lady members, sixty per cent are married to accountants. Only nineteen per cent of the lady members who have travelled off the island are married, so there is no evidence that they are leaving to follow a husband's employment. It seems more likely, that, once having qualified, they are applying their recently acquired taxation knowledge to fleeing from the country that educated them, at no little cost, to a country whose tax structure is perceived as being more friendly to high earning professionals.

Employment classification

Figure 5 shows that more than half of the women members are employed as professional accountants with thirty per cent working in industry. There is a category of membership called 'special', which is a reduced subscription available to members who apply to council on grounds of special circumstances. The most prevalent special circumstance claimed by the women members is 'child minding'. There is also a case of one woman member who has been awarded 'special' classification for a period during which she is serving as a voluntary worker overseas. Figure 6 gives more detail on this employment classification, showing that by far the largest grouping of women members is in the 'audit/tax senior' category. The second largest grouping is 'financial controller/management accountant'. There are disappointingly few women in the top executive positions such as finance director or partner. A cross analysis of these classifications by age indicates that it is the younger members who hold positions as 'audit senior' and 'assistant accountant', however the indications are that the women are not moving into the top positions in the professional offices and in industry as their age increases. There is some tendency for the women over twenty-five to operate as sole practitioners from home, or to go into academic positions. More than half of the single women are in the income bracket £17,501 upwards, whereas only thirty per cent of the married women find themselves in that bracket. There is a tendency for those women who have worked overseas to have a higher income. Women with children are invariably in the lower pay bracket, and there is a high correlation between the number of children and the pay: the more the children the lower the income!

Of the large professional offices, Craig Gardner & Co. boasts the highest proportion of women trainee accountants in their annual intake, with almost fifty per cent, while the other large offices take between twenty and thirty-eight per cent women. All the professional offices adopt the view that they wish to employ the 'best people', and their sex is immaterial to the decision. However, they all express disappointment at the ability of the qualified women accountants to 'stay the course' and move up through the ranks of manager, principal manager, and director to that final golden throne in the sky marked 'partner'. Coopers & Lybrand have a female partner and although Craig Gardner also have a female partner, she is not a chartered accountant. The number of female managers, principal managers and directors is universally reported as disappointing.

That women are, at present, not making their way to the top executive posts is incontrovertible. The reason is slightly more complex. The possible explanations would include:

- That women are discriminated against.
- That women are less successful because they are less able than men.
- That women see their jobs as a means of providing funds for them to engage in activities that really attract them.
- That motherhood causes women to divert attention from their careers.
- That women are not as ambitious as men.
- That women are attracted to fields that pay less, for example, charitable work, lecturing, etc.

Discrimination

Even though most female managers are regarded as extremely competent, men, particularly in industry, think that they will eventually leave, either to have children or because the tensions of work will become too much. Both are legitimate concerns. A woman on the fast ascent corridor is under intense pressure. Many corporate types believe that she gets much more scrutiny than a man and must work harder to succeed. This is a view held by a majority of Irish lady accountants surveyed. The pressures increase geometrically if she has small children at home. Discrimination is not, however, perceived as a major problem by Irish lady accountants. When surveyed, thirty per cent felt that they had never suffered any discrimination, sixty-eight per cent felt that they had suffered occasional discrimination and two per cent felt they had experienced serious discrimination. The degree to which discrimination was experienced did not vary with the marital status of the women. Women who are in the higher salary ranges are less likely to perceive sex discrimination but women with children are more likely to report experiences of discrimination.

Ability
The examination statistics at all levels indicate that women are certainly not less able than their male counterparts. Research has concluded that male and female managers do not differ in the way they manage technical and human resources. Women's assertiveness and leadership qualities are the same as those of their male counterparts.

The 'balanced' approach to life
The jobs that seem attractive to women as they move into the post-qualifying period are those that would combine successfully with interests outside a career. Women seem to be anxious to seek an answer to the question: 'Is there life after qualification?' A man, on the other hand, appears happier, after qualification, to bury himself even more deeply into the furrow of his career, spending the daylight hours in a frenzy of meetings, business trips, reading technical data, writing complex reports and supervising a swarm of yuppies all slavering after his job, and then arriving home under a ton of work that must be completed before the dawn ushers in the next day of unrelenting sweat-soaked toil. Men, of course, can combine this with a family. It is still the social norm for the wife of a successful accountant to provide the domestic cushion essential to support the high flyer on his ascent to heaven. Women, on the other hand, seem happier to exercise their profession in a less pressurised manner, freeing up part of their day to sample the delights of their new-found professional salary, or to socialise or to establish relationships with husbands and children. The consequence of this is, of course, that they do not achieve the glorious career pinnacle that is the reward of devoted undivided attention to the job.

Motherhood
It is an inescapable biological fact that motherhood detracts considerably from the time that a young professional mother can devote to her career. Seventy-three per cent of the lady members attributed the small proportion of their number who succeeded in reaching the upper echelons of industry and the profession to motherhood. There is evidence, however, that these professional mothers do not want to give up their profession completely and are anxious to find ways and means of combining a career with motherhood. Facilities such as crèches, part-time working and flexi-time all offer women a means of achieving this objective.

The 'balanced' approach: Geraldine Barnwell, B.Comm., A.C.A., of the National Institute of Higher Education. Her 'other life' is her home.

Ambition

Half of the lady members surveyed would classify themselves as 'ambitious' or 'very ambitious'. Thirty-five per cent regard themselves as 'reasonably ambitious', with fourteen per cent 'not ambitious'. (One per cent didn't know). There is very little evidence of girls 'drifting into' accountancy. Most respondents indicated a positive decision to enter the profession. I was relieved to see that no one was attracted to accountancy by the prospect of being sent down the country in the dead of night with a gang of men of nefarious intent.

Jobs with flexible hours

It is undoubtedly true that jobs with flexible hours, including charitable work and lecturing attract women. Women do not necessarily put in fewer hours, but they like jobs which allow them to put in the hours when they are at their maximum output.

The profession's response

The attitude of the Irish professional offices to women accountants is one of absolute and meticulous non-discrimination towards women. Women have exactly the same chance of being employed (unless they are obviously pregnant); of being offered training programmes; of getting plum jobs; of receiving salary increases; and of succeeding in the promotions race as their male counterparts. Exactly *the same*. None of the offices has a policy to cater for its women accountants. They expect the women to fit into the policy which has developed to cater for the male accountants. None of the offices has an affirmative action programme in relation to its female employees, and none saw any need to consider such a programme. None of the Big Eight offices had considered part-time work, although Cooney, Bannon & Corrigan have two lady members of their professional staff who work part-time (apparently very successfully). Job-sharing, job-splitting, flexi-time or work from home via a computer link are not offered by any of the large firms. None has a policy of including women in the interviewing or promotions process. Nowhere were there any crèche facilities, paternity leave or parental leave for sick children, although all the offices support women wishing to take maternity leave and in some instances give well in excess of the statutory minimum support. A spokesman for one of the offices described paternity leave as a 'charter for skivers' and said it would be introduced over his dead body! Other offices were more benevolent and indicated that, while they wouldn't like to see paternity leave as a 'right', they quite often allowed the chaps to stay at home for a couple of days to serve the champagne to the visitors who called to deliver presents for the new baby.

Craig Gardner is currently considering the area of support for lady accountants, who, having had their families, wish to return to the profession.

One of the partners indicated that the issue of retraining women to return to work is a very live issue and that they hope to have a policy in relation to this area within the next two years. In 1986, SKC's UK bedfellows, Peat Marwick Mitchell announced a positive policy for mothers returning to work. The degree of success or failure of this scheme will be carefully monitored by the Irish offices.

So, despite impressive progress at the entry level and in middle management, women are having trouble breaking into senior management. In the United States, women complain of discrimination, ranging from sexual harassment to inadequate feedback. In Ireland, the complaint is not about discrimination, but about the lack of an affirmative action programme. However, something of a semantic chasm separates men and women. Women think of an affirmative action programme as a vigorous effort on the part of companies to ensure that women are treated equally and that sexual prejudices are not permitted to operate. Men think of the term as 'reverse discrimination', giving women preferential treatment. The reality is that with our economy lagging, companies are more worried about surviving and making money than about how their women managers are doing, and that, therefore, companies and organisations with affirmative action plans are very thin on the ground. While many male accountants feel that there is not an issue, that women will become partners just as easily as men if their qualifications and dedication to the job are the same, there is a belief amongst women that such an attitude is part of the problem, indeed that it is the central problem.

The American Institute of Certified Public Accountants has identified 'the issue of strengthening the upward mobility for women in public accounting' as a future issue. The AICPA is making efforts to increase the participation of women on its committees, and proposes to engage in further research into the issue. The Irish Institute has no such plans, and Irish Institute committees are conspicuous for their lack of female representation. There are three lady chartered accountants and one lady lawyer on the thirty-six Institute committees who constitute 1.7 per cent of the total membership of the committees.

Conclusion

Men, since the inception of the Institute, have built a complex social network around themselves. The network consists of other men, who were boys together, who played and grew up together, who went to school and university together, and who continue to do business together. Women have, historically, been left out of this network. They have built up another network, equally complex and useful to them — a network of handmaidens to surround the men whose business success was critical to the provision of food and shelter for them and their children. With the gradual introduction of mixed education and increasing numbers of women taking professional qualifications, the male network will slowly open out to include women, and society will accept as perfectly natural the spectacle of women in top executive and professional posts. But this will take time. Women could speed up the process with a little gentle encouragement. Very soon the supply of young people will contract and it will be necessary to keep the highly qualified young women whom the profession and industry are presently losing. The more interesting phenomenon may well prove to be the opening out of the female network to include men who wish to take an active part in the home making, child rearing and secretarial support roles which have been closed to them!

The Institute of Chartered Accountants in Ireland from its inception was a trail blazer in relation to women. In this, its centenary year, it would be appropriate for the Irish Institute to examine the issue of women in the profession. Discrimination in Ireland is not perceived as a major problem, but women still regard motherhood as a major barrier to the progression of their careers. This, of course, is an issue with much wider social implications; but as we move towards an era where the baby boom is petering out and where there will be fewer suitable graduates to train into the profession, we should be looking at the issue of keeping the women in the profession and facilitating them over the early years of motherhood. They are highly skilled and competent young professionals with years of expensive training and education behind them, and with many skills and talents which can augment and complement the skills which male executives can offer. It is surely wrong to offer them a choice of motherhood or professional advancement, when with some planning and a suitable action plan which can assess their special needs, they could be kept fruitfully in harness in the difficult years which face our economy as we enter our second hundred years.

There is one golden rule to bear in mind always; that we should try to put ourselves in the position of our correspondent, to imagine his feelings as he writes his letters, and to gauge his reaction as he receives ours. If we put ourselves in the other man's shoes we shall speedily detect how unconvincing our letters can seem, or how much we may be taking for granted.

Inland Revenue Staff Instruction

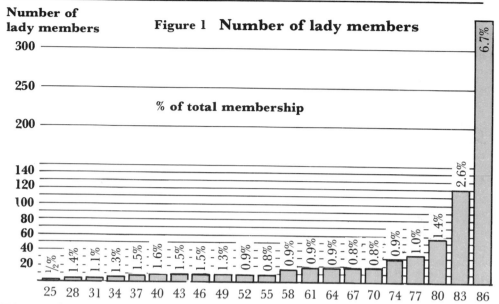

Figure 1 **Number of lady members**

Figure 2

Ratio of women to total in professional occupations (extract)

	%
Nurses.	88.6
Other medical professionals	77.9
Teachers	61.5
Professed clergymen and nuns	57.7
Social workers	54.3
Pharmacists	42.6
Medical practitioners	25.1
Authors, journalists and editors	25.1
Actors, entertainers and musicians	23.1
University professors and lecturers	20.6
Judges, barristers and solicitors	19.7
Chemists and other scientists	14.8
Dental practitioners	13.3
Draughtsmen	10.2
Surveyors and architects	5.7
Veterinary surgeons	2.8
Chartered accountants	1.4
Engineers	1.3
Commissioned army officers	0.1

Source: CP 1981 Vol. 7, Table 3

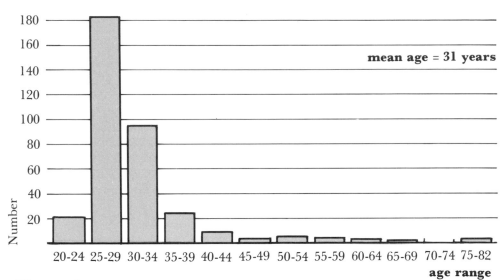

Figure 3   Age profile of lady chartered accountants

mean age = 31 years

Number

age range

20-24 25-29 30-34 35-39 40-44 45-49 50-54 55-59 60-64 65-69 70-74 75-82

Figure 4

Geographic spread of lady members

LOCATION	% OF TOTAL LADY MEMBERS	OF WHICH, MARRIED
Republic of Ireland	62%	22%
Ulster	16%	36%
UK	11%	21%
Europe	2%	13%
Overseas	9%	20%

Figure 5

Employment classification of lady members

CLASS	% TOTAL LADY MEMBERS	OF WHICH, MARRIED
Industry	30%	23%
Employee — Professional office	55%	15%
Practitioner	10%	41%
Retired	1%	33%
Special	4%	94%

Figure 6

Responsibility level of lady members

EMPLOYMENT CLASS	% OF CLASS
Industry	
Financial and management accountants	56%
Lecturers	12%
Bank managers and investment analysts	10%
Company directors	6%
Assistant accountants	5%
Internal auditors	4%
Company secretaries	3%
Assistant bank managers	3%
Trust administrators	1%
Employed in professional office	
Seniors	74%
Managers	14%
Assistant managers	5.5%
Supervisors	5%
Audit assistants	1%
Directors	0.5%
Practitioners	
Sole traders	74%
Partners	26%
Special leave	
For child minding years	93%
For voluntary service overseas	7%

What between the duties expected of one during one's lifetime, and the duties exacted from one after one's death, land has ceased to be either a profit or a pleasure.

Oscar Wilde, *The Importance of Being Earnest*

Editorial Introduction to 'Is business well served by the chartered accountant?'

By and large the emphasis of this volume has been on the practising profession. But since nearly half of the members of the Institute operate in areas outside the practising offices, it is appropriate and salutary to consider the adequacy of the training and experience of the chartered accountant to their needs.

Gerry is an eminent chartered accountant, and was the first president of the Institute from the industrial stream. He claims that it is many years since he was functioning as an accountant, and indeed this is so, for his talents have been devoted for a long time in the sphere of management, and he would have merited a place in our gallery of 'excellence' elsewhere in this volume had we not succeeded in securing him as a major contributor.

However remote he may be from the techniques of accounting, he has kept closely in touch with the developments in the profession, and the combination of that intimate knowledge and his wide experience in management assure the relevance of his comments.

There is nothing which will not yield to perseverance and method.

Edmund Burke (1729-97), *Letters*

Gerald P. Dempsey, B.A., F.C.A.

Gerald P. (Gerry) Dempsey has served business and the profession in a wide variety of positions during his career. After an economics degree in UCD he qualified as a chartered accountant in 1952. Following a little over a year in practice with Reynolds McCarron & Co. he joined Aer Lingus and commenced a thirty-two year career with that company. Starting as internal auditor he moved up to the top financial position in 1968.

In 1974 he became chief executive of the company's ancillary businesses, and thus led an 'entrepreneurial' team of private sector businesses within a public sector company. In 1986 he retired prematurely from Aer Lingus and is now a director of Waterford Glass plc in Ireland, Omni Hotels Corporation in the USA and the Guinness Peat Group plc in London, thus continuing the international flavour of his career. He is also a director of the International Fund for Ireland, Gilbeys Group of Ireland and Abbey Life (Ireland).

His links with the profession have remained close; he has lectured in accountancy in UCD and held the chairmanship of the Leinster Society of Chartered Accountants in 1971 and the presidency of the Institute in 1978.

Is business well served by the chartered accountant?

by Gerald P. Dempsey

MEN and women today who have acquired skills as chartered accountants are used by the business world in ways that could not have been envisaged 100 years ago. In the next few pages I shall assess the type of services which the accountant is called upon to offer, and which, indeed, to a very high degree he delivers.

In the first part I shall comment on the chartered accountant as he functions in business, either as the leader of the business, or as a part of the financial function, or as a non-executive director.

I shall then move outside the business and consider his independent function, as the auditor and as the provider of other financial services.

Finally I offer a few comments on the nature of the training and education which he gets, and on the type of environment within which he may have to operate in the next few years.

Within the business

The leader
It goes almost without saying that the critical job in any business is that of its leader. Clearly it is the most difficult, most challenging and most rewarding task in any organisation. If things aren't right at the top, no business can prosper for long.

It seems to me that regardless of whether the business leader is the original founder or a successor he must have entrepreneurial motivation. This is because business is essentially an enterprise rather than an organisation. Unless it constantly reminds itself of the need for enterprise it will become driven by organisational factors and will fail to flourish.

If in the leadership of a business there is a dominance of the attitudes of the accountant, or of the marketing executive, or of the engineer, to the extent that any one of those disciplines unduly influences decisions — then the business is unlikely to be operating at its optimum. The accounting attitude, emphasising control, prudence and balance, will tend to inhibit risk-taking. The marketing attitude may optimistically and buoyantly push sales at the expense of profit.

The engineering attitude may become absorbed in function, even the elegance of the thing designed and produced, with less concern for both saleability and cost. The business leader can have any, or none, of these disciplines: his purpose is to draw on them, use them, with a view to driving the business forward. Indeed, a leader with an accounting background, for example, although he may find that that discipline is a useful informant of his awareness, will be well advised not to use it much in his work. He will need to hire good accountants to deal with the accountancy work, while he devotes his time to the task of leadership. In fact, one of the worst mistakes he can make is to believe that he does not need a strong finance director because his own accounting ability will cover that function.

I have said that enterprise is the key. How can it be acquired? Can it be taught? I think not. It is something which thrives when the national atmosphere favours and actively encourages it. Here in Ireland we suffer from a negative business climate; we seem to feel guilty about success, play it down, knock it in others. In England success has been rather bad form: better to be a jolly good loser. However, the Thatcher era has been changing such attitudes. In the US, perhaps because of history, geography and cultural melding, they seem to have got it about right. Success is the *point* of the exercise. Self-trained, self-motivated entrepreneurs are expected, and accepted. Enterprise can flourish even in the absence of a favourable culture; but it is harder.

I look at those who have reached the top. They all seem to have several vital qualities: a tremendous drive and dedication to profitability and growth; constant awareness of the customer, of what the market needs; a facility with, even an appetite for, the key figures; and a desire, sometimes overly strong, to be the leader.

So, if it does not seem to matter greatly from what discipline the entrepreneur emerges, or indeed whether he emerges from *any* formal discipline, is there any particular advantage in having an accountancy training and background at all? With certain caveats I think that a knowledge of the skills of record keeping, balance sheet interpretation, numeracy, facility with figures generally, *is* a positive advantage. Of all the disciplines — legal, engineering, marketing, accounting — arguably accounting is the most useful, particularly in larger, more complex businesses. The engineer or mathematician or scientist, whose background has to a degree been theoretical and abstract, may find that his discipline is no great help in leadership. A balance sheet may be something of a mystery to him, and the esoteric accounting processes may be alarming. If that is so he may avoid making decisions having an accounting or financial impact, and may tend to delegate too much in that area. Therein lies a negative, since all business decisions have financial impact.

There are some major caveats. The entrepreneur with accounting skills must be capable of escaping from the detail. He must move from the floor to the ceiling. He must leave the details to his financial man. To the degree that he succeeds in escaping from the meticulous bonds of his training and habits, so he becomes free to exercise the imaginative expansion of his mind.

Also the longer an accountant stays with the auditing side of practice the less likely will he be able to emerge as a successful businessman — the harder it will be to make the jump. However, those on the consultancy services side of the professional practices can make the switch to industry more easily. Indeed, the consultancy practices have for some time been creating a pool of potential managers and entrepreneurs. Whilst this is so, I should like to offer a warning to young people, if they aspire to an eventual career outside the profession, that there is some danger in spending too much time (say more than five years) in advisory work. They may develop considerable skills in advising others how to do, but lose the capacity to do it themselves. They may, indeed cross this Rubicon without seeing it.

The financial officers
The financial function is critical to the continuity of any business. It is not the motor, not the driving force, but it is the bedrock from which flow confidence, soundness and sureness. No business can be soundly based without a strong financial function.

By 'strong financial function' I imply one which records accurately, interprets intelligently and sensitively, and provides effective means of financial control. To many in management the 'bookkeepers' are considered a nuisance — but good management knows that it is dependent upon the finance function for stability, rectitude and control. Further, without a sound internal accounting system the external audit will be less than satisfactory.

In Ireland there is a danger, particularly amongst the smaller companies (say those with a turnover of less than seven figures) to regard the recording function as essential, but to consider the interpreting and control functions as something of a luxury to be provided, perhaps, by the hired professionals. Many would consider that the cost of a full-time function in the interpretative/control sphere would be excessive. This is a false — and dangerous — economy.

The astonishing number of different treatises that have been published on Book-Keeping; the innumerable bankruptcies and suits at law, disputes, etc. that have been produced by false statements, errors and obscurity in accounts; the inconvenience, perplexity, and anxiety that is produced in every compting-house where books are balanced, are sufficient proofs that a system of Book-Keeping capable of preventing those errors is much wanted.

From 'An Introductory Address' in *Jones's English System of Book-Keeping*, Bristol (1706)

In the larger companies the people who control the financial function are the finance manager and the finance director. These two people stand a little apart from each other, viewing the world from somewhat different perspectives. The finance manager controls the finance function of the company, and as such occupies a senior managerial post in the company. He is expected to ensure that books are properly kept, set and monitor the controls and produce regular financial reports. The finance director sits on the board, and while supervising the financial function, is expected to guide the concern on matters of financial strategy.

If they are honourable men, both of them may expect from time to time to be faced with questions of ethics. If they are chartered accountants, the code to which they are expected to adhere exists, at least in outline, and in high aspiration. For example, Statement 1 of the 'Ethical guide for members', entitled 'professional independence' says:

> Professional independence is a concept fundamental to the accountancy profession. It is essentially an attitude of mind characterised by integrity and an objective approach to professional work ...
>
> Although a member not in public practice may be unable either to be or to appear to be free of interests which might conflict with a proper approach to his professional work, this does not diminish his duty of objectivity in relation to that work.

Nobody can deny that the financial manager concerned with his professional standards can be faced from time to time with agonising problems. His choices can be made more difficult by feelings of group loyalty and responsibility to an employer. If a financial manager feels that his colleagues are going down the wrong path what is he supposed to do? Consider those in the small groups who knew what was going on in the Guinness or Boesky affairs. Unfortunately, very frequently it is relatively easy for somebody emotionally unaffected to see the issues starkly and clearly. But for the person closely involved, there is the constant pressure of creative justification, of appeals to the environment of competitive practices. Issues most certainly became clouded. Is it expected of a man that he should risk his job and possibly his career? In many ways his position is very similar to that of the auditor, except only that usually his stakes are much higher. The auditor may lose one good job. The manager may lose all. Yet integrity and standards are at stake, and the role of the accountant/financial manager in industry may be the extremely difficult one of doing all within his power to keep his colleagues on the right side of the line.

He holds a position of trust at the head of a corporate function, and if he is aware that things are going wrong, he should at least report to those who ought to know, and having done so, his conscience may be clear. If, however, he is obliged to participate in a course of action which does not accord with his concept of professional ethics, and if he cannot persuade his colleagues to change direction, then it is hard to see how he can do other than dissociate himself entirely, if necessary by resignation.

The financial director on the other hand cannot ever escape from his responsibility merely by reporting. He is amongst the decision-makers and he has no choice but to stand up and be counted.

I have dwelt at some length on the ethics question. On a more positive note, I have to say that it is my experience that the chartered accountant performs well in these functions, and gives vital service to business. The stronger and the more pro-actively he interprets his role, the better will be his value.

The non-executive director

The accountancy profession in Ireland is well represented in the non-executive director function; and indeed very rapidly in recent years the function itself has acquired great importance. Possibly as a result of the shocks and scandals of recent years, and certainly swayed by the enormous pressures from regulatory bodies in these islands and in the US, most public companies have come to accept and welcome the concept of the non-executive director, or what they call in the US the 'independent director'. The contribution of the non-executive director has become a major aspect in the control and development of big businesses, and because of this there has been a demand that these people should bring to the board a range of high skills, adequate for the incisive assessment of matters of strategic import. Board tables are much less gentlemen's clubs than they used to be. The day when the managing director dominated the board, and resented interference from board members not involved in the management, is rapidly drawing to a close. The true role of the board as the protector of the interests of shareholders and other stakeholders is gaining wide acceptance.

The question of the best balance between executive and non-executive directors is not a subject for this paper. Suffice to say that it is an important subject, particularly for publicly quoted companies. In my view the role played by the non-executive director is a key one and the accountant is generally ideally suited to the role, particularly if his experience has largely been in industry rather than on the audit side of practice.

The emergence of the audit committee is another very significant phenomenon of the recent past. Indeed, the acceptance of the concept has taken a mere seven or eight years. Quite soon it may even become mandatory to have one. Whilst nobody suggests that the audit committee is a cure-all, it is a tremendously important, indeed a vital, link between the board of directors and the external auditors, each with its responsibility to the shareholders — a previously missing link. The audit committee should be made up entirely of non-executive directors, and almost always is. The finance director, the chief executive, the outside auditors — these are witnesses, and should not be members. Without a doubt, the accountants within the group of non-executive directors are the most natural people to take a major part in the work of the audit committee.

The independent accountant

The auditor

It is not necessary for me to stress the critically important role played by the external auditor. Nor need I dwell here on the growing responsibilities of the auditor and his exposure to legal action. Business cannot survive without the auditor. This is because for their development and growth businesses must enter into many critical relationships with other parties. These may be stakeholders, such as employees, owners, lenders, suppliers, customers, or possibly complete outsiders. In all cases financial reports play a vital role and mostly there is a need for verification and report by an independent accountant or auditor.

By and large industry and commerce are well served by the profession. On the auditing side, in my experience, it generally gets the service it should expect. I have, however, two concerns:

● There is a continued lack of evenness of standards within national boundaries, and between different countries. Nationally there are sharp differences, which coincide very approximately with the divide between the large and the small practices.

A number of the big 'international' firms are amalgamations of national firms often with varying traditions and outlook. The degree to which they have been able to ensure conformity of standards amongst their component parts seems to me to vary quite widely. When employing an auditor it is advisable to look behind the facade at the underlying structure, if that is possible, so as to assess what methods are in use to co-ordinate standards of practice.

It has been argued that because the smaller firm is generally employed by the smaller client company, the exposure of the various contractual parties is that much less, and that standards to be applied to the audit of larger companies are higher than those which should reasonably be expected to apply to the lesser league. I feel, however, that the stakeholders in large businesses and small ones are essentially the same — creditors, lenders, employees and owners — and that although when the business is small they may be fewer in number or in the extent of their exposure, taken individually they suffer proportionately the same as a result of bad professional work. They are entitled to expect from both the internal and the external accountants the use of the same standards of excellence as are deemed applicable to the larger businesses. The same SSAPs are relevant to all situations, and should be applied with the same rigour.

When dealing with the continent of Europe another difficulty emerges, which is more fundamental and structural. Despite the introduction of accounting directives and considerable improvement in harmonisation, there still remains a strong divergence owing to very different cultural and legal backgrounds. The concepts of 'true and fair', and 'going concern' have meant very little in the major European accounting context.

Reading the accounting statements of Germans or Italians, one realises that the language — the accounting language — is not the same. One is not, in fact, looking at sets of figures as they would be prepared in the Anglo-Irish tradition. On numerous occasions I have found it necessary to set about a translation, not only of the words, but also of the figures — even of the concepts. In considering potential acquisitions of French and Spanish companies, I have found myself profoundly uneasy with the figures as presented and with the absence of what I would have regarded as a recognisable audit certificate, and have therefore had to have the figures restated in what was to me a recognisable form. That sort of thing is seriously inhibiting to business dealings within Europe and between continents. One feels more comfortable — on more solid ground — when dealing with accounts prepared in the tradition with which one is familiar.

● My second worry is that there is not enough input into the making of accounting standards by business — and I am talking here not of the accountants in industry, but of the leaders of the business world, the entrepreneurs. Their voice is not sufficiently loud. Hence many of the standards express an excessively regulatory mode of thought. Unfortunately the Boeskys of this world — when they are found out — bring in their wake a great wave of regulatory thinking. 'We must stop these practices at all costs. Batten down the hatches. Pass more laws. Employ more inspectors.' But this is not the way to go. Enterprise will not flourish in an excessively regulatory society. We have seen in the past few years that where accounting standards are complex, restrictive and difficult to understand, industry reacts negatively. We have seen even, sadly, some of the larger companies taking a sort of cocky pride in non-compliance. So I would make a plea for a greater role for the non-accountant business man in standard-setting.

The provider of financial services

In my opinion industry and commerce have been tremendously well served by the other side of the practising profession — the side giving expert advice in the fields of taxation, finance, management services, corporate strategy, and company law and practice. A need has been perceived, and it is good that the profession has risen to the challenge of meeting it. It will remain good as long as standards are maintained. At present any business is well advised to turn to the trained professionals, rather than to many of the undisciplined, self-styled, 'consultants' offering their services to the market.

Tax advice must take a pre-eminent place. Generally it feels non-productive and not wealth creating work but regrettably it is a totally necessary service. Almost all business decisions are influenced in some way by the taxation consequences.

The area of mergers and acquisitions has tended to be dominated by the merchant bankers, which means that in some cases it is necessary to employ two sets of advisors, the bankers and the accountants, thereby adding substantially to cost. If the larger accounting firms more seriously challenged this market, and created departments adequately skilled in this specialised field, business would be better served.

Training and education

I take a basic point of view — perhaps it might be regarded as reaction-ary — that training to be an accountant should be that and nothing else. He should not be trained *for* industry, or for that matter, *for* practice. Professional integrity and ethical standards are likely to be best protected and enhanced if he is trained as an accountant to be his own master. What he intends to do with his career thereafter is a second consideration. A number of people may become chartered accountants by being articled in industry, but I imagine that the number following that route will tend to be quite small. The syllabus should cover what is essential for all accountants to know and should be updated fre-quently to be sure that concepts which are evolving very rapidly should be adequately covered — for example, the developing thinking concerning the role and structure of the board and of the audit committee.

If I were to be asked to select just one aspect of the training of an accountant which I would consider inadequate, I think I should say 'communication'. The skills of communication are fundamental to all forms of reporting; and I think that accountants are often not the best at displaying these skills. In our complex world a premium attaches to those who have acquired communication skills — skills of saying what needs to be said in clear and economic terms, of add-ressing the needs of the hearer or reader in a language to which he can relate. Basic schooling does not seem to give it. Both at school level and in the course of subsequent training a greater emphasis seems to be given to the acquisition of knowledge and skills other than the skill of communication.

Facing the future

Elsewhere in this book is an essay on technology. There may be seen the incredible acceleration in technology, particularly in the communications field. It will not be necessary in the future that the accountant should know all the available technology, but it is necessary that he should be friendly with it, and know how to put it to his service.

Then again he must live with the concept that the market for accounting thought is world wide. The environment in which he lives, and in which we all live today, is an international one, and while we should all be poorer without our regional differences, we cannot avoid or evade our function as citizens of the world. Business will be best served by accountants and the accounting firms which are aware of these facts and have geared themselves to live with them.

The profession in Ireland

There is less need to argue the case for a separate Irish profession than there is for a separate profession in Scotland, for Westminster's writ does not run in Dublin. The fact that Dublin's does not run in Belfast has not prevented the Institute of Chartered Accountants in Ireland from maintaining its position as the senior body of accountants both north and south of the Ulster border, and thereby commendably demonstrating that frontiers have no more importance than people choose to attach to them. But to ask the Irish Institute to ignore Ireland's position as an independent republic would be unrealistic, in the light of history.

The Irish profession faces some special problems, mostly stemming from the fact that Ireland is a small yet divided country. The existence of two jurisdictions, two educational authorities, two sets of statutes adds to the problems that would in any case beset a professional body with fewer than 2,500 members, to focus on Ireland's chartered accountants for a moment. The relative smallness of the Irish Institute makes it difficult for it to provide a full range of services to its members economically, and the ease of manoeuvre which a small body can normally enjoy is in this case reduced by the need to respect the sensibilities of members on both sides of the border.

David Solomons, *Prospectus for a Profession,* 1974

Accountants at play: golf

Accountants at play: the Christmas party

Diarmuid Ó Cearbhaill, M.A., B.Comm., H.Dip.Ed.

Diarmuid graduated in languages and commerce at University College, Galway, and subsequently studied at Oxford and Louvain. He worked as an economist at the Department of Finance before returning to Galway on his appointment as Léachtóir le Geilleagar agus Tráchtáil. He served two terms as dean of the Faculty of Commerce at UCG. His recent publications include the editing of *Galway: Town and Gown, 1484-1984* and several studies on regional and community development. In 1986 he was appointed Fulbright Scholar in Residence-Economics at Reed College, Portland, Oregon.

Outline

Accounting terminology and conversions set the general context for an initial discussion by Diarmuid Ó Cearbhaill of some business issues and complexities associated with the use of minority languages by some forty million persons within the EEC. In his more detailed consideration of the Irish scene he draws attention to the difficulties involved in trying to preserve the use of Irish while seeking to develop and industrialise Gaeltacht areas. Similar problems and issues have arisen in the case of other linguistic minorities e.g. Scottish and Welsh. Business education through Irish at secondary and third levels, including the provision of modern textbooks, forms the basis of preparation for the practical use of that language, ranging from Gaeltacht areas to the European Bureau for Lesser Used Languages whose accounts are expressed in ECUs. Initiatives of universities, state bodies and research institutes in publishing sophisticated accounts and major business reports are cited. The implications of information technology for enterprises conducting their business through Irish are also stressed. In conclusion, the motto of a German translator is recalled for accountants using minority languages or major dialects, as they strive for the right blend of accuracy and flexibility.

The use of minority languages in business

by Diarmuid Ó Cearbhaill

Úsáid mionteangacha i gcúrsaí gnó

SAMHLAÍTEAR faoi chuntasóirí, de ghnáth, gur dual dóibh a bheith cruinn, beacht, gonta. Chuige sin uile, is áil leo caighdeánú a thrasnaíonn teorainneacha teanga sa riocht is go mbíonn an téarmaíocht cuid mhaith mar an gcéanna ó thír go chéile. Thug údar an ailt seo sampla fánach dá leithéid sin faoi deara i dtéacsleabhar Fraincise dár theideal *Le Cash Flow*, a d'fhreagródh don téarma *Sreabhadh Airgid* sa nGaeilge. Fiú más nós coitianta é ag lucht na dteangacha domhanda aithris dá réir a dhéanamh ar a chéile i dtaca le téarmaíocht tráchtála, an fearr dóibh sin a úsáideann mionteangacha Eorpacha glacadh scun scan le téarmaí simplí sothuigthe an Bhéarla agus na Meiriceánach, nó earball dúchasach a chur le béarlagair gnó atá bunaithe go minic ar phréamhacha Laidne nó Gréigise? Sin, nó téarmaí a chruthú as an nua muna bhfuil focal feiliúnach ar fáil cheana féin sa mhionteanga atá i gceist?

D'ainneoin meatha ina lán cás, tá úsáid mionteangacha Eorpacha agus tuiscint orthu i bhfad níos forleithne agus níos coimpléascaí ná mar a shílfí ar an gcéad amharc. Níl sochaithe chomh himeallach ná réigiúin chomh scoite amach ó chaidreamh eachtrach is a bhíodh fadó, agus tá a dteagmhálacha tráchtála leis an domhan mór i bhfad níos coitianta i saol athraitheach ár linne féin ná mar a bhíodh anallód. Dá bharr sin uile, tá gréasán casta de mhionlaigh a bhfuil a bheag nó a mhór d'eolas acu ar theangacha neamhfhorleathana an Chomhphobail Eorpaigh (CE) agus a chleachtaíonn iad go rialta nó ó am go chéile i dtír amháin nó níos mó. Maíonn Dónall Ó Riagáin, rúnaí ginearálta an Bhiúró Eorpaigh do Theangacha Neamhfhorleathana, go labhraíonn suas le 40 milliún saoránach de chuid an CE — nó duine as gach ochtar — teanga neamhfhorleathan nach príomhtheanga an bhallstáit í ina bhfuil cónaí orthu. Ar na náisiúin bheaga atá i gceist tá Éire agus Lucsamburg, mar aon le pobail eitneacha mar na Briotánaigh, Freaslannaigh agus Catalónaigh.[1]

Léiríonn tuarascáil a d'ullmhaigh an *Istituto della Enciclopedia Italiana* do Choimisiún an Chomhphobail (1986) a dheacra is atá sé léargas uileghabhálach d'fháil ar stáid na mionteangacha seo agus a n-úsáid.

Is follasach, ámh, go mbaineann éagsúlachtaí móra leo i dtaca le labhairt agus scríobh ó theanga go chéile. Tagann débhéascna (diglossia) i gceist nuair a labhraíonn duine teanga amháin ar ócáidí áirithe lena mhuintir, lena chairde, agus é ag plé le cúrsaí talmhaíochta, mar shampla, ach go labhraíonn sé teanga 'eachtrannach' i gcúinsí faoi leith eile, mar shampla ar ócáidí oifigiúla, le strainséirí, agus é ag plé le cúrsaí tionscail. Bheadh a leithéid sin coitianta i roinnt de na monarchana Gaeltachta.[2]

Aithníonn an tuarascáil thuasluaite laigí geilleagracha úsáideoirí mionteangacha i dtaca le teirce acmhainní, dífhostaíocht agus eisimirce. Eascraíonn teannais agus aighnis faoi fhéinrialú, réigiúnachas agus 'coilíneachas' ó rialtais lárnacha agus ó fhoinsí idirnáisiúnta. Maireann dúcheisteanna buana maidir leis na comhréitigh chearta is gá a aimsiú idir forbairt gheilleagrach a chur chun cinn, ar thaobh amháin, agus meath mionteangacha a sheachaint de réir mar a thréigeann mionlaigh a bhfód dúchais nó de réir mar a ghlacann siad le gnásanna an mhóirimh i gcúrsaí geilleagracha agus tráchtála, ar an dtaobh eile.[3]

Tarlaíonn conspóidí uaireanta faoi earcú bainisteoirí, teicneoirí agus ceardaithe riachtanacha ón nGalltacht agus a dtionchar siúd ar úsáid na Gaeilge i monarchana Gaeltachta. Braitheann an tionchar úd, dar ndóigh, ar a gcoibhneas leis an bhfoireann iomlán ó chás go chéile. Má tá codán ard de Ghaeilgeoirí ó dhúchas ar mheitheal oibrithe, is fearr an seans go bhfanfaidh an Ghaeilge in uachtar ar an láthair oibre. Is cosúil gur ísle i bhfad an glanchostas *per capita* a roinneann le cruthú fostaíochta i miontionscadail Ghaeltachta atá bunaithe ar acmhainní agus scileanna áitiúla ná an t-ualach a leagann tionscail mhóra sheachtracha ar an gcáiníocóir ginearálta. Bíodh is nár éirigh le cuid acu go n-uige seo, is fearr a thagann siad le caomhnú na teanga Gaeilge, ach dóthain díobh a bheith ar bhonn slán.

Sampla suntasach eile dá leithéid seo is ea cás na Breatnaise, a chuaigh i léig go mór de réir mar a tharla forbairt thionsclaíoch i gceantair áirithe sa Bhreatain Bheag tar éis an Dara Cogadh Mór. Ceapadh feidhmeannaigh agus teicneoirí nach raibh cumas acu sa Bhreatnais chuig postanna i dtionscail mhóra nua a tháinig in ionad roinnt de na sean-mhiontionscscail sa riocht is nárbh fhéidir an teanga úd d'úsáid feasta.[4]

Maidir le hAlbain, bhí na húdaráis patuar, ach thoilíodar i ndiaidh a chéile le húsáid Ghaeilge na hAlban sa chóras oideachais, ar an raidió agus ar theilifís ag an BBC. Mar chuid de na chéad thionscnaimh athbheochana i measc lucht gnó, thosaigh an Clydesdale Bank agus an Bank of Scotland ag soláthar seiceanna dátheangacha dóibh sin a d'iarr iad.[5] Ar an Oileán Sgiathánach tá treoir leanúnach tugtha ag fir ghnó mar Iain Noble maidir le húsáid Ghaeilge na hAlban. Sa bhliain 1983 thug Roinn Oideachais na hAlban aitheantas foirmeálta do chúrsa dioplóma i staidéar gnó ag an tríú leibhéal sa choláiste ag Sabhal Mór Ostaig — cúrsa a mhúintear trí Ghaeilge na hAlban.

Tá *Faclair Eorpach* (1982) curtha ar fáil ag Coimisiún na gComhphobal ina bhfuil mórán téarmaí thar a bheith cosúil nó ar aon dul le focail atá i nGaeilge na hÉireann, e.g. *aonad, cunntais, malairt, easbhaidh, di-luachadh*. Freagraíonn *séideadh* don téarma *boilsciú* atá againn ar *inflation*.

Maidir le hoiliúint trí Ghaeilge i dtaca le cúrsaí gnó abhus, múintear roinnt mhaith ábhar mar eagras gnó, tráchtáil, cuntasaíocht agus eacnamaíocht i scoileanna ag an dara leibhéal, ach ar mhionscála. Le cúlú ginearálta A-scoileanna ó na caogaidí i leith, tá líon na ndaltaí laghdaithe go mór. Tá an scéal duairc céanna le n-aithris faoin tríú leibhéal, cé go bhfuil an geilleagar fós á theagasc trí Ghaeilge i nDámha na nDán agus na Tráchtála i gColáiste na hOllscoile, Gaillimh. Múintear roinnt cúrsaí gnó trí mheán na teanga sin ins na coláistí réigiúnacha i nGaillimh agus i Leitir Ceanainn.

Cibé ar bith faoi na clamhsáin a bhíodh dá gclos fadó faoi easpa téacsanna feiliúnacha i nGaeilge le haghaidh staidéar gnó agus tráchtála nuair a bhí líon na mac léinn i bhfad níos mó ná mar atá ar na mallaibh, ní gearánta dá macasamhail anois sa mhéid is go bhfuil faoi dheireadh i bhfad níos mó téacs nua-aimseartha agus téarmaíocht chuí foilsithe ag an nGúm. Más maith is mithid.

Ag an leibhéal praiticiúil, tá úsáid na Gaeilge i gcúrsaí gnó le feiceáil in imeachtaí na gcomharchumann ins na ceantair Ghaeltachta agus dar ndóigh i seirbhísí Údarás na Gaeltachta agus ranna stáit, agus i dtuarascálacha agus i gcuntais bhliantúla cuideachtaí státurraithe. Tá soláthar déanta le fada an lá ag Gael-Linn ar raon mór gníomhaíochtaí. Tá samhail shoiléir shofaisticiúil den chaoi inar féidir gnó iomlán a reachtáil trí Ghaeilge le fáil i gcáipéisí den tsórt a

If any man were to ask me what I would suppose to be a perfect style of language, I would answer, that in which a man speaking to five hundred people, of all common and various capacities, idiots or lunatics excepted, should be understood by them all, and in the same sense which the speaker intended to be understood.

Defoe

hullmhaítear do chruinniú ginearálta bliantúil *Chomhar,* a chuimsíonn cuntais iniúchta ar a n-áirítear cuntas sochair agus dochair, clár comhardaithe agus ráiteas ar fhoinse agus úsáid mhaoine, maille le nótaí faoi pholasaí cuntasaíochta, sócmhainní dochta agus cuntais bhainistíochta.

Léiríonn an cás sin gur féidir cuntais chasta choimpléascacha a láimhseáil go paiteanta agus go beacht trí mheán ár gcéad theanga ach an toil a bheith ag lucht gnó agus ag an bpobal chuige. Sí an toil sin croí na ceiste. In áit béal bocht a dhéanamh den scéal, cuimhnímis go bhfuil stádas éigin bainte amach ag an nGaeilge ar leibhéal idirnáisiúnta, bíodh is nach teanga oifigiúil oibre den CE í. Mar atá mínithe ag an Riagánach in 'Osamharc Éireannach ar Theangacha Neamhfhorleathana an CE' (1986), tá an leagan Gaeilge de na conarthaí éagsúla chomh bailí agus chomh hoifigiúil is atá leaganacha ins na naoi dteangacha oifigiúla oibre. Tá socruithe áirithe ann maidir le déileáil le comhfhreagras Gaeilge agus le húsáid na teanga sa Chúirt Bhreithiúnais.[6]

Sroicheadh cloch mhíle úr i gcúrsaí iniúchóireachta sa bhliain 1986. I bhfómhar na bliana sin, thapaigh iniúchóirí an Bhiuró Eorpaigh do Theangacha Neamhfhorleathana, Binder Hamlyn, an deis a thug an biúró dóibh don chéad uair riamh chun sé leagain de chuntais iniúchta a eisiúint, i nGaeilge, i mBéarla agus i bhFraincis, agus iad uile in ECU agus i bpuint Éireannacha (féach an t-aguisín leis seo, a bhaineann le clár comhardaithe 31 Nollaig 1985).

Is ceannródaithe iad ollscoileanna agus forais taighde áirithe abhus agus i gcéin i dtaca le húsáid mionteangacha ina gcuntais bhliantúla agus ina dtuarascálacha teicniúla. Mar shampla, is trí Ghaeilge a láimhsigh agus a d'fhoilsigh Coláiste na hOllscoile, Gaillimh, cuntais ioncaim agus caiteachais de bheagnach £19 milliún i 1985-6. Tá sé de nós ag Coláiste na hOllscoile, Aberystwyth, leagan cuimsitheach Breatnaise dá chuntais bhliantúla a sholáthar. Is díol suime, freisin, a bhfuil foilsithe le blianta beaga anuas i mionteanga ar a dtugtar Galego maidir le geilleagar, sochaí agus airgeadas Ghalicia na Spainne. Tugann tuarascáil a d'eisigh an *Centro de Información Estadística* i Santiago faoin teideal *Galicia en Cifras* léargas eile fós ar an gcaoi gur féidir, sa chás go gcuirtear chuige i gceart, gnéithe coimpléascacha de chúrsaí gnó a chíoradh go críochnúil cuimsitheach i dteanga nó fiú i gcanúint atá lasmuigh de raon príomhtheangacha ár linne.

We must not always judge of the generality of the opinion by the noise of the acclamation.

Edmund Burke (1729-97), *Letters on a Regicide Peace*

Leis an mborradh leanúnach atá faoin teicneolaíocht faisnéise, is cinnte go bhfuil athruithe bunúsacha i ndán don chuntasaíocht maidir le bailiú, scagadh agus léiriú sonraí gnó. Ní foláir do chuntasóirí agus do chomhairleoirí gnó a úsáideann mionteangacha na deiseanna úra sin a, thapú chun leas iomlán a bhaint as an sciobthacht agus an solúbthacht is dual do a lán gnóthaí beaga beoga i dtaca le cumarsáid, riaradh agus pleanáil, go háirithe nuair a bhíonn siad ag freastal ar mhargaí áitiúla.

De bhrí go ngoilleann constaicí na hiargúltachta agus díbharainneachtaí scála ar mhonarchana agus ar mhionghnóthaí a bhrathann ar mhionlaigh fhánacha ar nós na Gaeltachta, tá sé thar a bheith tábhachtach go rachaidís siúd i mbun na dteicníochtaí is oiriúnaí agus is éifeachtaí dóibh. Toisc ríomhairí agus saoráidí cumarsáide a bheith i bhfad níos saoire agus níos 'cairdiúla' ná mar a bhíodh, tig le mionghnóthaí caighdeánú agus cóiriú chun a gcumas iomaíochta i gcoinne corparáidí agus cuideachtaí móra a neartú. Maidir le straitéisí atá bunaithe ar chórais faisnéise, ní foláir dóibh díriú ar na cleachtais chaighdeánacha margaíochta agus cuntasaíochta is gá i ngnó ar bith, bíodh sé beag nó mór. Laistigh de chrann geinealaigh faisnéise a chuimsíonn buncheisteanna mar cora láithreacha agus fáistineacha an mhargaidh agus an fhadhb an bhfuil brabús á ghnóthú, beidh ar an mionghnó réitigh a lorg ó bhrainse na gcuntas a thabharfas faisnéis iomlán don bhainistíocht lárnach faoina bhfuil ag tarlú d'ioncam agus do chostais. Chuige sin uile, níor mhiste do chuntasóirí an tsaoithínteacht a sheachaint agus iad ar thóir an chruinnis in úsáid na Gaeilge. Meabhraídís an chomhairle a thug Gearmáineach iomráiteach fadó i dtaca le haistriúchán ó theanga go chéile. B'é a mholadh siúd ná go mba chóir a bheith chomh dílis agus is féidir, agus chomh saor agus is riachtanach! ●

Foinsí eolais

1 D. Ó Riagáin 'Osamharc Éireannach ar Theangacha Neamhfhorleathana an CE,' *Comhar*, Lúnasa 1986.
2 John Hume 'Parlaimint na hEorpa agus Todhchaí na dTeangacha Neamhfhorleathana', *Comhar* (Forlíonadh Eorpach), Samhain 1981.
3 D. Ó Cearbhaill (ed.), *New Approaches to the Development of Marginal Regions*, I, Galway 1986, 300-39.
4 M. Stephens, *Linguistic Minorities in Western Europe*, Gomer Press 1976, 161-2.
5 *Ibid*, 72-3.
6 *Linguistic Minorities in Countries belonging to the European Communities*, Summary Report prepared by the Istituto della Enciclopedia Italiana, Rome 1986.

Is mór ag údar an ailt seo an chabhair a fuair sé ó Dhónall Ó Riagáin agus ó Thadhg Ó Ceallaigh, Oifig Eolais an CE.

Aguisín
An Biúró Eorpach do Theangacha Neamhfhorleathana

Clár comhardaithe 31 Nollaig 1985

	1985 ECU	1985 ECU	1984 ECU	1984 ECU
TREALAMH		3,196		1,860
SÓCHMHAINNÍ REATHA:				
Fiachóirí i Cuntais isteach	1,812		42,571	
Banc agus airgead	36,175		5,604	
	37,987		48,175	
DÓCHMHAINNÍ REATHA:				
Creidiúnaithe/Cuntais amach	2,101		2,359	
SÓCHMHAINNÍ REATHA GLAN:		35,886		45,816
		39,082		47,676
COMHDHÉANTA MAR A LEANAS				
Cúlchiste Ioncaim		39,082		47,676

Sínithe thar cheann an bhoird:

DÓNALL Ó RIAGÁIN

MÁIRE UÍ GHÓGÁIN

Stiúrthóirí   ● ● ●

Subject:
How to produce 'true or fair' accounts when inflation makes the Consumer Price Index soar:

In 1914	2½ — C.P.I. (Base 1982)
1922	5
1978	50
1982	100
1986	127

Cornelius F. Smith

A minority language used by all accountants

Styles of reporting

Hard times for the Dublin Hop Stout Company according to the Directors' Report of 1895, which suffered a loss of £601 9s. 7d.:

'The new issue of Ordinary Shares referred to in last year's report was only partially subscribed for (the Members of the Board being almost the only subscribers for them); this greatly hampered the Company's operations and contributed to the non-success of season's trade.'

As a result of that failure the Company decided to issue £3,000 Debentures, but '£2,800 of this amount have been issued and taken up (with a trifling exception) by the members of the Board alone — indeed since the commencement of the business the chief burden, financial and otherwise, of this heavy (and to them novel) business has fallen on the shoulders of the Directors. They have for years devoted a vast amount of time and labour in carrying on the business, and have received no remuneration of any kind whatsoever.

In June last a serious trouble arose. The brewing of Hop Bitters, which had been fairly satisfactory for about a year previously, went suddenly wrong, and continued so for a period of about two months. Mr Bayly — who, of course, was the responsible head and manager of this department — failed to discover the cause of this fatality, so that we were compelled to discontinue the manufacture of this drink for a time. This has been a most serious loss to the Company, as besides losing the trade at the best period of the year — when expenses were at their highest point, and having the bulk of what was sent out returned at great expense and damage to our reputation — there was the final loss of having the various brews in question ultimately destroyed.

Owing to these unfortunate and unforeseen reverses and losses, your Directors sometime since, after mature consideration, decided that it would be quite out of their power to continue the business as at present constituted. They personally solicited offers from English and Scotch Capitalists in the trade for the business as a going concern. . . . They are pleased to be able to state that they have now a substantial offer . . .'

Good. Good. Maybe it was hardly fair, anyway, to expect the Directors to succeed in the direction of a business that was so 'novel' to them!

A very different style — in fact surely unique in Company reporting anywhere — was used by the late Sir Basil Goulding, Chairman of Fitzwilton Ltd, in 1975. It is possible only to give a flavour of what he choose to call his 'Bones':

II

The very most you can say about the past year is that it is passed.

Things were not always thus. There was a time, an' it not half-past, when God was in his heaven and all was right with the world — well, with its export markets. I cannot tell, without pink flushes, of the profit that fertiliser division was to make up to but a few months before it didn't half make it.

Thenabouts, too, the debilities of the picked pocket set in, inflation the stealthy stealer. By the droughty year-end a man hadn't the financial strength to stake his kid to a coke, nor the physical to finish, in his cheap anorak, the do-it-yourself glass, brick and paint job he had had to constrict from a contractor.

But I am wyandotting around like a leaderless citizen in deep litter; one of many.

III

In ancient Greece the world series was contested for years between the Lapithae and the Centaurs, a running battle 'later conceived of as mankind versus mischievous monsters' (O.E.D.).

In latterday civilisation (ha!) the monstrous encounter has been between the Presumptions and the Realities.

Incredible and sudden and flashing victory to the Realities — whom Presumptions had confidently presumed to parry indefinitely — has left a battlefield of stretched warriors, slain or crumpled.

Consider. There had not within a fifty year consciousness been a reversal of presumptio ad absurdum. There had come to sedimentary assumption the expectation of what I offer as a short slick definition of inflation: 'acquiring the means of acquiring things (money) without regard to the making of the things acquirable (goods and services)'.

It was Presumptions that first shot their own bolt, that promoted the Arab oil stick-up, that later accompliced in the Moroccan phosphate shoot-out, and that had mounted the Scandinavian timber mugging.

The Presumptions were that the supplies available to meet boundless requirements were boundless; and that in markets bound to boom one should boom on boundless. These two cohabited to breed a screwball of price-yeast: no need to inform, here, how oil and energy were transfigured; no need to tell farmers how phosphates, nitrogen and potash helicopted; nor to lecture construction men on how the timber autogiro lost its rotor and plummeted.

IV

The purpose of this homily, as prissy as any other, is to attribute the direct consequences that we have met upon to their right cause, the crassitude of mankind, and thereby to rescue them from the backed-up drains,of class antagonism.

Unemployment, redundancies, closings, bankruptcies, are not the consequence of cannibal capitalism ravening on missionary work-flesh.

Whilst it suits some to flash beguiling glimpses of class porn, the true fall of events is fully and inevitably accounted for without those charms . . .

V

When, from foreign devilry as it seemed, the price of energy and raw materials and, from our own, wages and salaries took off as from Cape Canaveral the price of the products that they made left earth's atmosphere too.

Earth and farmer, amongst others, watched them go with chagrin. Of the two earth changed not, remains as fecund if fertilised, as niggard if not. If this summer has not taught it next winter will.

Farmer was like and worse. For at the very instance that his costs clumped his markets emaciated, his meat minced.

Inevitabilities. He sold not neither did he buy. So the fertilisers he bought not sold not. Then worse. The money that made the goods go round keeled over when they didn't. The wages that made the goods go up were quenched. The men that made the goods toiled not, were driven to spin.

Emotional responses propose themselves, humanity seconding. It would be nice if they could be elected. But the hard lesson of today is that Realities have made a military coup and are clearing the streets, the tank versus the sling. No market, they dictate, if your product is too dear and your customer's product too cheap.

More inevitabilities. Cost of production must be crewcut, we biting back our aims to live like great, like greater, to living like lesser for a while (Fitzwilton topsmen have lately renounced pay rise, even cost-of-living).

Today's nap, only somewhat overstated, is: 'If you're offered a job, take it for half the money and twice the output.'

VI

Let us catch up, as Jove, this bolt of events, hold it temporarily sconced, and go chase (unlike Jove) that other bolter, the counterpart of the working man, working money.

Now working money is a queer artist; meaning, starkly, that it is unartistic; it attends strictly to the mundane, leaves the earth only by error of tread, not by elevation of thought.

More precisely, for Fitzwilton, working money — a main slab of it — has always been the trencher from which the raw materials of foreign kitchens were fed to our voracious stomach.

Came, of a sudden, a state of obstruction; couldn't digest because couldn't pass, or vice versa; no sales no make.

Now blockage in the alimentary canal of a manufacturer can set up hypertension in the nervous system of bankers, and titillation in the tastebuds of the newsmen.

And, lo, it was so.

I write rather too close to the lather of events: so that it is hard to declare, with the tramp metal of aroused viewpoints affecting my compass, whether others mis-judged our strength or we misjudged its use.

Perhaps the true sequence, to be unfair to all, was one of over-reaction to under-treatment.

And so on. One could quote for pages with continuing delight.

Index

Acknowledgments

The following organisations have financially sponsored the preparation of this volume and their assistance is gratefully acknowledged:

Allied Irish Banks plc
Anglo Irish Bank Corporation plc
Bank of Ireland
Barclays Bank plc
Carroll Industries plc
CRH plc
Glen Dimplex Ltd
Guinness & Mahon Ltd
Hibernian Insurance Company Ltd
Hill Samuel & Co. (Ireland) Ltd
Irish Life Assurance plc
Jefferson Smurfit Group plc
Northern Bank Ltd
Smurfit Paribas Bank Ltd
Trustee Savings Banks
TSB (Northern Ireland) plc
Ulster Bank Ltd
Waterford Glass Group plc

The editor and publishers thank the following for the use of photographs:

The Financial Times p. 31; An Bord Iascaigh Mhara/Irish Sea Fisheries Board p. 35 (top); Waterford Glass Group plc p. 35 (bottom); The Irish National Stud Company Ltd p. 36; Bord Fáilte Éireann/Irish Tourist Board p. 55; Harland & Wolff p. 59 (top and bottom); J. Allan Cash p. 93 (top and bottom), p. 184 (top); Derek Spiers/Report p. 105 (large); Office of the Taoiseach p. 105 (inset); Telecom Éireann p. 184 (bottom); The European Parliament p. 129 (top); IBM Ireland Ltd p. 190; Dr D.G. Byrne, Department of Computer Science, Trinity College, Dublin p. 199, pp. 201-4.